DOWN FOR THE COUNT

The Shocking Truth Behind the Mike Tyson Rape Trial

◆

Mark Shaw

with commentary by
ESPN's Charley Steiner

SAGAMORE PUBLISHING
Champaign, IL

Production Manager: Susan M. McKinney
Dustjacket and photo insert design: Michelle R. Dressen
Editor: Sara Chilton
Proofreaders: Brian J. Moore, Phyllis L. Bannon

**Publisher's Cataloging in Publication
(Prepared by Quality Books Inc.)**

Shaw, Mark. W.
    Down for the count: the shocking truth behind the Mike Tyson
rape trail / Mark Shaw.
    p. cm.
    Includes index.
    Preassigned LCCN: 93-84245.
    ISBN: 0-915611-78-3

    1. Tyson, Mike, 1966 —Trials, litigation, etc. 2. Trials
(Rape) —Indiana—Popular works. I. Title.

KF221.T97S53 1993   345.772'02532
                                     QBI93-686

Printed in the United States.

I dedicate this book to: Chris, my wife and best friend, whom I love very, very much; our children: Kimberly, Kevin, Kyle, and Kent, who always bring a smile to my face; and my canine buddies: Bach, White Sox, Peanut Butter, Duffy, Snickers, and Milk Shake, who love me whether I feed them or not.

◆

CONTENTS

◆

ACKNOWLEDGMENTS

◆

I want to thank my lovely wife, Chris, for her countless hours in front of the computer, and for her excellent suggestions for this book. Special thanks also go to Susan McKinney, the wonderful editor at Sagamore Publishing for her great comments and suggestions, and to my colleague and friend Donna Stouder for taking what I write and correcting the grammar enough so people can read it.

Special thanks to Charley Steiner, the award-winning broadcaster at ESPN not only for writing "Going, Going, Gone," the riveting chapter describing Mike Tyson's sentencing hearing, but also for his friendship and valuable collaboration during our coverage of the trial. I also want to express my gratitude to David Brofsky and Bob Eaton at ESPN for allowing me to work with such a first-class television network, and to Gene Policinski, Jon Saraceno, and G.E. Branch III for assisting me with my column for *USA Today* during the trial.

Thanks also go to Law Professor Thomas Schornhorst at Indiana University and to Director John Gallman at Indiana University Press for their dedication to making the book the best it could be, and to my friends at ABC affiliate WRTV in Indianapolis for working with me during the trial.

Thanks to Joe Gelarden of *The Indianapolis Star*, Art Harris of *The Indianapolis News*, Ron Borges of *The Boston Globe*, Wally Matthews of *Newsday*, Earl Gustkey of *The Los Angeles Times*, E.L. Shipp and Phil Berger of *The New York Times*, and Jon Saraceno, among others, for allowing me to witness firsthand what true professional journalism is all about.

My gratitude also goes out to attorneys Owen Mullin, Rick Kammen, Bob Hammerle, Professor Schornhorst and Judge Sam Rosen, whose valuable advice assisted me with the legal points made in this book.

Thanks also to special friends Scott and Janice Montross, Mickey and Janie Maurer, Pete and Alice Dye, Doc and Becky

Howard, Ray and Terry Browning, Mike and Anne Horii, Judy Deputy, Mike and Carol Hundert, Jack and Marilee Leer, Sandy and Linda Alderson, Dave and Nancy Foley, Ted and Bonnie Key, Sam and Joan Rosen, Andy and Fran Rogers, Mike Stipher, Kathryn Galan, and the entire Fred Roark family, among many others, who have always shown me what true friendship is all about.

Special thanks to Debbie Paul and Sam Stall at *Indianapolis Monthly Magazine*, and to my wonderful family of new friends at Sagamore Publishing, who have made the publishing of this book such a special event for me.

Thanks to my literary agents, Frank Wiemann of the Literary Group and Matthew Snyder of Creative Artists Agency, who believed that a lawyer/television personality/legal analyst/rancher/dog lover could also write.

Special thanks also to my sisters, Anne and Debbie, and my brother, Jack, for their support, and my parents, Marvin and Vera Shaw, who pointed me in the right direction when I was growing up.

Above all, thanks to the good Lord who has allowed me to experience so many special blessings during my life on his earth.

PREFACE

---◆---

In the period of a year that began in the fall of 1991, five national events resulted in trials or hearings that captivated the imaginations of millions of people around the world.

In October of that year, Federal Judge Clarence Thomas was charged with sexual harassment by University of Oklahoma Professor Anita Hill during his Senate confirmation hearing for the Supreme Court. Later in 1991, one of the famed Kennedy clan, William Kennedy Smith, was prosecuted in Palm Beach, Florida, for the alleged rape of 30-year-old single mother Patty Bowman.

In January of 1992, famous boxer Mike Tyson was tried for the "date rape" of 18-year-old beauty contestant and college student Desiree Washington in Indianapolis, Indiana. During the summer months that followed, four L.A.P.D. officers were charged in state court with savagely beating motorist Rodney King in Los Angeles. Finally, in the fall of 1992, 17-year-old Lemrick Nelson, Jr. was prosecuted for killing Jewish scholar Yankel Rosenbaum in the Crown Heights section of Brooklyn.

Four trials and one hearing, five emotionally-charged, high-profile cases. Five international media events. Four "not guilty" verdicts, and only one conviction—that of Michael Gerard Tyson, who was sentenced to six years in state prison for the rape of Desiree Washington.

Why was Mike Tyson convicted and not the others?

Was the deck stacked against him when pro-prosecution Judge Patricia Gifford was selected to preside over the case? Did alleged victim Desiree Washington hoodwink the jury into believing her cry of rape?

Was there a concerted effort by overzealous prosecutors to conceal critical evidence from the jury? Did the conservative, midwestern jury convict Tyson based more on guesswork than the actual evidence in the case? Would Tyson's famed appellate attorney Alan Dershowitz's personal attacks on Desiree Washington, and his scathing remarks concerning the Indiana court system prevent Tyson from gaining a reversal of the conviction?

In fact, did the entire criminal justice system fall short in providing Mike Tyson with a fair trial, and a chance to clear his name on appeal?

These questions and more loom large as one begins to try to understand the fateful circumstances that led to the shocking rape conviction and imprisonment of the 25-year-old Tyson, who rose from the slums of Brooklyn to earn the coveted title of heavyweight champion of the world. Examination of the Tyson trial and appellate records, and expert legal analysis of the trial proceedings show many striking similarities—and as many crucial differences—between the Tyson trial and the four other cases.

In the end, there is much to learn from Tyson's trial and conviction. When placed in perspective with the mood of the country toward blacks and celebrities in general, and with the specific facts and circumstances that separate Tyson's case from the other events, it is not at all surprising that only Mike Tyson went "Down for the Count."

PROLOGUE

◆

It was 1:15 p.m. on Monday, the tenth day of February 1992. Seated around a rectangular table were 12 strangers who had been brought together for only one purpose: to decide for the world whether 25-year-old Michael Gerard Tyson, once the heavyweight boxing champion of the world, was guilty of raping 18-year-old Miss Black America beauty contestant Desiree Washington on July 19, 1991.

Included on the jury were eight men and four women, 10 whites and two blacks. Among them were Ken, a black behavioral specialist who later would say "the case was rigged"; Michael, a computer services expert who became known as "Kentucky Lucky" when he was crowned the jury pool champion; and Steve, an auto parts manager who had stunned Judge Patricia Gifford and the rest of the courtroom by bravely raising his hand to get permission to go to the bathroom right in the middle of big-time defense attorney Vincent Fuller's final argument to the jury.

Strangers 17 days before, the 12 now had more than one common bond that had brought them closer together. All had survived a terrible fire at their hotel on the fifth day of the trial that killed two firefighters and a businessman.

While the 12 had agreed with one juror's statement that Mike Tyson was to be judged as if his name was Smith or Jones, all of them knew that the world was watching their verdict with great anticipation. Would Mike Tyson walk out of court a free man, or have the words "convicted rapist" associated with his name for the rest of his life?

As the 12 assembled to begin their deliberations, the first order of business was to elect a foreman. Closely gathered around the table in the small, cream-colored, sparsely furnished jury room located adjacent to Judge Patricia Gifford's courtroom, the jurors voted as most courtroom observers had predicted. Tim, the note-taking IBM salesman who had taken it upon himself to pass out breath mints to fellow jurors during the trial, would be their leader. This was in spite of the fact that one juror had labeled the ex-Marine to be "much more conservative than the rest of us, more straight, a real redneck."

The members of the jury then turned their attention toward what procedures they would use to evaluate the testimony of forty-five witnesses and the significance of more than 100 exhibits that had been presented at trial. To some jurors' surprise, however, the group seemed less interested in tackling the evidence than in learning each other's current opinion about whether Tyson was guilty or not guilty.

Therefore, less than 15 minutes into the deliberation process, and before there was any discussion of the evidence presented at trial, a first vote was taken. Small slips of notebook paper were distributed to each juror, who wrote guilty or not guilty on the paper. The slips of paper were neatly folded up, and placed in a bowl in front of the jury foreman.

Foreman Tim then drew the slips from the bowl one at a time, and spread them out neatly on the table for the jurors to see. All eyes focused on the papers, and there was a profound sense of suspense as the jurors awaited the results of this first vote. Six members of the jury had voted to find Tyson guilty, and six had voted to find him not guilty. Less than nine hours later, these twelve would become one when the final vote was taken, and that verdict would be guilty on all three of the counts against Tyson.

When the jury foreman informed the judge that they had reached a verdict, court personnel began to contact the various participants in the trial. Word spread quickly and the courtroom began to fill up. At 10:29 p.m., Mike Tyson came into the courtroom, flanked by Don King and by his bodyguard and confidant, John Horne. No defense lawyers were present. Now deadly serious, Tyson made his way to the counsel table and sat there alone like a mortally wounded animal. That picture of Tyson all alone would become etched in everyone's memory. It was a sad moment.

At 10:35, first local counsel Jim Voyles and then Tyson's chief counsel, Vincent Fuller, and the other lawyers marched in. Prosecutors Greg Garrison and Barb Trathen were already seated, and finally Judge Patricia Gifford entered the courtroom.

Judge Gifford began, "State of Indiana v. Michael Tyson. Show State by Greg Garrison and Barb Trathen. Defense by Vincent Fuller, Kathleen Beggs, Lane Heard, and James Voyles. I understand the jury has reached a verdict. State ready? Defense ready? All right, bring in the jury."

Four minutes later, the first juror entered the courtroom. From the expressions on all 12 faces, there was no doubt of the decision: all of the 12 were stone faced, and none looked at Tyson.

When the jurors were seated, the judge asked whether a verdict had been reached. Juror #9, Tim, rose from his seat in the back row and announced, "Yes, we have." He then handed the three verdict forms to the bailiff.

Judge Gifford took the forms and looked at them one by one. Then, at 10:46 p.m., she looked straight ahead and read the forms slowly.

As to count I, we the jury find the defendant Michael Tyson guilty.

As to count II, we the jury find the defendant Michael Tyson guilty.

As to count III, we the jury find the defendant Michael Tyson guilty.

1

◆

GUILTY

When Mike Tyson first heard the word "guilty" spoken by Judge Patricia Gifford, his head cocked to the side as if he had been hit with a thunderous right cross. He whispered "Oh, man," and slumped down in his seat.

Most trial observers who had watched the events that transpired between the day when Tyson was suspected of rape through the final arguments by the prosecution and defense to the jury, had no doubt that a guilty verdict was to be expected. Despite only minimal evidence to prove him guilty, Mike Tyson would fall victim to those who failed to act in his best interest, and become tangled in a web of bad decisions, miscalculations, and an ill-conceived trial strategy that would ultimately land him in prison.

Anyone familiar with the trial process knows that cases are won and lost, not based solely on the evidence, but also on many critical peripheral factors that influence the jury. Similar to the election process, trial strategies are planned with only one purpose in mind: to influence each juror toward the desired point of view.

In most cases, and certainly in this one, actual evidence becomes merely a bit player in the theatrical drama that is presented in the courtroom. For the duration of a trial, the judge, the attorneys, the accused, the accusers, and even the jurors become actors on a stage where a defendant's very freedom hangs in the balance.

In the Mike Tyson case, both the Marion County prosecutor, Jeffrey Modisett, and Tyson's manager, Don King, were faced with difficult decisions to make as a result of rape charges. Both Modisett, representing Desiree Washington, and King, representing Tyson, would implement complicated game plans for their champions. Those game plans would involve the selection of the players for the trial, the makeup of the prosecution and defense teams, and the strategies to be employed.

Both Modisett, a first-term prosecutor in Marion County, Indiana, and King, the flamboyant, controversial, ex-convict (King was found guilty of manslaughter in the beating death of a man; he was later pardoned) who ruled Tyson's life, knew very well what was ultimately at stake.

For Modisett, the dubious challenge of prosecuting one of the most famous black men in the world was not one that he looked particularly forward to. When he first heard of Washington's allegations of rape against Tyson, Modisett called his political advisers together to discuss the many pros and cons of the case. On the one hand, prosecuting Tyson would certainly propel Modisett's name into the national limelight and provide him with more high-profile publicity than he could ever have imagined possible.

An unlikely politician to begin with, after a narrow victory in his race for prosecutor against Republican Drew Young, the Democratic Modisett now had higher ambitions on his mind, just as his predecessor, Stephen Goldsmith, had before he became mayor of Indianapolis. While the potential for a boost to Modisett's political career certainly existed if he could topple the ex-champ, there were several obvious downsides to the case as well.

Tyson was in fact a very popular man, especially in the black community. In spite of his disastrous performance in Tokyo, which resulted in the loss of his heavyweight crown to bumbling Buster Douglas, Tyson's stock was on the rise again, and he was scheduled for a $30-million bout with heavyweight champion Evander Holyfield.

To the black community that Modisett courted politically, Tyson was one of a very few bonafide black heroes. His break from the ghettos of Brooklyn was well documented, and Tyson was a huge favorite with the media. Wherever he went, Tyson was front page news, and Don King made sure that his precious breadwinner was ready and willing to appease the press. Successful prosecution of "date rape" cases was tough enough, but an attempt to lock up Tyson would indeed be formidable.

To successfully prosecute the case, Modisett knew he would have to gun down a heavyweight team of defense lawyers who would be the best that money could buy. Tyson was estimated to be worth between $80 and $100 million, and Modisett believed King would provide the boxer with first-rate representation.

At the meetings Modisett held prior to filing charges against Tyson, discussions centered on the overall political effect that the Tyson trial, if there was to be one, would have on Modisett's political career. Even though Washington's case against Tyson was initially considered to be a weak one, in the end the actual strength or weakness of the case was secondary to this main issue.

In the end, however, Modisett found the perfect politician's answer to his dilemma as to whether or not to prosecute Tyson. After all the viewpoints of his various political advisers were taken into consideration, he decided he would send the case to a special Marion County Grand Jury under Indiana Code Section 35-34-2-14 for consideration. By doing so, Modisett figured he couldn't lose. If the six members of the Marion County Grand Jury decided to charge Tyson with rape, so be it. And if they didn't, so much the better, since privately Modisett was telling his advisers that he would just as soon see the case go away.

The special grand jury was appointed on August 13, 1991. Delighted with his decision, Modisett then assigned Deputy Prosecutor David Dreyer to handle the presentation of the evidence. Desiree Washington was told of the decision, and Dreyer began to prepare for a hearing before the grand jury.

In fact, Modisett and Dreyer might very well have been free of the burden of Tyson's case had it not been for an incredible piece of luck that ironically came their way from the nationally famous lawyer that King would choose for Tyson.

To Don King, the charges against Mike Tyson were just another in a long series of scrapes with the law that threatened the ex-champ's career. In spite of attempts to segregate Tyson from any potential disaster that would end his boxing career, King knew of Tyson's personality and unpredictable mood swings that made him a gentle soul one moment and violent the next.

These mood swings, King believed, were a direct result of Tyson's early years in the Brownsville section of Brooklyn. An early-age product of a broken home, Tyson was headed straight to hell until a gentle man named Bobby Stewart at the Tryon School for Boys took a liking, not only to the young Tyson, but to his potential boxing prowess as well. When Stewart introduced Tyson to the legendary boxing trainer Cus D'Amato, who had squired Floyd Patterson and Jose Torres, Tyson was saved from a life that would have surely ended in prison, if not in an early violent death.

When Tyson's talent took him to the upper echelon of the boxing world, King decided to try to steal the young champion away from his managers, Bill Cayton and Jim Jacobs. King's efforts to get his hands on Tyson were finally successful, and the King/Tyson era began.

When King first informed "Iron Mike" of the potential rape charges against him, Tyson sluffed them off with disinterest. King, however, a veteran of such skirmishes, realized the danger that might lie ahead. He knew   that this was not New York, or L.A., or any other "liberal" city where Tyson was to be charged. Long-time relationships with members of Indianapolis's black community told King that Tyson would be judged in an 80 percent white, ultra-conservative, Dan Quayle-type city where the Ku Klux Klan had deep roots. While King was confident the rape charges by Washington were just another attempt by a scorned woman to get a piece of Tyson's millions, he still recognized that his client needed the advice of a highly skilled legal defense professional who could run those hon-yocker Indiana prosecutors out the door. Money, of course, would be no object.

King, like Modisett, realized the high-stakes game to be played. If Tyson was convicted, he would not only go to prison, but his million-dollar boxing career would in all likelihood be over, and King would lose his only sure breadwinner and a large cut of those potential millions as well.

With millions to utilize in Tyson's defense, King began to evaluate the atmosphere Tyson might head into if in fact the case were to go to trial in Indianapolis. Unlike Palm Beach, where a white defendant would go on trial based on charges by a white woman in a nearly all-white city; or Simi Valley, where white policemen would be tried on charges that they savagely beat a black motorist in Los Angeles, right in the middle of an ultra-conservative, white county; or in Brooklyn, where a black youth would be on trial for killing a Jewish youth in a mixed-minority neighborhood; Tyson was to be tried in a conservative city with blacks comprising only one-fifth of its population.

King apparently considered retaining a black attorney to represent Tyson, and also contacted famed Los Angeles lawyer Howard Weitzman, who had successfully represented such well-known clients as John DeLorean and Magic Johnson. Fitting the lawyer to the atmosphere of the city where Tyson was to be tried was a difficult decision for King, who knew that even the black community was split down the middle as to Tyson's guilt.

The family advisers to William Kennedy Smith went through a similar process in the selection of the attorney to defend him. Also with unlimited millions at their disposal, the advisers carefully considered the list of the most famous lawyers in the country before their final selection of Miami lawyer Roy Black. Apparently every well-known attorney from F. Lee Bailey to Gerry Spence to Weitzman was considered, but in the end the Kennedy Smith family advisers chose someone who was well known in the area.

Unlike Vincent Fuller, who would be Don King's choice, the 46-year-old Black had extensive county court trial experience. Considered a rising star in Florida's legal defense community, Black was regarded by his peers to be a studious, personable, and imaginative trial attorney who knew how to play up to the jury. Lawyers who knew him told reporters that Black was a master at cross-examination, and highly skilled at dealing with sex crimes—cases in which the outcome often depends on the cross-examination of the accuser.

Both in the Rodney King state case and in the Bensonhurst trial, defense lawyers were also chosen who fit both the racial makeup of the city and the facts of the case. In the Rodney King case, the four policemen all chose white attorneys with conservative appearances to defend them, and Lemrick Nelson's family selected black attorney Arthur Lewis, to handle his defense.

In the final analysis, however, the selection of an attorney to represent Tyson ended up to not be a difficult one for King. Fiercely loyal to those who had befriended him in the past, King picked up the phone and called the prestigious offices of Williams and Connolly in Washington D.C. When 61-year-old Vincent J. Fuller, lawyer extraordinaire, came on the phone, King knew he was talking with not only a man he could trust, but also a prestigious lawyer who would be the perfect warrior to save Tyson from the arm of the law.

King had complete confidence in Fuller's ability because Fuller had freed King from the arm of the law as well. When the IRS charged King with tax evasion in 1984, King brought Fuller into the case to save him from prison. In a Philadelphia federal courtroom, King had watched Fuller's brilliance at work. Without ever putting King on the stand, Fuller had won a swift acquittal on all charges.

What was good enough for King would be right for the ex-champ as well, King reasoned. Little did he know that this decision to hire Fuller and his band of big-time Washington barristers, would be the first, and perhaps most significant, step that would ultimately lead Mike Tyson straight to prison in March 1992.

Unlike federal trials, which are held under more formal circumstances utilizing stricter Federal Rules Of Procedure, state cases involving rape and other felonies are held in "down and dirty" county criminal courts. While Fuller had extensive experience in federal court, he had little in the county court system, where King knew Tyson would be tried.

The term "down and dirty" evolved due to the nature of the county court system, which besides being overcrowded and thus gridlocked beyond hope, parades its accused through the revolving doors like cattle headed for slaughter. Some county court systems are worse than others, but as many as 75 to 100 cases can be handled each day in each court.

Most county courts involve a "good ol' boy" network, which means that since the same lawyers normally practice in the same courts before the same judges day after day, everyone knows everyone else on a first-name basis. Thus, judges are more inclined to give a break here or there to the lawyers they know, or to look the other way if a court rule is violated.

Nowhere is this more true than in the six-county criminal courts that operate in Indianapolis, where a handful of experienced trial attorneys ply their trade. If someone wants to obtain the services of one of these "connected" lawyers, they will do so

through either the public defender system, which is very political, since the judges usually appoint political cronies or party
favorites to serve as public defenders, or by hiring (at a substantial fee) well-respected defense attorneys such as Jim Voyles,
Owen Mullin, Rick Kammen, Robert Hammerle, Arnold Baratz,
or Voyles's partner, Denny Zahn.

The six criminal courts in Marion County that share the
heavy felony caseload are manned by six judges who do their
best to move the cases through the system as quickly as possible.
When the distinguished Judge John Tranberg in criminal court
#1 retired, Judge Patricia Gifford became the most sought-after
judge by most of the well-known defense lawyers. This was in
spite of her background as a prosecutor, for most realized that, of
the six judges available, Gifford at least kept up on case law, and
for the most part would give them a fair shot during a jury trial.

In turn, with both a personal and professional acquaintance of the skills of many of these attorneys, Gifford knew what
to expect when they practiced in her court. Their familiarity with
the judge, her rules, and how far she would allow them to drift
from those rules was always an important part of their strategy.

In these "down and dirty" county criminal courts, the
attorneys "work their cases" from the moment they are hired.
Utilizing their familiarity with the court procedures, and their
personal relationships with the important court personnel (clerk,
bailiff, court reporter, court deputies, etc.), they will attempt to
position their cases in the most advantageous manner, not only
to protect the rights of their client, but to achieve the ultimate goal
of gaining a dismissal of the charges, or an acquittal.

The first rule of thumb for any decent defense lawyer is
to stall the case as long as possible before actually having to go
to trial or plead the case out. Besides allowing sufficient time for
payment (known in legal circles as the "rule in Shelley's case"),
a crafty lawyer knows that delay after delay can only be to his or
her advantage. Witnesses may die or disappear; the victims may
change their minds or move away; people's memories suffer
with time; and the prosecutor's office may be more inclined to
offer a better plea bargain on an older case than on a new one
whose gory facts are still fresh in everyone's minds.

County criminal court lawyers are obviously a different
breed than those fancy, three-piece-suit lawyers who practice

only in federal courts. More known as "seat of your pants" attorneys, because of their ability to be imaginative or change directions and always land on their feet, these theatrical county lawyers also pride themselves on being able to "read" a jury. This ability comes from years of being a trial lawyer, for— unlike a federal court lawyer, who may try two cases a year— the county criminal court lawyer may very well try two cases in one week.

Owen Mullin, long the kingpin of Marion County Court defense attorneys, wrote the book on how to manipulate a case through these courts. Mullin was especially imaginative and innovative in dealing with county court juries, and always espoused the theory that the jury made its decision based as much on their like or dislike for the defendant's attorney as on the defendant him- or herself. Mullin thus advocated the "we" theory: A defense lawyer must personalize even the most repulsive defendant by speaking to the jury as if the two are a team.

Mullin always made certain that he knew the names of all of the jurors, and when he began his final arguments, he always went down the line and addressed each juror as if they were longtime friends. He also knew that it took only one of those jurors to save his client, and so he would tailor his last words toward the particular juror whom he felt was most sympathetic to his position.

In addition, Mullin—a great strategist—believed it imperative that he get the jurors to think about everything *but* the evidence. The old warrior also realized that he must provide the jury with a good, believable reason for acquitting the accused since they would need one when family and friends asked them why they had voted not guilty.

This type of experience, and the knowledge of the workings of the county criminal courts that goes with it, are the tools of the trade for any competent criminal defense lawyer. In a case where a famous celebrity would be on trial, Don King must have known, from his own days at odds with the law in the Cleveland, Ohio county courts, that Tyson would require someone who could lock horns with a local judge who was more inclined to believe the prosecution's line of thinking. Moreover, if he was to choose an "outsider," King must have realized the necessity of making certain that the "outsider" would work hand in hand with a local lawyer so as to take advantage of that attorney's understanding of the workings of the local courts.

Whether King ever considered these factors in the choice of Vincent Fuller is unknown, but when decision time came, Tyson's promoter and protector chose a lawyer who had little or no county courtroom experience, had little or no sex crimes defense experience, and would end up shoving his local counsel to the sidelines like a bad-hands wide receiver.

In spite of being nationally known as a white-collar crime, silk-hat-type attorney, Vincent Fuller apparently decided that rape charges in a state courtroom were no different than tax evasion charges in a federal courtroom, and so he was quick to accept the case. Flanked by partner Kathleen Beggs and associate Lane Heard (neither of whom had any county courtroom or sex crimes experience), Fuller began to plan step one in the defense of his new, famous client, Mike Tyson. He would reportedly charge $500 an hour plus unlimited expenses for his work, with the final bill totaling nearly a million dollars.

When Prosecutor Modisett learned of Fuller's potential appearance in the case along with Voyles, a shock wave went through the sixth floor offices at the City-County Building in downtown Indianapolis. Some in Modisett's office thought that the first-term prosecutor might buckle under to the pressure of having someone as prestigious as Fuller in the case, but in the end, Modisett stood fast in his belief that the case should be heard before the Marion County Grand Jury.

The more Deputy Prosecutor David Dreyer learned about the case, the more he felt that the chances for an indictment were at best 50-50. Charged with convincing five out of the six jurors that there was enough evidence to indict Tyson, Dreyer prepared his case carefully, based on the testimony of Washington and of Virginia Foster, the black driver of the limousine that transported Tyson and Washington from the Omni Hotel to the Canterbury Hotel where the alleged rape occurred. Medical testimony and other corroboration for Washington's story would be presented as well, but for the most part Dreyer knew that the believability of Washington would be the telling issue that would either trigger the grand jury to charge or not charge Tyson.

Within three weeks of the hearing, the prosecutor's office received the surprise of their lives. Fuller's office informed them that Tyson, who of course did not have to testify because of his right against self-incrimination, would do so voluntarily. More than that, the ex-champ would appear even though no immunity would be given Tyson so that if he was indicted, any statements could be used against him.

Modisett and Dreyer could hardly believe the good luck that had come their way. First, Tyson, who had a history of awkward, often dismal appearances in courtroom proceedings, would now tell his side of the story, allowing the State to hear Tyson's account of the encounter with Washington. Tyson would, of course, be subject to cross-examination, and the state would see firsthand what type of witness he would make if a trial were held.

Vincent Fuller, of course, must have known of the risks involved with permitting Tyson to testify in his own behalf. Unlike defense lawyer Roy Black, who never allowed William Kennedy Smith to say one word about the alleged rape incident before he testified, Fuller apparently felt that he and Tyson and King could go into the grand jury and knock out the State's case with one blow. Against the advice of his Indianapolis local counsel, James Voyles, Fuller readied his client for an orchestrated media event purported to put an end to Tyson's problems with Desiree Washington once and for all.

On August 18, 1991, Tyson testified before the grand jury. On August 19, 1991, the grand jury voted to indict Tyson on one count of rape, two counts of criminal deviate conduct, and one count of confinement. If convicted, the ex-champ faced up to 64 years in prison.

2

♦

TRIALS AND TRIBULATIONS

Even though the Clarence Thomas Supreme Court confirmation hearing and the William Kennedy Smith rape trial were held well before the Mike Tyson trial, both cases may have had a profound effect on the eventual outcome of the Tyson trial.

Most people had never heard of Clarence Thomas or Anita Hill prior to the hearings, but the strong accusations by Hill and the equally strong denials by Thomas would make world headlines during the week of October 6, 1991. Held in front of an all-white "jury" of United States senators in Washington, D.C., the two black combatants squared off in an action-packed Senate chamber before a mesmerized international television audience who chose sides in defense of his or her champion.

Supposedly at issue in the hearings was the question of the overall fitness on the part of Judge Thomas to serve on the United States Supreme Court. However, the allegations of sexual harassment by the quiet law professor from the University of Oklahoma propelled the hearings to national prominence when Hill accused Thomas of harassment in the form of uninvited and unwelcomed sex-related conversations with her while she was employed at the U.S. Department of Education.

While there was no actual judge or jury sitting in judgment of Thomas's guilt or innocence, in the end the senators (and the viewing audience) would express their opinions as to whether

Thomas or Hill was the more believable. Likewise there were (perhaps unfortunately) no prosecution or defense teams to face off in the hearing, and thus it was merely the senators who questioned Thomas and Hill.

Whether racial motives entered into the proceedings is pure conjecture, but the spectacle of seeing a black woman accuse a black man of sexual harassment in front of an all-white group of senators was indeed a peculiar scene. No real rules of evidence, as in a court of law, were utilized, and such factors as motive and reputation were admitted, eventually affecting the believability of both Thomas and Hill.

When the Senate panel finally brought in its "verdict," Clarence Thomas's believability would win out, whether based on politics or on the actual evidence brought forth. Later the full Senate would confirm his nomination. Anita Hill would return to her post at the University of Oklahoma, having made an incredibly important impact, not only on the right of a woman to speak up about sexual harassment, but on the future of women in American politics as well.

Just two months later, on December 3, 1991, a jury would be picked in West Palm Beach, Florida, to decide the guilt or innocence of William Kennedy Smith, the son of Jean Kennedy Smith and the nephew of John, Robert, and Edward Kennedy.

Before Dade County Circuit Court Judge Mary Lupo, Smith answered charges that he raped a Palm Beach woman, Patty Bowman, at the Kennedy estate in the early morning hours of March 30, 1990. While the trial would be televised, Ms. Bowman would keep her identity a secret until after the trial.

The lawyer faceoff in this case was indeed a classic one, as tough-minded Moira Lasch took on the wealthy, theatrical, and intellectual defender of the privileged, defense lawyer Roy Black. From the outset, the two advocates locked horns time and time again as they sought to gain the upper hand prior to the trial— which would involve virtually no minorities in any role.

During the eight days of trial, the momentum seemed to swing back and forth, especially following the emotional testimony by Bowman when she described Smith's rape of her on the sand down in front of the estate. Smith also would electrify the courtroom with his vivid account of the incident. Whether it was the brilliance of Black, the sub-par performance of Lasch, or perhaps the overall weakness of the case itself, the jurors swiftly acquitted Kennedy Smith (after deliberating only 77 minutes) of all charges on December 11, 1992.

With these two events as a backdrop, the Mike Tyson trial began on January 27, 1992, just 47 days after the Kennedy Smith verdict. Speculation arose as to what effect the not-guilty verdicts for Clarence Thomas and William Kennedy Smith would have on the Tyson case. One allegation of sexual harassment by a black woman against a black man and one rape charge by a white woman against a white man had been heard and discounted. Now, a jury in the Midwestern city of Indianapolis, Indiana, would sit in judgment of the charge of rape by a black woman against one of the most famous black men in the world, former heavyweight boxing champion of the world Mike Tyson.

Following the Tyson trial, two other explosive cases would be heard by juries, one in Simi Valley, California, and another in Brooklyn, New York. Although neither of the cases involved sexual harassment or rape charges, the two cases would provide interesting comparisons with the Thomas/Hill hearing, the Kennedy Smith case, and the Tyson trial.

In the early months of 1991, millions of television viewers all over the world watched in shock as an 82-second videotape was played over and over on television. Shot by amateur photographer George Holiday, that tape shows a black motorist, Rodney King, being repeatedly beaten about the body with fists and nightsticks by several members of the Los Angeles Police Department. Public outcries over the beating came from President Bush and fellow law enforcement officers as well as from civil rights leaders who deplored the actions of the police.

With convictions of the four police officers charged practically a foregone conclusion, the trial began on March 5, 1992, in Simi Valley, California, a very conservative city 75 miles north of Los Angeles. Before Judge Stanley M. Weisberg, black prosecutor Terry White faced four white defense lawyers who argued to the six-men, six-women jury (ten whites, a Latina and an Asian-American) that their respective clients were justified in using the necessary force to take the delirious King into custody.

After 29 days of trial, the world was astonished when all four officers were acquitted of all charges, and set free. Public reaction was quick and forceful, with deadly riots taking place not only in the streets of Los Angeles, but also in Minneapolis, Chicago, and other major cities in the country. Federal civil rights charges against the policemen were filed within days after the verdict, but that action could not quell the deep distrust for the legal system in the black community.

In Brooklyn, there was another highly explosive case awaiting trial before Jewish Judge Edward Rappaport. Rioting following the tragic death from an auto accident of seven-year-old Gavin Cato by a Hasidic Jew led to the brutal cold-blooded murder on August 11, 1991 of Yankel Rosenbaum in the streets of Crown Heights. Even though bloody money and a bloody knife had been found on his person, and he had allegedly confessed after being positively identified by Rosenbaum prior to his death, 17-year-old Lemrick Nelson's conviction was not assured. Differing versions of what occurred by the policemen assigned to the case in effect put the police on trial, even though the evidence was overwhelming against Nelson, unlike that in the Tyson case.

In late October, black defense lawyer Arthur Lewis was able to convince the largely black jury that his client should be acquitted. Jurors later said that they did not believe the police account of the incident. Nelson's acquittal sparked outrage in the Jewish community, where more than 700 angry Hasidic Jews poured into the streets of Crown Heights in protest of the verdict.

Headline-making charges of sexual harassment, two allegations of rape, an unprovoked attack on a defenseless motorist, and a vicious cold-blooded murder, all in less than a year. Media from around the world would capture all of the sordid details for everyone to see, but none more so than the around-the-clock, circus sideshow presentation of the Mike Tyson trial.

3

◆

THE GAME
IS ON

Now that Mike Tyson had been indicted by the grand jury, Prosecutor Jeffrey Modisett and Tyson promoter and confidant Don King again made certain critical decisions that would greatly affect the outcome of the case.

Under normal circumstances, the Tyson matter would have been presented to the regularly selected Marion County Grand Jury. Due to its high-profile status, however, and other more important factors, Modisett had chosen to utilize his power by convening a special grand jury to consider the case.

That decision had not been made without careful consideration by the prosecutor. In Marion County, a case can come before one of the six judges in three ways. Felony charges that come through the municipal court system without the need for an indictment are distributed among the judges on a rotating basis, 50 at a time. If the felony charge requires an indictment, it is then heard before the grand jury. If the indictment is returned, the case is then assigned to the presiding judge for that term as one of the 50 cases.

The third way a case can come before a specific judge occurs if the prosecutor convenes a special grand jury to be presided over by the selected judge. Thus, when Modisett convened the special grand jury and selected Judge Patricia Gifford to oversee it, he guaranteed that she would ultimately hear Tyson's case.

Incredible good fortune shown down on Modisett in this situation, since the judge who was presiding over the "batch" of cases for that term was also none other than Judge Patricia Gifford.

Counsel for the defense would later argue on appeal that the prosecutor had in effect gone "judge-shopping" by convening a grand jury that would be presided over by Gifford. While purposely sidestepping a direct accusation that Gifford had any personal prejudices in the case, Tyson's appellate counsel would allege that the judge was not randomly selected as prescribed by law. Unfortunately, random selection would not have made any difference in Tyson's case, due to the fact that Gifford was the presiding judge over the current batch of 50 cases, and would have been the trial judge whether a special grand jury was called or not.

The defense's concern over having Gifford preside at Tyson's trial was well-founded. While the judge did enjoy a reputation among her peers for fairness and unquestionable judicial ethics, it was no secret that Gifford was also very prosecution friendly, especially when it came to rape cases. Indeed, Patricia Gifford's background made her a very controversial judge in the Mike Tyson rape trial.

The 54-year-old Gifford was born in Indianapolis, the daughter of an Army colonel. Gifford graduated from high school in Athens, Georgia, and then attended the College of William and Mary. Once graduated, she taught school in Indianapolis, and then moved to West Germany where she was a teacher at Army Dependent Schools.

Apparently unsatisfied with teaching, Gifford then opted for law school at the Indiana University School of Law in Indianapolis, continuing the line of lawyers in the family that included her grandfather and an uncle. Upon graduation, she spent several years in the Marion County prosecutor's office where she was a specialist in rape cases. Her first courtroom skirmish was against famed lawyer F. Lee Bailey, whom she soundly defeated.

Gifford is given credit for initiating the legislation that culminated in the passage of a strict rape shield law, which broadly prohibits the introduction of evidence relating to a rape victim's sexual history. The purpose of the Act is to recognize that the accused and not the accuser is on trial, and to encourage alleged victims of rape to come forward and not fear humiliation from defense attorneys' questions regarding their sexual conduct. Questions relating to victims' sexual pasts are therefore prohibited so a jury will not be prejudiced against the victim due to allegations regarding her moral character or lack thereof. While the rape shield law has for the most part been effective, many defense attorneys believe that it allows prosecutors to present the victim as a holier-than-thou witness, when just the opposite may be the case.

After her days as a prosecutor, Patricia Gifford first ran for judge as a Republican in 1978. Mother of one college-age daughter, she and her husband, Bob, an aspiring actor, have for the most part kept a low profile during her term in office, although Gifford has never been afraid to speak her opinion when an important issue comes to the forefront.

Known as a judge who exercises strict control over her courtroom, the judge's tough demeanor hides a soft-spoken, friendly woman who says she believes in the rights of the underdog. Despite her white hair and somewhat icy appearance, Gifford can be jovial and even funny at times when trying to put an uncomfortable witness or young attorney at ease.

When asked after the Tyson trial why she wanted to be a judge, Gifford told *Indianapolis Monthly* Magazine ,"I think I have the ability to weigh both sides and make a determination. I have compassion for people, and I can weigh those things that affect them. I also can have the compassion for the victims and yet not let it influence me beyond what the law says should be done."

Gifford's sentencing record prior to the Tyson trial indicated that she had been extremely tough with convicted rapists when excessive violence or a weapon were used. However, in situations comparable with Tyson's, where no weapon was involved, the judge's record of average seven-year prison sentences was in fact below the 12-year average for all of the criminal courts.

It is not clear whether Gifford ever considered not accepting the Tyson case due to her background. But when she finally did agree to try the Tyson case, she leaned on the experience gained by her counterpart in the William Kennedy Smith case, Circuit Judge Mary Lupo. Known as a strict disciplinarian, the 43-year-old Lupo had built up a reputation as a stern judge who, like Gifford, exercised complete control over her courtroom.

To an outsider, Lupo sometimes gave the appearance of being unsure of herself on the bench, but those who practiced in her court knew that she was a no-nonsense judge. Unlike Gifford, who was felt to favor the prosecution, Lupo had a reputation for being equally fair to both the prosecution and the defense. As a result, neither the family advisers for Kennedy Smith nor State's Attorney David Bludworth needed to base their choice of trial attorney on this factor. Similar situations existed both in the Rodney King case, where Superior Court Judge Stanley Weisberg was known to be impartial, and in the Bensonhurst case, where Judge Edward Rappaport had a reputation for fairness to both sides.

Such consideration can be vital to the success of either the defense or the prosecution. Depending on the issues, the inclinations of the judge can be as important as any other factors that would decide the outcome. Some judges are known more for their kindly manner than their judicial prowess, and the attorneys must anticipate the attitudes of a judge toward different situations or legal challenges before even the pretrial hearings.

In the William Kennedy Smith case, for instance, one of the main pretrial matters to be decided involved whether other alleged instances of sexual assault or attempted rape by Smith would be allowed to be presented at trial. Admissibility of an alleged confession by Lemrick Nelson in the Bensonhurst case was a pretrial issue for Judge Rappaport, and in the Rodney King case, the judge was asked to rule on whether allegations of assault or battery by the police officers charged with beating King could be introduced at trial.

The decisions handed down by the court concerning the critical pretrial motions often dictate the eventual outcome of the trial. In fact, when Judge Lupo ruled against the prosecution, and decided that similar sexual allegations against Kennedy Smith could not be introduced at trial, many legal experts believed that the State's case was doomed to failure.

Jeff Modisett knew that Judge Patricia Gifford was, for the prosecution, the perfect person to try Mike Tyson. In fact, Modisett's chances to gain a conviction of the ex-champ were enhanced, not only by Fuller's unwise decision to put Tyson in front of the grand jury, but also by the fact that with Gifford at the helm, Modisett would have an ally in blocking the defense's strategy. In fact, during the trial, legal experts believed that the former prosecutor-turned-Judge would time and time again allow the defense small, frequently insignificant victories while giving the prosecution the major ones. With the knowledge that Gifford would be firmly in control, Modisett now needed to turn his attention elsewhere.

The strategy of the prosecutor's case in chief was, in reality, a simple one. Desiree Washington's testimony, along with corroborating evidence from limousine driver Virginia Foster and certain medical testimony, had convinced the grand jury to indict Tyson. While he knew that convincing 12 jurors of Tyson's guilt would be much more difficult, in light of the anticipated defense effort to in effect put Washington and her motives on trial, Modisett was comfortable with his case and the chances to gain a conviction that might have a positive effect on his political aspirations.

Even though he questioned the famed Fuller's risky decision to send Tyson in front of the grand jury, Modisett knew from sources on the East Coast that Fuller would indeed be a formidable trial lawyer. Discussions were again held with members of Modisett's political advisory group about the various trial lawyers available to prosecute Mike Tyson.

Modisett was faced with a somewhat similar dilemma as that faced by Florida State's Attorney David Bludworth in the Kennedy Smith case. There, Bludworth was forced to make a decision whether to prosecute a member of one of the most famous families in the world. Like Modisett, Bludworth needed to show that, even though Kennedy Smith was a famous person just like Tyson, he would receive no favorable treatment.

Unfortunately for Bludworth, his office seemed to relish the thought of a showdown with Kennedy Smith, and therefore heightened expectations of a conviction. Bludworth purposely chose an experienced sex crimes female lawyer, 40-year-old Moira Lasch, to lead the prosecution team. A career prosecutor, Lasch headed up the felony division of the Palm Beach Prosecutor's Office, gaining a reputation as its number-one trial lawyer.

Bludworth also chose Lasch because he did not want the political risk of trying the case himself. Facing re-election, Bludworth knew from his political advisers that, while it was important that he be perceived as carrying out the duties of his office by prosecuting Kennedy Smith, he also needed to distance himself from the case in the event of a disastrous outcome.

Such was also the situation faced by Los Angeles District Attorney Ira Reiner in the Rodney King state case. When deciding who to name as chief prosecutor, Reiner faced the same sort of political questions that faced both Modisett and Bludworth. On the one hand, Reiner knew that most people perceived the case as a "slam-dunk" one, with the eventual outcome already decided due to the explosive videotape of the beating.

Beneath the surface, however, Reiner realized that, while the black community and millions of Americans were calling for justice, the Los Angeles Police Department and its officers would be watching the case closely as well. Faced with trying to please everyone, Reiner chose veteran black prosecutor Terry White to handle the case, believing that both his experience and his race would stifle perceptions that he would not pursue the case to the fullest extent of the law.

In the Tyson case, Modisett immediately discarded himself as an option, based both on his lack of experience as a trial lawyer and on the continued feeling on his part and those he trusted that the Tyson case was a very delicate political matter. The most obvious choices to try the Tyson case were David Dreyer, his chief deputy; Mark Jones, a skillful trial lawyer on staff; and Carol Orbison, a sex crimes prosecution expert who had a very impressive conviction rate.

As the decision deadline drew nearer, however, Modisett's attention was suddenly turned in a different direction. A former deputy prosecutor, Greg Garrison, had become a "special, for-hire" prosecutor, and had gained excellent reviews across Indiana mainly for his ability to successfully prosecute big-time drug dealers. Although he was impressed with Garrison's resume and his plan to convict Tyson, Modisett knew the selection of the 44-year-old Garrison would be a controversial one. Some members of Modisett's staff would resent the pistol-packing Garrison (he normally carries a gun), and wonder why an outsider had to be brought into the case.

It was not difficult to assess what Garrison's aspirations were for taking the case. The $20,000 he would receive was certainly no great deal for him, and most colleagues knew that he was in the case solely because he hoped for fame and fortune (and ideally new work as a special prosecutor), if he could secure a conviction of the celebrity Tyson.

Despite Garrison's great abilities as a trial lawyer, Modisett also knew of the risks of having perhaps the right man for the wrong job. In a case where the only issue was to determine whether Washington was telling the truth, the prosecution would be bringing in a man with the reputation of being a loud-mouthed, bombastic, abrasive, cowboy-boot-wearing, slicked back red-haired gunslinger to prosecute a case that Modisett wanted to be low key.

More than that, the selection of Garrison would obviously give off the impression that Modisett felt he had no one in his office competent enough to handle the case. In the end, inner-office politics may have only played a small part in his decision, but his choice of Garrison appeared to indicate that he had no confidence in Mark Jones, who was the first man selected for the job, or in Carol Orbison, an expert in prosecuting sex crimes cases.

While Modisett later said that the responsibility of running the entire prosecutor's office prevented him from personally trying the case, he may have fallen into the "they have a high-powered, big-time lawyer, so we better have one, too," syndrome. However, such a decision could have been a disastrous one.

Whatever the reason, Modisett hired Garrison, and then appointed Barbara Trathen, a serious-minded deputy, to be his co-counsel. Modisett would still call the shots, but Garrison and Trathen would be his foot soldiers.

Disappointed, but not completely devastated by the grand jury setback, the Tyson defense captain, Vincent Fuller, now found it necessary to formulate his game plan for the trial of his famed client.

To be successful (and he was sure he would be to the point of overconfidence), Fuller apparently believed that the keys to the case were to: 1) show that Tyson had a reputation as a womanizer who used bad language and sexual innuendoes to alert his intended prey of his intentions; 2) prove that Desiree Washington clearly knew of Tyson's intentions; 3) persuade the jury that Washington was willing to have consensual sex with Tyson because she hoped for a long-term relationship; and 4) demonstrate that Washington filed rape charges against Tyson because he treated her like a one-night stand, and was only after his money.

In order to play out his strategy, Fuller had made it clear to local counsel James Voyles that he (Fuller) would be in charge, and that Voyles would end up doing little significant work before or at trial. In fact, Voyle's respected partner, Dennis Zahn, refused to become involved in the case due to this factor.

Fuller's decision to basically "go it alone" was made in spite of background information Voyles gave to Fuller about Gifford's prosecutorial inclinations, and the need to pursue a personal relationship with the judge so she could become comfortable with the out-of-state attorneys.

Vincent Fuller would be in charge of the case because there was no other way for him. Fuller's firm, Williams and Connolly, was the former home of famed attorney Edward Bennett Williams, who was not only known as a great lawyer and orator, but also as one of the principal owners of the Washington Redskins football team. Located on Twelfth Street in the heart of Washington, D.C., the firm had built its reputation for being experts in practice before federal courts, and with federal departments and agencies.

Vincent J. Fuller is right at the top of the list of attorneys on the Williams and Connolly stationery, and is widely known as the patriarch of the firm. He was born in Ossining, New York, on June 21, 1931, and records indicate that he was admitted to the bar of the District of Columbia and the U.S. Court of Appeals for the District of Columbia in 1956, and then in New York in 1962.

Fuller received a Bachelor of Arts from Williams College in 1952, and a law degree from Georgetown Law School in 1956. His resume lists his memberships in the District of Columbia Bar, New York State Bar, American Bar Association, American Board of Criminal Lawyers, and American College of Trial Lawyers.

Fuller is known as a practical, businesslike, highly organized lawyer. Most of his clients had been upper-income, white-collar businessmen, yet he had also carved out a different sort of reputation through his well-conceived insanity defense of John Hinkley, who was charged with shooting President Ronald Reagan.

Hinkley, who was charged with shooting President Ronald Reagan.

Fuller's constituents say that no one can organize and implement a trial strategy better than Fuller. A relentless advocate known for his booming voice, Fuller can intimidate a witness with merely his forceful presence, while carefully eliciting the critical information needed to clear his client. Unlike Roy Black or Arthur Lewis, however, Fuller had virtually no prior experience in the county court system. He also had absolutely no trial experience defending persons charged with sex crimes.

Fuller's best efforts had come during the John Hinkley trial and later on when he defended Don King and chose not to risk putting his client on the stand. The acquittal verdict in King's case amazed most observers, who truly believed that Dandy Don was headed back to prison.

Fuller's outward appearance fit his "professor" image perfectly. Always dapper in $600 conservative suits, at trial Fuller looked every bit like a scholarly, peaceful gentleman ready to give a speech on international politics. With "granny" glasses, a square jaw, and swept-back dark hair speckled with gray, Vincent Fuller's appearance contrasted sharply with that of the rugged, tough-looking Tyson.

One of Fuller's sidekicks, 41-year-old Lane Heard, was born in Houston, Texas. Heard graduated *summa cum laude* from Yale University with a Bachelor of Arts in 1973, and received his law degree, also from Yale, in 1978. He had also graduated from Cambridge University in 1972 where he was a Phi Beta Kappa. A tall, thin, unassuming man, Heard's quiet manner belied a reputation for being a master inquisitor at trial. At Fuller's side, he appeared to be a perfect complement to Tyson's chief counsel.

Perhaps the most unusual member of the team was 35-year-old, matronly Kathleen Beggs, who received a Bachelor of Arts degree from Wellesley College in 1979 and later earned her law degree from Harvard in 1982. Beggs seemed an odd choice to join Fuller and Heard. Less experienced than either of them, Beggs was apparently chosen to counteract the appointment of Barb Trathen for the defense.

Burly local counsel James Voyles was a natural choice to join the defense team. Voyles's teddy-bear appearance concealed a fierce advocate who was highly loyal to his clients.

Better known for his ability to negotiate "good deals" for those clients through successful plea-bargains than for his actual trial work, Voyles had ascended to the number-one position among defense lawyers in the state of Indiana.

Modisett, Garrison, and Trathen in one corner, with Fuller, Heard, Beggs, and Voyles in the other. Judge Patricia Gifford would referee the high stakes showdown, while Mike Tyson would merely sit and await his ultimate fate.

4

◆

PRETRIAL POSITIONING

The pretrial positioning by the prosecution and defense may have been more eventful than the trial itself. At least that was the observation of those legal experts who attended the pretrial hearing—one that was filled with back-and-forth jabs between the lawyers.

To begin with, the final pretrial hearing in the Tyson case marked the first real confrontation between Vincent Fuller and Greg Garrison. At issue were six motions:

1) Defendant's motion to exclude certain FBI evidence pertaining to the case;

2) Defendant's motion to dismiss based on error in selection system for both grand and petit jury panels;

3) Defendant's motion to supplement voter registration roles with additional list of jury panel participants;

4) State's motion to reconsider Court's ruling to exclude Dr. Eugene Kilpatrick, a rape trauma expert, from testifying about the defendant's behavior with the complainant's 911 call shortly after the rape occurred;

5) State's motion to exclude defendant's request to add eleven new witnesses to witness list;

6) Defendant's motion for continuance of the trial.

While the defendant's motion to dismiss based on prejudicial error with the selection process for the grand and petit jury was denied, the allegation of impropriety in selecting the petit jury (the trial jury) did point out a potentially fatal flaw in Indiana's system. By using voter's registration rolls, the defense was able to show that, of the 179 people called as potential jurors for the Tyson case, 160 were white, and just 19 were African-American. Of the 101 total finally assembled after disqualifications, 90 were white and only 11 were African-American. Despite some confusion as to the statistics and some embarrassing errors by defense lawyer Kathleen Beggs in attempting to qualify certain statistical documents for admissibility (all regarding the authenticity of the documents presented as evidence), the petition did point out a basic unfairness of the Indiana system.

Most of the rest of the hearing centered on Fuller's smoke-screen motions regarding requests to have additional witnesses appear at the trial. A useful defense ploy, the witness motion deflected the attention from the only real issue with which Fuller was concerned, that of the judge's previous ruling to exclude the testimony of Dr. Eugene Kilpatrick, the rape trauma expert from South Carolina.

In one of the three or four confusing mistakes made by Greg Garrison and the prosecution prior to the trial, the deadline for filing notice for all witnesses had passed when the State filed a request for Dr. Kilpatrick to testify at trial. Immediate objection was made by the defense team, and Judge Gifford summarily denied the witness request motion.

The State then filed a motion for reconsideration based on the fact that the late request to have the doctor testify was based upon their recent knowledge of a previously undisclosed 911 call made to police by Desiree Washington shortly after the alleged rape. Unfortunately, through a series of errors by the prosecutor's office, the call and subsequent tape were unknown to the prosecution until it was disclosed by Washington during testimony in a deposition given by her on January 7, 1992. The State's petition for reconsideration said that the 911 call, alleged to have been some 13 minutes long, was very crucial to the State's case since Dr. Kilpatrick could testify as to the alleged victim's state of mind during the call.

To this argument, Fuller basically said bullshit. He pointed out that the motion had not been filed until the 14th of

January, a week after the deposition. He also pointed to the fact that the prosecution had known of Dr. Kilpatrick since November, had talked with the defense team about him, and then had said that they would not in fact use him as a witness.

No thought was apparently given by the defense to requesting a change of venue due to pretrial publicity, as was done in the Rodney King case. Whether the motion would have been granted was far from certain, but the defense must have believed that the more conservative outlying areas around Indianapolis would not bode well for Tyson.

The hearing produced derogatory remarks from the prosecution to the effect that the defense team was "paranoid" and prone to believe that a conspiracy existed against Tyson by the local police, FBI, and the prosecutor's office. The judge without explanation, however, decided that the order banning the witness would stand.

Throughout the hearing, Fuller seemed to observe closely the demeanor of Greg Garrison, trying to get a bead on what type of courtroom presence the fiery prosecutor could be expected to assume. Well aware of Garrison's hair-trigger temper, and his temptation to lose his cool, Fuller carefully watched his advocate's presentation of the evidence, looking for his well-known tendency to overstate his position on issues that were not at all critical to the outcome of the case.

For his part, Garrison, already a bit puzzled by Fuller's inexplicable decision to take Tyson to the grand jury, also observed his counterpart in an attempt to decide for himself whether Fuller was the highly skilled lawyer that he had been built up to be.

Prior to the first day of testimony, five important pretrial matters still awaited decisions from Judge Gifford. They were:

1) A petition to exclude a WISH-TV Channel 8 tape that contained an inflammatory Tyson statement ("I should have killed the bitch when I had the chance") at a press conference (by defense) (granted).

2) A petition to exclude a garment worn by Desiree Washington during rape attack (by defense) (denied).

3) A petition to exclude any reference to Tyson's criminal history (by defense) (granted).

4)   A petition to exclude the past sexual history of Desiree
      Washington (by prosecution) (granted).
5)   A petition to exclude Desiree Washington's counseling
      experiences which were begun as a result of the violent
      behavior of her father toward her mother (by prosecution)
      (granted).

Of these motions, the most intriguing was the one involving allegations that Desiree Washington had received counseling
after her father allegedly attacked her mother at their home.
Apparently, a domestic disturbance between the two had resulted in the arrest of Donald Washington, but later the charges
were dropped.

The Channel 8 tape also might have had an enormous
impact on the trial had it been seen by the jury. Most viewers who
saw the tape (Tyson says during a news conference, "I should
have killed the bitch," to no one in particular), when it was shown
on a nightly newscast were shocked by Tyson's strong words, but
the judge continued her strong pattern of disallowing any evidence that wasn't extremely relevant by granting a defense
motion to exclude the tape.

Prior to this hearing, another hearing had been held,
which proved to be more important than perhaps it first seemed.
Fuller and his cohorts had privately expressed great displeasure
with the method by which the prosecution was able to, in effect,
"judge-shop" and wind up with the pro-prosecution Gifford as
trial judge.

To that end, instead of filing a Motion for Change of
Judge, as they had a right to do, the defense filed a Motion for
Random Selection of Judge, which outlined the defense opposition to the manner in which a prosecutor can all but guarantee his
or her desired choice for trial judge by filing a motion for a special
grand jury in that judge's court. Citing federal violations of a
defendant's rights under the United States Constitution to a fair
trial, the defense argued that the selection process "not only
creates the appearance of impropriety, but also violates a
defendant's right to due process of law."

The defense pointed out in the motion that "any system
in which the prosecuting attorney can pick and choose which
judge will hear which case creates a serious appearance of

unfairness to defendants." It went on to say that "even if the particular judges chosen are without bias and are of unquestioned integrity and ability—and we have no reason to question Judge Gifford on any basis—the mere fact that the system allows such manipulation by the prosecutor creates a potential for abuse and undermines the public confidence that undergirds the criminal justice system."

In simple terms, the argument meant that while there was no reason to suspect that Judge Gifford would be biased, the system was intrinsically unfair to any defendant, in this case Tyson.

The prosecution's response was to argue that the defendant's motion was based on "general grounds," and the selection process, even if judged to be unfair, would have made no difference in Tyson's case since the trial judge would have been Gifford anyway, since the cases from the general grand jury were being assigned to her court during the time when Tyson was indicted.

Judge Gifford issued a five-sentence denial of the motion, and with that ruling, and the others made at the pretrial hearing, appeared to have stopped the defense cold in their efforts to alter the course of the trial proceedings.

Preliminaries out of the way, it was now time for the main event. The hordes of media representatives readied their cameras and notebooks for action, and the attorneys turned their attention toward the important process of jury selection.

5

◆

PICKING THE JURY

In anticipation of the trial, both the prosecution and the defense had carefully scripted game plans for what type of jury they wanted to sit in judgment of Michael Tyson. In formulating those plans, the respective counsel kept in mind age-old doctrines regarding jury selection that have been true since the beginning of the trial process itself.

The prosecution knew that to convict the ex-heavyweight boxing champion of the world, they would have to convince all 12 jurors, for all verdicts are required to be by unanimous vote. And they would have to convince all twelve jurors that Tyson was guilty beyond a certain standard, i.e., reasonable doubt.

The defense team, on the other hand, in order to gain acquittal for their client must only convince one juror that the prosecution has not met this important burden of proof. If that is done, they will at least gain a mistrial, and if that one juror can in turn convince his or her fellow jurors toward that position, a verdict of acquittal is possible.

Defining "reasonable doubt" has never been easy, even in the precise language offered by a judge during the final instructions to the jury before the deliberations begin. Some jurors believe reasonable doubt means removing *all* doubt, while others lean more toward the actual definition, centering around doubt that would have to be removed before one decided such important matters in their lives as the purchase of a home or the change of employment.

Defense lawyers defined reasonable doubt in the William Kennedy Smith case as "an abiding faith . . . something you hold tightly." Prosecutor Moira Lasch described finding "guilt beyond a reasonable doubt as never wavering or vacillating."

Each attorney involved in the case must gain, from experience, a sense of the type of juror they feel would be most sympathetic to their client. In a rape case, the prosecution will lean toward very conservative, take charge, generally male jurors who will stand up for law and order and vote their conscience no matter what sympathy they may hold for the defendant. Male jurors are most times preferred in a rape case because studies have shown that women are less inclined than men to believe women who charge rape. "Take charge" individuals are also preferred by the prosecution rather than wishy-washy types because of the difficulty people have in actually voting to convict someone, no matter what the evidence may be.

The defense, on the other hand, usually will seek out more women jurors in a rape case, and hone in on individuals who have more liberal views of life in general and the criminal justice system in particular. The defense will also try to seat jurors who are less strong in their beliefs, with the hope that in the end they will have more trouble making up their minds, and perhaps be unable to cross the difficult line of a guilty verdict.

Many cases are also decided simply on the relationship that the attorneys build up with the jurors throughout the trial. Once the trial starts, the attorney and the client become one, and the jurors will begin to shape their viewpoints based on an overall reaction to both. Thus, in this case, prosecutors Garrison and Trathen and Tyson's accuser Desiree Washington become a team, as would Vincent Fuller and Mike Tyson.

From the very first words out of the judge's mouth, the jurors will begin to formulate their opinions of both teams. Because first impressions are most critical, the prosecutors and defense counsel must watch, not only the tone and content of what they say, but what they wear, where they sit, how they relate to their clients, the manner in which they interact with the judge, and the feeling they receive when questioning the prospective individual jurors.

The prosecutor and defense also begin to try their cases through preliminary questions to the prospective jurors. With their respective main strategies in mind (prosecution—lack of consent/forced rape; defense—consent, etc.), the attorneys pose hypothetical questions to the jurors that are intended to establish thoughts in their minds that will trigger a certain response once the facts of the case are revealed during testimony.

Many attorneys have turned to jury specialists to aid them in selecting a jury. One such firm in Florida was hired during the jury selection process in the William Kennedy Smith case. These jury experts compile data regarding each juror, and then, through extensive research and systems analysis, provide essential data to the attorney that gauges how a certain juror might vote based on a specified set of facts and circumstances.

In the Kennedy Smith case, jury consultants Cathy Bennett and Robert Hirschhorn utilized questionnaires that they had developed just for that trial. Roy Black contended that the defense had to overcome two large obstacles, pretrial publicity and the strong negative feelings about the Kennedy family, in dealing with selection of the jury, and that the questionnaires helped them secure pretrial information regarding these subjects.

To expose any biases of the respective jurors, Black used open-ended questions to elicit strong inner feelings they might not want to reveal. Black also did not take notes during the questioning, and instead concentrated on the answers given and on his personal feelings about whether he felt that a particular juror would be an ally or enemy of Kennedy Smith.

"If you're open and honest with them, and show them that you're human, they'll start to like you," Black told reporters covering the trial. "However, if you come out there with a big ego, and act overbearing and supercilious, they'll cut your legs out from under you."

While the experts can be useful, an experienced trial lawyer, like Black, most often relies on his or her own gut feelings toward particular jurors as to whether they should be retained as jurors. Jury selection is, after all, a people-picking process, and all the computers in the world cannot predict precise human behavior.

In the Rodney King state case, prosecutor Terry White said after the trial that he did not get one juror he wanted for the case that ended up with the acquittal of the four officers. White said that "the six-man, six-woman panel would have been a perfect jury in a criminal case with a civilian defendant, but could not have been worse for a case in which law enforcement officers were charged."

In the King state case, the judge had granted a change-of-venue motion, and the trial was moved from Los Angeles, with its variety of ethnic groups, to Simi Valley, where the population was almost entirely white. White, a black man, said that he and his staff rated the 264-member panel of prospective jurors from one to five, with one being best, and that they had only 27 "one's," or "two's," on the list due to the strong pro-law enforcement attitude in the region.

White also reported that there were only half a dozen blacks on the panel, and that, because of the order in which their names were called, just two were ever really considered for selection by the prosecution.

Nevertheless, the makeup of the jury was so hostile toward the prosecution that there was probably little chance of a conviction. Almost incredibly, several of the jurors were either relatives of police officers, had worked in law enforcement themselves, or were security guards. No wonder the prosecution faced an uphill climb from day one of the trial.

In the Bensonhurst case, the trial was held in a predominantly black and Hispanic neighborhood, and the final jury contained six blacks and four Hispanics.

Regardless of whether scientific analysis or gut feelings are used, many lawyers, in fact, believe that jury selection is merely a crapshoot, and that luck plays a big part. In fact, experienced trial lawyers fear the potential juror who doesn't say much more than the ones who tend to go on and on concerning their feelings about this or that subject. More defense lawyers have been hoodwinked by what jurors don't say than by answers they freely offer.

In picking a jury, court rules permit challenges for "cause," which means an answer from a juror clearly indicates a bias or prejudice that causes him or her to be disqualified by the court, and "preemptory" challenges, which are a number of challenges given to each side allowing lawyers to disqualify and excuse a juror for any reason at all.

In anticipation of the trial of Mike Tyson, some 100 jurors in and around Indianapolis had been notified by mail to report to the City-County Building. Among the questions that were sent to all prospective jurors in the case were the following:

Have you been a member of the National Organization for Women or other groups interested in women's issues?

Have you ever had any involvement with boxing?

Do you consider yourself to be more of a "thinking person" or a "feeling person?"

People called through a computerized random selection process of registered Marion County voters were also asked numerous questions about their personal background, education, and family, as well as their opinions on other issues relevant to the case.

Potential jurors were asked whether they, family members, or friends had been victims of domestic violence, involved in a lawsuit, arrested or convicted of a criminal offense, involved with law enforcement in any way, or if they had studied psychiatry, sociology, or related subjects. One of the more unusual questions was: What three people, living or dead, do you admire most?

The prospective jurors were asked what they had read or heard about the William Kennedy Smith rape trial and about the rape allegations against Tyson. They were told to respond if they or any family member knew anyone from a list of 95 potential witnesses or others associated with the case. And they were asked about their impression of lawyers, knowledge of the Indiana Black Expo and the Miss Black America pageant, their sources of news, and their participation in any school or professional sports.

With pretrial matters completed, on January 27, 1992, Marion County Criminal Court Judge Patricia Gifford said the words, "State of Indiana vs. Michael G. Tyson, case # 49G049109CF116245." Prosecutor Jeffrey Modisett and his deputies, Greg Garrison and Barbara Trathen, began selection of a jury that they hoped would convict Mike Tyson for the crime of rape, criminal sexual deviate conduct, and confinement.

While Greg Garrison's reading of the statutes to the prospective jury was quite formal, everyone was quick to note that Mike Tyson was charged with sexual acts that were normally not discussed in everyday conversation. Alleged acts such as oral sex and use of a finger to stimulate sexual excitement made it clear that the evidence to be heard would be very sensitive, and in fact very embarrassing for both Tyson and Washington.

One wonders what the prospective jurors thought of all of this as they sat waiting to be questioned. All of them tried to avoid Tyson's eyes, but from time to time they would sneak a glance at the celebrity.

The stone-faced Tyson himself looked as if he wondered where the hell he was, and why he was in this position. He sat almost dazed in a seat behind his counsel, doodling on a pad of paper as he watched proceedings that could take away his freedom and destroy his career.

As question after question was asked of the jurors, the strategies to be employed by both the prosecution and defense became clearer. Prosecutor Greg Garrison focused in on such issues as:

1)   What elements constitute the crime of rape?
2)   What elements constitute the crime of sexual deviate conduct?
3)   What elements constitute the crime of confinement?
4)   The defendant has the right to a fair trial, but so does the prosecution.
5)   "No" means "no" means "no"!
6)   A defendant in Indiana can be convicted on the testimony of just one witness.
7)   A woman is in charge of her own body.
8)   Bad judgment should not be held against a person who is raped.
9)   A celebrity must abide by the same rules as other people.
10)   The William Kennedy Smith trial has no relationship to the Tyson case.

While each of these issues were discussed, it was clear that the main thrust of the prosecution's case was to involve "No means no." In spite of some bad judgment on the part of Washington, this lady had said "no" to Tyson's advances. When Tyson ignored this, and in turn confined her to a bed, committed deviate sexual acts upon her, and forced her to have sex, he broke the law. Short, sweet, and to the point.

Questions presented to the prospective jurors by Vincent Fuller provided a preview of the defense's intentions as well.

Those questions involved:

1)   Reasonable doubt is doubt based on reason, and involves decisions one would make of only the highest concern to everyone.
2)   Consent is an absolute defense to rape.
3)   Consent can be expressed or implied.
4)   Expressed consent means verbal consent.
5)   Implied consent means giving the impression of consent by actions or by the facts and circumstances surrounding the alleged actions.
6)   Implied consent can also come from silence or from not objecting to an act.
7)   An 18 year old is an adult, and has to be judged as one.
8)   Young black people relate to each other differently about sex than white people do.
9)   A boxer is not to be judged more violent than others just because he's a fighter.
10) Media hype is just that, and not to be judged as evidence.
11) A celebrity does not have to be a role model, and thus judged by a higher standard than others.
12) A person can make a false accusation just as easily as a true one.
13) The defendant is not required to provide any evidence whatsoever in his defense.
14) Go where you shouldn't go and you get what you deserve.
15) Differing versions of a witness' testimony destroys his or her credibility.

During jury selection, celebrity names floated through the air. Besides Tyson, Don King's name was bandied about. Jurors were asked if they had heard of King, and most answered that they knew he was a "promoter."

Magic Johnson and Pete Rose were also mentioned. The defense inquired of a potential juror whether he felt Pete Rose was unfairly singled out for prosecution. Objection was made, and sustained. Magic's name also came up since one juror said he was a hero. Upon further questioning, he admitted that while Johnson was a hero of his, he probably got what he deserved when it was discovered he had AIDS.

Robin Givens was brought up as well, solely to determine whether anyone had any knowledge of her name. Probably to her chagrin, nobody did, except for one juror who recalled that when Robin filed for divorce from Tyson, she said she wanted nothing and then proceeded to try to cash a $100,000 check on his personal account.

Due to its recentness, the Kennedy Smith case was an issue. In fact, the defense requested that the judge ask about that case in her preliminary questions, and she did so. Most jurors admitted knowledge of the case. Some had followed it very carefully. All knew of the date-rape allegation. Some agreed with the verdict, others did not.

Whether knowledge of the William Kennedy Smith case in this trial would end up prejudicing Tyson's case could only be guesswork. Would a jury, after listening to testimony, decide Tyson was falsely accused as Kennedy Smith was, and thus acquit him, or be able to find enough differences between the testimony of the accusers, and therefore find him guilty? The defense strategy to associate Tyson with William Kennedy Smith might backfire, but they were betting that once the evidence was heard, a similar verdict would result.

One topic of interest centered on the effect that the attitude of the black community would have on the eventual outcome. Such was not a united effort, to be sure, but several prominent black ministers had organized rallies in support of their fallen hero. Ironically, while many, including Tyson's lawyers, were questioning the unfairness of the potential racial makeup of the jury, some reports circulated from the jury pool that many blacks did not want to be on the jury, fearing perhaps undue pressure to acquit Tyson no matter what the evidence.

During jury selection, Tyson continued to doodle figures on a legal pad, but seemed to pay little attention to the proceedings. He did consult with his attorneys during their helter-skelter conferences regarding selection of the jury, but actually seemed distant and removed from the events surrounding him. His behavior during the jury selection was indicative of similar behavior by Tyson at a press conference or weigh-in before a big fight. During those times, Tyson would almost appear to be asleep, or at the least "not with it," according to those familiar with his prefight behavior.

Perception of the lawyers and their performance during the jury selection varied. Legal expert Jim Drucker thought Fuller was attempting to take on the role of the kindly professor, and intended to educate the jury. Charley Steiner of ESPN disagreed, believing Fuller's impersonal touch was placing a barrier between Fuller and Tyson and the jury. Earl Gustkey of the *Los Angeles Times* found Fuller's style "very businesslike," but Joe Gelarden of the *Indianapolis Star* thought his methods indicated a "federal courtroom manner that might not work in the down and dirty atmosphere of a county criminal court."

Without the guidance of a jury selection expert, the defense seemed very disorganized. A respected local attorney, Rick Kammen, understood that the defense team had consulted with the same experts that Roy Black used in the Kennedy Smith case, but that they were dismissed when the "defense didn't like what information they received from the experts."

Courtroom observers believed that the final selection process by the defense was really done on a helter-skelter basis. A deputy sheriff assigned to the court said that "too many cooks" were the problem, and I personally heard the defense attorneys in a "What do you think? Well, I don't know. What do you think?" type of exchange when it came time for final selection.

For two-and-a-half laborious days, the judge and the attorneys asked question after question of the prospective jurors, trying somehow to determine their sensibilities to the issues most important to either side. Most of the questions bordered on the boring: political philosophies, work-related discussions, past experience with the criminal justice system, and so forth.

Probing of intimate matters was required of selected jurors where necessary. One man was forced to admit to imminent bankruptcy, while another was embarrassed to reveal that his wife had been raped by a black stranger prior to their marriage. Most said they would not be embarrassed to discuss the female genitals or talk about vulgar terms if necessary. One juror admitted that many of his co-workers would describe him as "hateful," and another that he had to attend counseling classes due to a court-related arrest. People were asked whether they knew any lawyers, most gave a quick "no," followed by a smile.

Reservations the defense had about racial imbalance of the jury proved valid. Consistent with the fact that only 22 percent of the population of Marion County was black, three of the 12 jurors were black (later on in the trial one black juror would be excused); making the final count ten white and two black jurors who would deliberate the case. Male and female mix was on balance with eight men and four women.   The jurors' ages raged from 21 to 55, but most of the them were in their 20s and 30s.

When all was said and done, 12 regular jurors and three alternates were chosen and then sequestered for the remainder of the trial.   As a former defense lawyer, I tagged the jurors as: "leaders" (those prone to lead fellow jurors in the deliberations), "followers" (those who would be swayed easily by fellow jurors), or "unknowns" (those difficult to predict).

The jurors finally selected and sworn in were:

1) **Joanne** — White, female, about 40, married, small children at home. Her husband worked at Allison Transmission in Indianapolis and was a firefighter. She felt that the media hype for the trial was to be "expected." A follower.

2) **Ken** — Black, male, 25, married. Worked as a behavioral specialist with handicapped students in the Indianapolis Public Schools. He said he had seen Tyson fight, and that he loved sports. He appeared very laid back, and perhaps a bit too nonchalant about becoming a juror in the case. Probably a follower.

3) **Beth** — White, female, 31, single. Worked for the Indianapolis Chamber of Commerce. Believed that young people look up to celebrities, and thought that celebrities would want to set an example for young people. Unknown.

4) **Walt** — White, male, early 20s, married. He was a truck driver for Pizza Hut who seemed to give all the answers that someone would give if they wanted to be a juror in a famous case. A leader.

5) **Steve** — White, male, about 30, married. A parts manager at a body shop. A big fan of Indiana University basketball, he reads the sports section of the newspaper first. Follower.

6) **Neil** — White, male, 21, single. Lived with his parents in a southern suburb of Indianapolis. A t-shirt designer at a local printing shop. Definitely a follower.

7) **Nancy** — White, female, 31, single. Worked for a title company. Had few opinions about anything. Definitely a follower.

8) **Rosie** — Black, female, 39, single. An underwriter with an insurance company. Worked at a booth at Black Expo, which coordinated the Miss Black America Beauty Contest. Somewhat shy and reserved. Tough call—seemed well respected. A leader.

9) **Tim** — White, male, 37, married. A marketing manager for IBM in Indianapolis. He had served in a noncombat capacity in the Marines. His wife was a nurse in the cancer critical patient ward at Indiana University Hospital. With his strict discipline in the Marine Corps and conservative outlook, the fact that the defense passed on him was a great surprise to legal experts following the trial. Definite leader and possibility to be jury foreman.

10) **Dave** — White, male, 55, married. A UPS truck driver who worked nights, driving back and forth to Ohio. He admitted that he faced the threat of imminent bankruptcy. He coached youth baseball, so the other jurors nicknamed him "Coach." Seemed to have lived a hard life, and could relate to Tyson's dilemma. The oldest member of the jury, his morals as to young people's sexual appetites could be different than his fellow jurors. Unknown.

11) **Chuck** — Black, male, 36, married. Unemployed, but formerly worked in some capacity for the law firm of Ice, Miller, Donadio and Ryan. Had been a juror in two cases involving murder and robbery charges;   in both instances the defendant was found guilty. He did know about Robin Givens's relationship with Mike Tyson, and believed that the wrong verdict was reached in the Pete Rose case. Unknown.

12) **Chuck** — White, about 45. A Vietnam veteran, worked for a medical equipment company. He served on three criminal juries in the 60s and 70s, and remembered that in two of them the defendant was found not guilty. Unknown.

13) **Michael** — White, male, 44, single. Worked for Indiana Bell Telephone. Somewhat shy, he had been a boxing fan, but only until heavyweight champion Muhammed Ali left the ring. A follower.

14) **Matt** — White, male, 23, single. Worked as a sales manager. Thought celebrities should definitely act as role models for youngsters. A follower.

15) **Sandy** — White female, 52. A political conservative, she worked as a customer service representative. Potential leader.

By 11:00 a.m. on the 29th of January, all 15 jurors had been selected. Twenty-five percent of them were black, 75 percent men, 25 percent women. Could Mike Tyson get a fair trial from these 12 strangers?

6

---◆---

FOR OPENERS

Experienced trial attorneys believe that 90 percent of the case is over when the lawyers have concluded their opening statements, since most of the jury members will make their decisions based on the first impressions of the evidence as discussed in the lawyers' opening statements.

The opening statement before a jury is each side's chance to fully present its case. While a judge will instruct the jurors that nothing the lawyers say can be construed as evidence, there is no question that the statements have a tremendous impact on the outcome of the case.

To begin with, it is the first chance for a juror to size up the attorneys. First impressions are critical to jurors' perceptions of whether they can believe the attorneys, or whether they will in all likelihood disregard most of what the attorneys say.

The "trust factor" can be compared to that of a politician. Standing before a jury, the lawyers essentially are giving a campaign speech, promising to prove this or that as the trial moves along. Often attorneys will advocate not only what is positive about their cases, but what they consider false and misleading about their opponents' cases.

While a lawyer is bound to stay within the facts of the case, as they are most favorable to him or her, usually an attorney will exaggerate wherever possible to pound home the points that he or she believes will secure a vote toward his or her client.

Since the case is still fresh and exciting to jurors, and their minds haven't yet been convoluted with day after day of testimony, court rulings, and frequently confusing exhibits, they probably pay as much or more attention to these statements than to any other testimony during the trial.

In effect, the respective counsels map out their cases to follow the strategies that they have devised to fit the evidence that will be presented at trial. As a rule, though, jurors don't seem to hold counsel to their promises as much as one would think, and so the very first words out of the lawyers' mouths may very well decide the outcome of the case.

So as Prosecutor Greg Garrison addressed the jury with his opening statement, his intent was to outline his entire case against Tyson.

For Garrison, such a statement was long awaited, especially in view of the number of rumors that had been circulating about the State's evidence against Tyson. The prosecutor's office, unlike that of the one in the William Kennedy Smith case, had not publicly boasted about its case against Tyson.

"Washington's life experience," Garrison pointed out, "was shaped by her father." Mr. Washington was a "follower of boxing and a fan of Mike Tyson," and Desiree watched Tyson fight and watched him "use his fame and prominence to dispatch opponents." The prosecutor then went on to outline Washington's story for the jury, and attempted to portray his client as being unprepared to handle schemes like the one Tyson would involve her in. Garrison ended the summary of his evidence by telling the jury, "Over and over again, you'll believe this in your head and your heart."

Garrison's statement was effective, although predictable. Leaving his bombastic style at the doorstep, he merely set the stage for Washington's testimony, and made certain not to promise too much, too soon.

Defense Attorney Vincent Fuller now rose to the podium. Dubbed "Foghorn Fuller" for his staccato baritone delivery, Fuller acted as if nothing he had heard from Garrison surprised him. He reminded the jury of the age-old canons involving presumption of innocence, reasonable doubt, and the State's burden of proof. From behind a podium, Fuller said in his professorial style that there was no question that sex had occurred, but the sex was consensual. The barrister went over the theories behind what constitutes expressed and implied consent, saying, "Expressed consent is truly rare."

Fuller also described briefly his client's background and that of the accuser, pointing out that Tyson had little education while Washington was mature beyond her years. Fuller launched into his description of the events of July 18 and 19, with obvious differences from what Garrison had told the jury.

Fuller suggested to the jury that in fact Washington was the one who had pursued Tyson, and not the other way around. She was looking for a "long-term relationship," Fuller told the jury. "She was after Tyson."

Fuller then made a statement, and repeated it, that sent shock waves through the courtroom. Against the accepted practice of most experienced trial lawyers, Fuller said "He will tell you," and then, "Tyson will tell you," intimating, perhaps even promising, the jury that they would hear from Tyson himself.

Describing the sexual encounter in vague terms, Fuller expounded the theory that Washington became upset after the sex act when Tyson wouldn't walk her down to the limousine. "It was devastating to Miss Washington," Fuller told the jury. "She left not raped, but disillusioned." The defense lawyer then told the jury that Tyson treated Washington like a "one-night stand," and that "the motive for the rape charge is money." Fuller said that witnesses would say that Washington talked about Tyson, saying, "He's got money; did you see what Robin Givens got out of him?"

Fuller pointed out that Washington had hired civil lawyers sitting in the audience ready to "follow this case. If Tyson is convicted, she can file a lawsuit that will make her a wealthy woman," Fuller said.

Fuller's statement was much more risky than Garrison's. By promising that Tyson would testify and that the jury would find Washington to be motivated by money and fame, he needlessly made promises to the jurors that would have to be kept.

However, the opening statements showed that the positions of the two sides were clearly drawn. If one believed Garrison, the victim was a naive, goody-two-shoes kid, who was lured in by Tyson and raped. In Fuller's eyes, the victim was a scorned lover who decided to get back at Tyson by taking millions of dollars from him through a civil lawsuit.

Mike Tyson sat attentively as both attorneys discussed his encounter with Washington as if he weren't even in the courtroom. Fuller stood behind his podium, distancing himself from the 12 most important people in the world to Mike Tyson. Never once did he come near Tyson, or indicate any affection or camaraderie with his client. Jurors were not seeing a defense team at work, only a foghorn barrister from another state who had made a cold-fish first impression.

7

◆

DESIREE'S STORY

In the Mike Tyson trial, there was, in the final analysis, going to be only one issue that would decide the outcome of the case. Either the jury would believe Desiree Washington, or they would believe Mike Tyson, in their respective accounts of what really took place on a queen-sized bed in room 606 of the Canterbury Hotel on the night in question. Other testimony would take up much of the eight days of trial, but it would all be secondary to the key testimony of Washington, and that of Tyson if he chose to testify.

Just as in the Clarence Thomas / Anita Hill confrontation; in the Kennedy Smith case, where the "believability battle" was between Smith and Patty Bowman; in the Rodney King case, where the famous videotape would be weighed against the testimony of the police officers; and in the Bensonhurst trial, where the physical evidence against Lemrick Nelson would be matched up against the testimony of police officers, the stage was set for the jury to hear from the woman who had the courage to bring charges against the formidable Mike Tyson.

Taking advantage of the rape shield law that protected Washington from inquiries into her sexual past, prosecutors Garrison and Trathen deliberately portrayed Tyson's accuser as a shy, naive college student who insisted on keeping her identity secret to protect her privacy. Such would of course be in sharp contrast to Tyson, whose mean look and propensity for violence was well documented.

In fact, preconceived attitudes regarding "truth telling" are a direct result of the initial perceptions that are gathered from simple physical appearance. Defense lawyers are always concerned whether their clients can beat the predisposition among jurors that they "must be guilty or they wouldn't be there." As a result defense lawyers spend much of their time in close contact with the defendant, either with their hands on their shoulders or in close for personal conversation. The smart lawyer does this to show the jurors that the gruff-looking defendant isn't a vicious animal that should be locked up forever.

Initial perceptions, through physical appearance or demeanor, often are the most important element in whether a person will be believed in a criminal trial. Desiree Washington would be portrayed as a young, small, reserved childlike woman who could not anticipate the rough actions of a large, violent man like Mike Tyson. William Kennedy Smith was projected as a singled-out relative of a famous family, a studious, aspiring doctor who couldn't possibly have raped Patty Bowman, a woman with a spotted background.

Rodney King's large size and weight, and surely his color in all likelihood influenced the jurors in his case to believe four white police officers, who were much smaller in stature. Anita Hill's strong personality and striking appearance may very well have been held against her when compared with the more rotund appearance and pleasant demeanor of Clarence Thomas. When Hill proved a worthy match for the senators with her intellect, it only served to reinforce the perceived resentment against her.

These types of factors would be important as to whether Washington would be believed, but before she was called to testify, the State of Indiana called to the stand Kycia Johnson, a 20-year-old Miss Black America Pageant contestant from Oklahoma.

A roommate of Desiree Washington during the pageant, Kycia Johnson told the jury that she first saw Mike Tyson at the rehearsal in the Omni Hotel. She also said that Desiree was one of the four girls who participated in a promotional video with Tyson.

Johnson said she saw Tyson and singer Johnny Gill talking with Desiree and her roommate Pasha Oliver near one of the poles in the rehearsal hall room. She also said she saw Desiree pull out a piece of paper from her purse and give it to Tyson.

When she talked to Desiree later, Washington told Kycia "I'm going out with [Tyson] tonight."

Johnson then described an early-morning phone call from Tyson to the girls' hotel room. Washington finally went out, Johnson told the jury, but when Desiree returned, she said, "He's such a creep, such a jerk; he tried to rape me."

Johnson also told the jury that Washington wasn't the same after the incident. She was "quiet, more distant, and she was staring into space, thinking about something."

The round clock on the wall in Criminal Courtroom #4 showed 1:45 p.m. when the 12 jurors and all of the media from around the world got their first close look at the 18-year-old former Miss Black America Beauty Pageant contestant from Coventry, Rhode Island, who had accused Mike Tyson of rape.

In anticipation of her testimony, and continuing her portrayal as the innocent victim of a brutal crime, Desiree Washington was dressed in a carefully selected conservative gray suit with a white blouse. Her long black hair was parted to one side, and she seemed outwardly calm as Marion County Deputy Prosecutor Greg Garrison began to lead her through the events of the week of July 12, 1991.

Exhibiting a low-key, matter-of-fact manner, Washington, who had kept her identity secret, told the jury she was now a first-year student at Providence College in Rhode Island. She went on to say that her high school background at Coventry High School had brought her many honors, including being named social committee chairman and receiving the Outstanding Sophomore Award. During her senior year she had been one of 34 high school students in the country selected for a Hugh O'Brien Scholarship to visit the Soviet Union for two weeks in 1990.

Washington said she had begun to enter beauty pageants in 1989. She won the local Coventry pageant that year, and in 1990 was named Miss Black Rhode Island. Washington said she entered beauty pageants because she was "tired of blonde haired, blue eyed" women always being the winners.

Testifying without a single glance at Tyson, Washington then told of her work with the Big Sisters Organization, which began when she met a foster child who "touched my heart." She also told of being a Sunday School teacher and an usher in church.

Responding carefully to Garrison's narrowly focused questions, Washington told the jury that she had qualified for the Miss Black America pageant by winning the Miss Black Rhode Island competition. Upon arriving in Indianapolis on July 12 for the competition, she had gone to the historic Madame Walker Theatre in downtown Indianapolis to meet with pageant officials. Washington told of the preliminary activities for the pageant and of beginning her day at 4:00 a.m. Rehearsals for the talent competition and for promotional videos were then followed by appearances at stores and businesses that were backers of the pageant. Washington also met the two pageant contestants with whom she would share a hotel room, Kycia Johnson and Pasha Oliver.

Successful in his quest to portray Washington as a model citizen, Garrison now began to carefully guide Washington toward the fateful first meeting with Tyson. In answer to his concise questions, Washington told the jury that on July 12 the pageant contestants were just finishing rehearsals at the Omni Hotel when Tyson and singer Johnny Gill came to the rehearsal studio with Rev. Charles Williams, an organizer of the pageant. The contestants began to flock around Tyson and Gill, but the director of the promotional video quickly made the girls scamper back to their dancing duties.

Later, when Tyson walked among the girls, Washington said Tyson told her, "You're a good Christian girl, aren't you?" At the urging of a pageant official who had Tyson sing a rap song for a promotional video, Washington said Tyson hugged her, and asked her out for a date. "Sure," Washington said she told the ex-champ, as she glared for the first time at Tyson.

After a photo session with Tyson (where at Tyson's insistence several contestants sat on his lap), the ex-champ had a conversation with Washington and her roommate Pasha Oliver. Desiree asked Tyson if, in effect, they could double date, with Pasha going out with Johnny Gill. Washington said Tyson told her, "That's fine with me."

At the opening ceremonies for Black Expo that evening, the contestants were lined up outside the Indianapolis Hoosier Dome in two rows. Tyson arrived with the Reverend Jesse Jackson, and Washington told the jury she saw them kneeling in prayer together. Later, Washington said, she showed Tyson two swimsuit photos of her and Oliver that she had purchased earlier in the day. The photos "showed us off as looking like twins," Washington said. Washington said Tyson was wearing a mustard colored shirt and a "Together In Christ" pin.

"Are we really going out?" Washington said she asked him, and Tyson "confirmed the date."

Washington said she then went to her hotel room, where she changed into an outfit that would later be a pivotal issue in the trial. Given to her by a pageant official in Rhode Island for good luck, Desiree explained, the outfit was a bit too big for her, especially in the chest area.

Washington then left for the Johnny Gill concert scheduled for that evening, telling the jury, "I didn't feel he [Tyson] would call anyway." Once there, she said that it was cold, and her roommate did not feel well. After going backstage to see the rap singer Yo Yo, she returned to the hotel room.

At 11:00 or 11:30 p.m., Washington did some stretching exercises, talked a bit on the phone and with other contestants, and then went to bed. At about 1:00 a.m., Washington's other roommate Kycia Johnson came into the room, and Desiree, Pasha, and Kycia made small talk. At about 1:45, the phone rang, and Kycia answered it. The caller was apparently Dale Edwards, Tyson's bodyguard. Kycia handed the phone to Washington, and, she told the jury, she began to talk to Tyson.

"Can you come out?" Tyson allegedly said. "I just want to talk to you."

"It's late. My hair is in rollers. I'm dressed for bed," Washington said she told Tyson.

"Oh, c'mon. We'll go sightseeing," Washington said Tyson told her.

Following this exchange, Pasha Oliver apparently asked Desiree to ask whether Johnny Gill was there. Tyson told Washington that Gill wasn't with him.

"Why don't you come up here?" Washington inquired, but her roommates told her they weren't fit to be seen.

Washington told the jury, "I did not want to go out by myself," and asked Tyson why "we couldn't go out tomorrow." Tyson then apparently explained that he had to leave later that day. Finally, Washington said she decided to go downstairs to meet Tyson in the lobby of the hotel. As an afterthought, she told the jury that she took her camera so that she could take pictures while they were sightseeing.

Washington then testified she went to the bathroom and changed into the same outfit she had worn to the concert. She also said she left on her pajama underpants.

Going down to the lobby, Washington told the jury, she went to the front door, but the limousine wasn't there. She then headed for the back door and saw the gold limousine.

The driver opened the door for her, Washington said. Tyson was inside, and he immediately "hugged me, and kissed me on the mouth. It startled me . . . he had bad breath." Washington's comment brought a laugh from Tyson.

"'Oh, you're not like these city girls; you're a good Christian girl,'" Washington said Tyson told her. Washington said Tyson then explained that "he had to pick up something," and a few minutes later, Washington found herself in front of the Canterbury Hotel on North Capitol Street.

Desiree said she followed Tyson into the hotel, and Tyson shook the hand of a young girl who said, "Ooh, there's Mike Tyson." When she asked Tyson about the girl, he said, "he was sick of it . . . that people were a pain in the ass." Washington testified she never saw any bodyguard either in the limousine or with Tyson. Once inside the lobby of the hotel, she and Tyson took the elevator to the sixth floor, and then to room 606.

When they entered the hotel room, "Tyson went straight to the bedroom and turned on the TV. He then made a phone call," Washington told the jury, but "I stayed in the living room." Next, Washington said Tyson told her "to 'come in here . . . I want to talk to you.'" She told the jury she said to Tyson, "I thought we were leaving," but then she went into the bedroom anyway.

Washington said that she sat on the lower right corner of the bed. Tyson was up at the top, beside the phone on the night stand. "Tyson," she said, "asked about my schooling in Rhode Island." He asked "If I was on an athletic scholarship." She said she told him, "No." She said she did tell him "I am a big sister," and he said "he had been a big brother." Washington then said that they talked about "his 200 pigeons." She said she told him, "That's interesting . . . I love animals."

"We talked for fifteen minutes," she told the jury. He asked about "my home life, and was I daddy's little girl . . . Spoiled?" He asked "if my family liked him." She said, "They haven't met you yet." Washington said he told her, "Parents don't like me."

"'Do you like me?'" Washington said Tyson asked her. Washington said she responded, "You seem O.K." Then she told the jury "his voice changed a bit, and he said, 'You're turning me on!'"

"I'm not like that," she said she told him. "Then he put his hands up to his face," Washington said. She told the jury she went to the bathroom, saying, "I want to use the bathroom, and then we'll leave." She said Tyson told her "OK."

Washington testified she didn't take her purse to the bathroom. She told the jury she urinated, and then found there was some discharge on her panty shield, indicating that her menstrual period was about to begin. Washington said she took the liner off, and threw it away. "I had a pad in my purse," she said, but "I figured I could put it on later."

Washington then testified that she washed her hands, and then came out of the bathroom. There, she said, "was Mike Tyson sitting on the side of the bed with nothing on but his underwear."

The courtroom became very silent, and the jurors seemed spellbound as Washington said, "I was terrified. 'It's time for me to leave,'" she said she told him. "'C'm here,'" Washington said Tyson told her, and then he "grabbed my arm," and put "his tongue in my mouth."

Tyson sat passively in his courtroom chair as the small woman said, "It was disgusting." Washington then said Tyson pulled back, but he said, "Don't fight me!" She told the jury, "I began to hit him, but it was like hitting a brick wall."

Washington testified that Tyson then pinned her down, placing his forearm on her chest. He removed her jacket, and the "bra" part of the outfit slid down easily. Tyson then pulled down the "jams," the lower part of the outfit. Her panties were last to come off, Washington said.

"Get off me," Washington said she pleaded, "please stop." She continued to punch him, she told the jury, and he continued to say, "Don't fight me!"

"Relax," Washington said he told her, "and then he put his two fingers in my vagina. . . . I felt a lot of pain, and tears came to my eyes," she said. "It was excruciating pain."

"You're hurting me," she said she yelled, "but he laughed like it was a game. . . . He licked me, and then he jammed himself into me." She told the jury she pleaded again, "I don't want to have a baby; I have a future," but she said he continued by saying, "Don't fight me, mommy."

"He was mean, evil," she told the jury. "I got on top, and started to try to get away, but he slammed me down again . . . He went on till he was done, and then pulled out, and ejaculated on the bedspread," Washington said.

"'I told you I wouldn't come,'" she said he told her. "'Don't you love me now?'"

"You disgust me," she said she responded, and he rolled off of her. She got up "fast," she told the jury, and dressed "fast."

"'You can stay if you want,'" Washington said Tyson told her. "What, so you can do this to me again?" she said she replied. Washington said Tyson responded, "You're a baby, a crybaby."

"Is the limousine still here?" she said she asked him. Tyson then telephoned downstairs, she told the jury, and then she said he told her, "Yes."

"Out the door I went, carrying my shoes," Washington testified. She said she saw a tall "dark-skinned" man in front of 604. He had "a smirk on his face," she recalled. Outside, Washington said she found the limousine. "You seem nice and I'll give you a ride," Washington said the driver told her. Washington told the jury, "I was crying."

Back at the Omni Hotel, Washington testified that she went up to her room. Washington said she told a roommate, "He tried to rape me."

Washington said she then took a shower because she "wanted to feel clean." Then she said that she went to bed. Next morning, she told the jury, "It hurt to walk."

"I was so sore, I couldn't even put in a tampon," Washington said. As to why she went on to compete in the competition, she emphatically told the jury, "I am not a quitter. I wouldn't be here right now if I were a quitter," seemingly very proud of her ability to carry on despite the rape.

Washington explained, "I started crying in the afternoon." She said she told Pasha, "He raped me."

Later that day, Washington talked to her mother, who was staying at the Days Inn near the airport. When she told her mother that Tyson had raped her, her mother told her she would immediately call 911. When her mother reached the county 911 instead of the city 911, because of the hotel's location, Washington said her mother called Washington back, and she then called the local 911 and made a report.

Washington said she was then taken to Indiana University Hospital. There, she told the jury, she saw "the victim assistance nurse, before the attending physician, Dr. Stephen Richardson, examined me." She admitted that she had had only one previous pelvic exam before and "pulled away when he began his vaginal examination." She said her legs "were shaking," and that the doctor said she should "have an AIDS test when she got home."

As to her performance in the rest of the competition, she told the jury she felt that she "performed badly, yet I still received a Top 10 finish."

Washington explained, "I still have problems with what happened to me . . . I slept with my mom after the incident . . . She still talks to me until I fall to sleep, even while I'm at college."

In a little less than an hour, Washington's story had been elicited by Prosecutor Garrison for the jury. He seemed pleased with himself and his chief witness, and there was no doubt in anyone's mind that Washington had told a very plausible story. One that could send Tyson to jail for more than 60 years.

8

♦

ATTACKING DESIREE

In any rape case, and especially those in which there is no eyewitness testimony to the event, it is essential to the prosecution that its chief witness be highly credible. Jurors usually have sympathy for a woman who says she has been raped, and if a plausible story is told that the jury can understand and relate to, then the prosecution will likely gain a guilty verdict.

Prior to trial, prosecutors Garrison and Trathen had carefully laid the groundwork for Washington's testimony. One month before the trial, the Marion County Prosecutor's Office had secured the services of veteran Indianapolis attorney Robert Hammerle, who also acted as the lawyer for another key State's witness, limousine driver, Virginia Foster, before and during the trial.

The 45-year-old Hammerle has been a criminal defense lawyer for the past 17 years. His wife, Monica, also an attorney, handles death-penalty, postconviction matters for convicted murderers.

Hammerle is known as a bright, somewhat unorthodox attorney who has been highly successful in the county criminal courts of Indianapolis. He has gained a reputation of being an innovative, seat-of-the-pants defense lawyer, who can be counted upon to provide his client with the very best defense available.

It was this reputation that brought Hammerle a new client in the winter of 1991. On the other end of the phone one morning was the owner of a brand-new limousine service in Indianapolis, Virginia Foster. Foster told Hammerle that in July of 1991, she had received a phone call from Indiana Black Expo officials requesting that her limousine service provide transportation for ex-heavyweight champion Mike Tyson during his stay in Indianapolis. She told Hammerle that not only did she take the job, but that she was in fact the limousine driver for Tyson on the very night when the alleged rape of Desiree Washington took place.

Foster was calling Hammerle because she was being badgered by every news organization in Indianapolis since she was now a material witness in the case. Apparently her decision to call Hammerle was prompted by a television story that had depicted Foster as being a "less than reputable person," according to Hammerle. The news report had charged that Foster had had her chauffeur's license revoked, and had been intoxicated when she was driving Tyson around town. Foster also told Hammerle that there were rumors that she had been paid off, and that she was going to leave town and disappear.

Once retained by Foster, Hammerle began to set the record straight. He took the offensive and called Bob Campbell, the news director of local television station WTHR, to complain on behalf of his client. Campbell told Hammerle that much of the problem stemmed from Foster's refusal to speak to reporters, and Hammerle made it clear that he would now help with the communication between Foster and the press.

Hammerle also telephoned the Marion County Prosecutor's office to make certain that they knew that his client was indeed going to testify for the State at trial. Hammerle said, "Foster then told me the same story that she would testify to at trial, including the fact that Tyson had tried to physically attack her and expose himself during the time they spent together in July."

Following his retention by Foster, in early November Hammerle then ran into prosecutor Greg Garrison in downtown Indianapolis. "Garrison asked whether I would be interested in participating in a mock cross-examination of Desiree Washington," Hammerle said. "We're going to bring her in," Hammerle said Garrison told him, "and we'd like you to participate."

"Several weeks passed," Hammerle said, "but sometime in December they delivered to me a copy of Desiree's first statement to police for my review. I didn't have much time to review it the night before I was to examine her, but my impression was that there must be much more, . . . must be an amplification of it . . . later in the grand jury . . . I thought this must only be one part of the puzzle. . . . There was a lot more I would have like to have known."

Hammerle, who was not paid for his work for the prosecution said he purposely did not meet with Washington before the examination because "I wanted to bring her in unprepared . . . give her a feel for what she would experience at trial. . . . I wanted to take her through a rigorous cross-examination."

The parties gathered for the cross-examination in Superior Court #5's courtroom on the fifth floor of the west wing of the City-County Building. In attendance were Hammerle, Washington, Washington's personal lawyer, David Hennessey, prosecutors Greg Garrison and Barb Trathen, detective Thomas Kuzmik, and three other police investigators. "Prosecutor Jeff Modisett came in later," Hammerle recalled, "almost as a courtesy call.

"No notes were taken, and the session was not taped. I believe this was done intentionally," Hammerle said. "Garrison sat at one table, and I sat at another along with prosecutor Barb Trathen so that she could give me any information that I might need for my examination.

"Garrison began by taking Washington through a preliminary direct examination," Hammerle said, "and my initial impression of Washington was that, although she was soft-spoken, the most striking thing about her . . . was that I was overwhelmed with, was her composure. She had a real lack of emotion, and a tremendous amount of composure.

"Several times during the questioning," Hammerle said, "we stopped, and Garrison or Trathen or Hennessey would say 'Here's what you're doing,' or 'I don't want you to do that, or say that', or 'don't move your eyes that way,' in order that Washington would learn how to testify at trial.

"I questioned her for several hours, and didn't pull any punches," Hammerle said. "Sometimes she would look at Garrison and say, 'Do I have to answer that?,' but I would interrupt and tell her that I was the one asking the questions and that she had to answer.

"I questioned her about her financial interest in the case . . . hiring lawyers . . . one who is in the courtroom today, but Dave

[Hennessey] wouldn't let her answer," Hammerle said. "I wanted to get into the reason she had hired counsel . . . but I wasn't allowed to . . . and so I dropped it. Dave claimed the attorney-client privilege.

"My overall impression," Hammerle said, "the most overwhelming thing . . . was that she did battle with me. I had heard that there was this 18-year-old, naive lady, but I came away with the feeling that, while it [rape] could have happened, I was dealing with someone much stronger who had a backbone and when it stiffened . . . wouldn't let me run over her. I couldn't figure out how this all fit with all the naive mistakes she was supposed to have made."

In the end, Hammerle recalled that he had finished his practice cross-examination of Washington by summarizing for her all of the improbables he saw in the case. "I began by saying to her . . . 'Look, you met Mike Tyson, and you saw him making all of these passes at girls . . . and then you gave him a picture of you in a bathing suit, and you still didn't think he had sex on his mind?' She said 'No.' Then I said, 'He called you in the middle of the night, and you went down to the limousine, and when you got in he kissed you, and it still never crossed your mind that he had sex on his mind?'" She told him no, Hammerle said.

"'Then you went to the hotel, and you went to his room, and you sat on his bed, and it never crossed your mind that he wanted to have sex with you?' She said, 'No.' 'And then he said, 'You're turning me on,' and you didn't think he had sex on his mind?' She said, 'No.' 'And then you got up and went into the bathroom and removed the panty shield . . .' and on and on. I kept asking her and she kept saying, 'No' . . . and it didn't make sense . . . but that was her story," Hammerle said, "and she stuck to it."

"I met Monica [his wife] for dinner afterwards, and I told her that I honestly didn't think they could get a conviction," Hammerle said. "I told her that this [rape] could have happened . . . she told an effective story, impressive . . . but that composure of hers tells me that she is very good at dealing with emotions. If she was acting the next day after the rape supposedly occurred, then as defense counsel I would say [to the jury], 'how in the world do we know she isn't acting in the courtroom?'" he went on.

"After I told Monica the information about the panty shield, I remember that my wife told me that story is one that no woman is ever going to believe," Hammerle said. "Monica felt that a woman who goes into a hotel room . . . up to the room . . . is in the safe haven area of the bedroom, and then goes to the bathroom and removes the panty shield . . . well, there isn't a woman who doesn't associate with that . . . that the woman is expecting sex," Hammerle continued, "and I agreed with that."

Hammerle also said, "I ran into Greg Garrison the next day in the City-County Building on an elevator. I waited until everyone was off the elevator, and then I said to Greg, 'You, my friend, are in a world of shit!' He just looked at me and went down the hall."

Whether Garrison agreed with Hammerle or not, he and Trathen felt that Hammerle's rigorous pretrial cross-examination had served its purpose, and had readied their client for the anticipated similar test from Vincent Fuller that lay ahead at trial.

After Washington had completed her testimony for the State, Vincent Fuller had to make a quick judgment as to how effective Tyson's accuser's testimony had been. If he felt she had merely wounded the ex-champ, then he would most likely clear up any minor inconsistencies and sit down. On the other hand, if he felt Washington had knocked Tyson to the mat, then he would pursue a more vigorous cross-examination so as to repair the damage she had caused the accused rapist.

Cross-examination of the State's key witness was of course critical, because it would be the only measurement the jury would have of the inconsistencies in Washington's testimony that, the defense believed, would make it unworthy of consideration by the jury.

A defense lawyer must, however, carefully choose the best means to uncover those inconsistencies. In real life, that means developing a strategy so that, slowly and methodically, momentum is built, question after question, until key errors in the witness's testimony are brought to the attention of the jury. Focus by the attorney on those key points is essential, for the jury must be able to easily recall significant concerns about the testimony that simply do not make sense, and thus discount the witness's credibility.

In a sex crime case, the strategy becomes even more of a delicate one, because any discussion of the sexual act is obviously very embarrassing for the victim. The defense lawyer must remember that, whether it's true or not, the rape victims truly believe what they say. Therefore, it is essential that the defense lawyer question the witness carefully, but with relentless vigor, to elicit the testimony desired.

In the William Kennedy Smith case, defense lawyer Roy Black was especially effective with this type of cross-examination. He analyzed the evidence produced by accuser Patricia Bowman, and then decided what the main points were that needed to be probed in defense of Smith. He focused on Bowman's removal of her stockings, and whether a rape would take place under the very windows where Kennedy Smith's mother was sleeping. Black then strongly confronted the accuser with questions about these important issues, while at the same time avoiding any possibility of upsetting the witness to the point where she would break down.

At the Thomas/Hill hearings, Senator Arlen Spector, a former federal prosecutor, questioned Anita Hill in a very strong confrontational manner, which seemed to offend not only her, but many who observed the hearings as well. Apparently Spector felt strongly that Hill was being less than truthful, but his risky decision to handle the witness as he did elicited sympathy for Hill even among her worst critics. In fact, Spector's unnecessarily rude manner almost ended up costing him his seat in the United States Senate.

While Bowman's demeanor (edgy, confrontational), and Hill's (very professional, aloof) differed from that of Washington's (calm, controlled), Fuller's main theory of defense apparently still basically rested with the issue of consensual sex. Would he therefore, concentrate on the consensual issue, or spend time attacking Washington's testimony on the basis of her knowledge of Tyson's bad boy personality, his continual use of somewhat crude sexual innuendoes, her dubious behavior in accompanying Tyson to his hotel room at 2:00 a.m., and the "greed, money-hungry, going to file a civil lawsuit for millions against Tyson" motive?

Vincent Fuller's cross-examination of Washington began with questions about her background, focusing in on her high school years and achievements. The defense lawyer first asked Washington about her training with modeling. She described how in 16 weeks she learned to "walk, work with hair and make-up, and to improve my public speaking."

Ironically, Washington testified that she had worked with a "date-rape" law proposal at her high school in Rhode Island. She and some other students had formulated a model legislative bill for a school project, and forwarded it to the State Legislature. "We never heard back, so the idea died there," she said.

At the rehearsals, Washington told the jury that someone with the pageant said to Tyson, "Just play with them a little," meaning that Tyson was to engage in some fun with the girls. Tyson did so, she said, and then told the jury, "All at once, he was staring straight at me, and then he asked me for a date."

Did Tyson say "I want you?" "No," Washington replied. When asked about whether she said "That's rather bold of you" when Tyson said "I want you," Washington told Fuller, "That's not what happened."

Washington then told the jury that, by seeing Tyson with Jesse Jackson at the opening ceremonies, she thought Tyson was a "good person." Did she hear Tyson utter a vulgarity, as heard by another contestant, when Jackson asked Tyson to come over? Washington said, "No."

Fuller then asked about the photographs Washington showed Tyson. Did he reply, "I have the advantage . . . now I've seen you in a bathing suit?" "No," Washington replied. She was then asked whether she said, "We're going out on a date, right?" Washington told the jury, "No, I didn't say that," but she did admit nothing was said about where or when they'd go.

Fuller then asked Washington about her interest in music that had sexual overtones. She testified that she was familiar with the music of the rock group Digital Underground, with "Sex Packets" being the main song she had heard.

Washington next talked about the incident backstage at the Gill concert, where she and her roommates ran into a pageant official, Alita Anderson. She admitted that Anderson had reprimanded her for being a "groupie," and told her that she should avoid being backstage.

In answer to Fuller's question about the meaning of the word "groupie," Washington astonished most courtroom observers by telling the jury that she had never heard of the word.

Apparently intent on establishing Washington's obsession with sex and sex-oriented music, defense lawyer Fuller turned his attention to the words of the music from Yo-Yo, the popular black rap group. "You can't play with my Yo-Yo" was singled out for the jury's attention, but Washington only admitted some interest in the song.

Turning back to the pageant itself, Washington then said that she was required every day to arise at 4:00-5:00 a.m., depending on which one of "my roommates arose first."

"Did you care about being out all night?" asked Fuller. "No." said Washington. "Did you have a hope of a relationship with Tyson?" Fuller continued. "Never thought I'd ever see him again," she replied.

Washington told the jury that Tyson had "begged" her to come down to the limousine, and once again that, looking back, she remembered his voice being "a bit strange."

"Weren't you alarmed when Tyson kissed you on the lips in the limousine?" Washington answered, "No."

In answer to the allegation that she had changed her story from her deposition when she said the bodyguard was with them, Washington testified that she was "traumatized, in a foggy state" and that she "couldn't remember."

Fuller then asked Washington whether she had given two different versions of her story concerning whether she went directly to the bedroom when she entered the hotel room. Washington admitted that she had told Detective Thomas Kuzmik of the Indianapolis Police Dept. that she had gone directly to the bedroom, but in court had said she'd waited in the living room until Tyson called to her.

After some questions about whether the garment that Washington wore on the night of the alleged rape had been altered either by her or her parents (Washington denied this), Fuller decided to question Tyson's accuser about whether she had intentions of filing a civil suit for money damages against the ex-champ.

Washington's testimony would become an issue after the trial was completed, when allegations would be made that

Washington was less than truthful in answer to Fuller's questions.

Washington remembered that it was a lawyer, Walter Stone, who called her and her parents and not the other way around. "You are going to need help with the media," she recalled him saying. "They are going to drive you crazy." Washington then stated that Stone had a conflict, but suggested a Providence, Rhode Island, attorney, Ed Gerstein.

Washington told the jury that Gerstein and a local Indianapolis lawyer named David Hennessey accompanied her to the grand jury testimony in August, and were there at trial with her as well. Fuller and Washington then had the following exchange:

Fuller:	Do you know what financial arrangement you have with Mr. Gerstein in representing you?
Washington:	No.
Fuller:	You have no idea whatsoever?
Washington:	No. He never said anything like that. He just said that he would help us with the media and that, you know, he was . . . I asked my parents if I could pay him back little by little.
Fuller:	Do you think he has some retainer arrangement with your parents?
Washington:	I don't know what retainer means.
Fuller:	Do you think he has some fee arrangement with your parents?
Washington:	I don't know.
Fuller:	Have you heard them explain or discuss with you a contingent?
Washington:	What's contingent mean?
Fuller:	Fee payable on a contingent that he's successful in some way.
Washington:	No. The only thing I know, they have to pay for his flights out here.
Fuller:	His expenses?
Washington:	Yes.
Fuller:	They are not liable to pay him anything else?
Washington:	I don't know what else they pay him.

Fuller did not ask directly whether Washington had entered into a contingency fee agreement (i.e., an agreement whereby the lawyer represents the client and takes no up-front fee, but instead a percentage of any monetary damages awarded the client), with Gerstein to represent her in any civil suit against Tyson.

Fuller ended his cross-examination of Washington by asking certain questions to indicate to the jury that she must have known of Tyson's sexual intentions:

Fuller: You never met Mike Tyson before July 18, 1991?
Washington: Right.
Fuller: Within minutes of the time when you first met him, he's hugging you?
Washington: Uh-huh.
Fuller: And you said, "Sure?"
Washington: Uh-huh.
Fuller: He awakened you at 1:30 in the morning, and you accompany him out, correct?
Washington: Correct.
Fuller: You join him in the limousine, and he hugged and kissed you?
Washington: Uh-huh.
Fuller: You willingly drove to his hotel?
Washington: Yes, not that I knew where I was going, but yes.
Fuller: And you willingly went to his suite?
Washington: Yes.
Fuller: And you went to his bedroom, and onto his bed?
Washington: Yes.
Fuller: You remained on that bed until Mr. Tyson made a statement which you understood to be an explicit sexual remark?
Washington: Yes.
Fuller: And then you proceeded to go to the bathroom, which is around the other side of the bed, and chose not to go out the door, which was directly across the end of the bed?
Washington: Uh-huh.

Desiree Washington's testimony was over. Prosecutor Garrison asked a few follow-up questions, but evoked no new information.

Analyzing Washington's testimony was difficult, because both Garrison and Fuller seemed to sidestep the most crucial questions surrounding what happened on the bed during the alleged rape. Both attorneys seemed more interested in the half-hour period leading up to the incident than the few minutes when the attack took place.

For Garrison the absence of such questions was predictable. He achieved his goal of presenting a credible witness who told a very plausible and believable story. Fuller's polite and less than forceful cross-examination was difficult to understand, especially when Garrison's direct examination gave him so many opportunities to probe Washington about what specifically happened in the hotel room between her and Tyson.

Fuller seemed to tap-dance around the incident itself, and also did not take advantage of Washington's propensity to provide more information than requested and to speak much more rapidly when put on the defensive. Twice, Tyson's defense attorney failed to perceive that Washington became very defensive when confronted with an inconsistency, and his failure to follow up let Washington off the hook.

One example occurred when Fuller was questioning Washington about her relationship with her private attorneys. Having argued to the jury many times that Washington's main motive for filing charges against Tyson was greed, Fuller never followed up on the specific agreement that Washington had with either Ed Gerstein or David Hennessey. Thorough follow-up might in fact have produced the agreement itself, which would have been a strong piece of evidence for Tyson.

Much like the mock cross-examination tactics employed by attorney Robert Hammerle prior to trial, Fuller needed to ask rapid-fire questions designed to put Washington on the defensive. Quick questions demanding explanations of inconsistent points or ones that seemed totally fabricated were needed to put Washington to the fire and see how she reacted.

Without inflaming her, Fuller could have easily given the jury a portrait of a woman whose background indicated more than the naive appearance she presented to the jury.

Questions could have been posed, for instance, about Washington's seemingly ridiculous comment that she didn't know what a "groupie" was. While unimportant on the surface,

this answer indicated Washington's purposeful attempt to portray herself as a goody-two-shoes who would never engage even
in consensual sex with Mike Tyson. Other evidence as well
seemed contrary to this image, but Fuller never saw fit to follow
up on it. Unlike Hammerle, Fuller could never uncover the
sophisticated, worldly side of Washington.

In addition, this failure to follow up or ask vital questions
on other occasions meant that Fuller never asked Washington
about many issues that were highly critical to the case.

Where were more probing questions about the panty
shield removal? How did Tyson accomplish oral sex with
Washington and still keep her pinned to the bed? Did Washington scream or not, and if she did, why did no one in the hotel hear
her? If Tyson is one of the strongest and most powerful men in the
world, where were the bruises on the frail 108-pound woman?
And on and on.

The failure of the defense attorney to question Washington more thoroughly may have been a result of his perception
that she was not an effective witness. Defense counsel never
wants to allow the prosecution's chief witness to tell her story
twice, because that only emphasizes that story more for the jury.

The defense may also not have wanted to risk browbeat-
ing Washington so as to inflame her already strong emotions
against Tyson. Fuller may, in fact, have calculated that such a risk
was not worth taking, in light of his confidence that Tyson could
defend himself against the allegations.

Fuller had certainly not poked as many important holes
in Washington's testimony as Black had done in the Kennedy
Smith case with Bowman. Fuller had only highlighted small
discrepancies in Washington's story whereas Roy Black was able
to make Patricia Bowman admit she didn't know why her
stockings were left in the car in the parking lot, or why Kennedy
Smith would commit rape on a beach just a stone's throw from his
mother's open bedroom window.

Fuller was also not able to do what the defense lawyers
accomplished in the Rodney King case, when they took apart, bit
by bit, the State's most important evidence, the videotape, by
breaking it down frame by frame to show that King had actually
fought back against the officers more than was previously realized. In doing that, the lawyers were able to neutralize the State's

case, and, with the absence of Rodney King as a witness, plant reasonable doubt in the minds of the 12 jurors.

Whatever Fuller's reasons for not examining Washington more vigorously, the testimony of Desiree Washington now formulated the issues for the remainder of the trial. The State would now attempt to corroborate her testimony as much as possible, and the defense would seek to contradict that testimony, while waiting for Tyson himself to make his grand performance on the witness stand.

9

♦

IN SUPPORT OF DESIREE

Confident that Desiree Washington was an excellent witness and impressive to the jury, prosecutors Garrison and Trathen now mapped out their strategy for the remainder of the State's case. Both knew that the defense would make motive a main issue, and therefore it was important to educate the jury as to the reasons why Washington's statements regarding her intent to simply "sightsee" with Tyson, and not to sleep with him, were truthful.

Garrison knew that most of the jury was still probably somewhat skeptical of why Washington would go to Tyson's hotel at 2:00 a.m. in the morning if it were not her intent to have sex. While Fuller had not pounded at his star witness like he expected, Garrison knew that he would have to show the jury the circumstances under which he believed that Washington had been tricked into going to the hotel room in the first place.

Believing that Washington had given the impression of being a naive, somewhat gullible, starry-eyed college freshman, Garrison thus set out to prove to the jurors that the tenacious, tricky Tyson had set a trap for Washington that she could not avoid. To do this, the prosecutor would take the jury on a journey that would clearly show how Tyson used his fame and fortune to virtually kidnap his intended victim.

Prosecutor Moira Lasch had intended to do the same thing in the Kennedy Smith case by portraying the defendant as a rich nephew of a famous family, a sex-starved night-club rover who had only one thing on his mind when he picked up Patty Bowman at the Au Bar nightspot in Palm Beach. Based on Bowman's testimony, which alleged that Kennedy Smith began to take his clothes off to go swimming when they got to the beach down in front of his estate, Lasch intended to force the jury into seeing that Smith manipulated Bowman into a compromising situation from which there was no escape.

If such could prove successful, the prosecution would then argue that nothing that Bowman did after that was in any way consensual, but a direct attempt by her to evade the advances by Smith. Even if the jury believed that she willingly cuddled with the defendant, when Bowman said "no" to his sexual overtures, that meant "no," and his forceful attack on her was indeed rape.

While Garrison knew that Kennedy Smith's subsequent testimony had wiped away that theory, he wasn't sure that Tyson would be as successful. William Kennedy Smith and Mike Tyson might both be famous, but that's where the similarity ended. Thus if Garrison could prove by impartial testimony that Tyson had lured Washington to his hotel room under false pretenses, the ex-champ would have to testify, and then Garrison would rip his story apart.

Garrison began to weave his story by bringing in Laticia Moscrip, the general manager of the Canterbury Hotel, who introduced phone records kept by the hotel. These records would prove to be important later in the trial to show what calls were made by Tyson and his bodyguard in the early morning hours of July 18, 1991.

Next, the prosecution called McCoy Wagers, the night auditor at the Canterbury Hotel. He testified that in the evening hours of July 17, a representative of Tyson, Dennis Hayes, had called with the reservations for Tyson. The reservation called for two rooms for the 17th through the 21st.

Turning to the night in question, July 18, Wagers said, "Tyson came into the hotel between 1:30 and 1:45 a.m." Wagers stated that Tyson was, "happy and smiling, cheerful, and said hello." A woman was two or three steps behind him, Wagers said.

The night auditor then testified that he saw Tyson's bodyguard, Dale Edwards, about 2:00 a.m. in the parlor of the hotel. "Edwards asked for an outside line to make a long-distance call," Wagers told the jury. He also said he had an important phone call coming in and that he wanted to know when that happened. Edwards then ordered room service for room 604, Wagers said.

The night auditor testified that Edwards asked for the phone numbers of different airlines, and that he gave him U.S. Air. Wagers said he never saw the "woman who had accompanied Tyson again," and only saw Tyson when he checked out at 4:00 a.m. Wagers said Tyson looked tired, and there were no smiles or hellos.

Next to testify was Chris Lowe, a bellhop at the hotel. Between "1:45 and 2:00 a.m.," he said, he saw Tyson, and that Tyson shook his hand. He also testified that the woman with Tyson was in the hotel only 40 to 45 minutes.

Vincent Fuller's cross-examination of Lowe produced testimony that the lady with Tyson had come out of the limousine first, followed by Tyson, and then by Edwards, the 6-foot, 300-pound bodyguard.

When Tyson and the bodyguard left in such a hurry, Lowe expressed concern about whether they had really checked out. He therefore went up to room 606 where he found "money on the table, and a shirt on the bed."

A critical State's witness, Virginia Foster, would be the next witness, but prior to her testimony a hearing was held regarding whether she could testify about Tyson's conduct during her hours as the limousine driver. In the hearing, the prosecution alluded to the fact that Foster would testify that Tyson had "lured" her up to the hotel room in a manner similar to that alleged by Desiree Washington. Tyson also was alleged to have tried to touch her, and to have exposed himself to her as well.

Judge Patricia Gifford ruled that, according to an Indiana case, such prior conduct by the accused could not be used when consent was alleged as a defense. Besides the question of whether the evidence would be relevant, Tyson was not denying that he had sex with Washington, only that the act was consensual on her part. The fact that he made advances on another woman against her will was thus ruled inadmissible by the court.

Owner of the Solid Gold Limousine Service, 51-year-old Virginia Foster said she held a master's degree and had taught in the Indianapolis public schools, where she also had worked with behavioral problems with young kids.

Foster first confirmed the phone call from Tyson to Desiree Washington's room at about 1:35 a.m. on July 18. She also stated two other important facts: 1) that "Tyson asked the girl to come out and talk," and 2) that "he was begging—he obviously wanted a woman," she summarized.

Foster then testified that she drove to the Canterbury Hotel, opened the back door, and "helped the lady out first." She remembered that "the lady had a real pretty hairdo; that was what stood out about her."

At 3:10-3:15 a.m., she saw the "lady rushing out of the hotel." Before Foster knew it, she was in the car, and the bodyguard came out and told Foster to take her back to the hotel. "Any conversation?" Foster was asked. "Yes," she said. "The lady said, 'I don't believe him—who does he think he is?'"

At the Omni, Foster said she helped the lady out of the limousine. Responding to questions concerning the woman's demeanor, she said that "her hair wasn't as neat; she looked frantic, in a state of shock, dazed, disoriented, couldn't focus." She seemed "scared," Foster said.

Back at the Canterbury, the bodyguard told Foster, "we'll be leaving." At 4:15 a.m., the bodyguard brought the luggage. The limousine proceeded to a West 65th Street address, the house of Tyson's girlfriend, singer B Angie B. They knocked on the door, but nobody was there. A call was then placed to the Holiday Inn South, to see if B Angie B was there. When Foster was asked whether she could make it to the Holiday Inn and then to the airport in time for the flight, she said "No," and the limousine sped off to the airport.

Indiana University Hospital Emergency Room physician Dr. Stephen Richardson took the witness stand after Foster. Dr. Richardson, an associate professor, testified that Desiree Washington had two small abrasions in her vagina, consistent with 20-30% of the injuries seen in sexual assault cases. This testimony in itself was critical, but then Richardson made a statement that may have ultimately decided the outcome of the case. Responding to Prosecutor Garrison's question about whether he had seen such injuries before, Richardson told the jury that only twice in 20 years had he ever seen those types of abrasions with consensual sex. Dr. Richardson went on to say that the abrasions could only have been caused by "forced or very hard consensual sex." On cross-examination, Richardson said, that in 20,000 cases, he had only seen two with like injuries where consensual sex was found.

As a follow-up to Doctor Richardson, the State produced a forensic crime lab expert, James Enoch. At 10:28 p.m. on July 22, 1992, some three days after the incident, Enoch had gone to the Canterbury Hotel to collect evidence.

Enoch testified that he was asked to look for the existence of body fluids on or near the bed in the room. Utilizing a UB ultraviolet light, which can detect the existence of saliva, semen, and perspiration, he probed the bedroom looking for physical evidence.

The room had, of course, been cleaned the night after the alleged attack. Enoch testified that he nevertheless was able to look at a section of the bed on the lower right hand corner where Detective Kuzmik believed the attack had occurred. When he used the UB light, it showed the fluorescence that indicated the presence of fluids.

Regarding other physical evidence in the room, the expert testified that he found a sequin along the wall that separated the bedroom from the living room. He photographed the sequin and then collected it as evidence.

While the jury seemed somewhat unimpressed by the technical aspects of this collection of evidence, they were interested in the sequin. Garrison showed the jury the outfit Washington wore on the evening in question and indicated where the sequin would fit with the dress.

Questions as to whether the tiny sequin was yellow or white were raised, with the expert saying that the actual color depended on the lighting where the sequin was inspected.

Defense lawyer Kathleen Beggs questioned whether the garment itself had been altered since the garment was sent back from Washington's East Coast home. The expert said he had no opinion.

"What about the spots on the floor? Any connection of those spots with either Mr. Tyson or the complaining witness?" Enoch was asked by Beggs. Again he said, "No."

The prosecution then called to the stand the investigating officer in the case, Thomas Kuzmik. Assigned to the sex crimes unit of the Indianapolis Police Department, he told the jury that he first met Washington on July 22 (three days after the incident) at the Child Advocacy Center at 251 E. Ohio Street in Indianapolis.

He described the woman as being "nervous and unable to focus. She would begin a sentence, and then trail off. She was apprehensive, confused, had problems keeping everything in sequence."

The detective told the jury that he asked Washington about whether she still had the clothing she wore on the night in question. She told him that her brother had taken it back to Rhode Island.

The inability of the detective to secure the clothing immediately and the fact that he saw Washington three days after the alleged attack would prove to be a thorn in the side of the prosecution. The fact that the panties and other clothes worn by the victim could not be examined immediately and without question of any alteration by Washington or her parents made it difficult for the jury to assess the physical evidence.

The question of whether the outfit had been altered would never be completely answered. The defense planted an idea that Washington's father may have torn the garment but such was never proven.

The detective's testimony did raise questions about the police procedures used in the case. Detective Kuzmik testified that he could have subpoenaed the clothing when Washington's father explained that the garment was on loan from someone who gave it to his daughter as a good luck charm for the pageant. Kuzmik also stated that he didn't want to have the garment cut, but sent as it was, but was overruled by the prosecutor. The garment evidence was thus altered when the father tore sequins from the dress and cut a patch away from it to send to Kuzmik.

The detective testified that nine sequins were sent from Donald Washington, yet only seven were in the envelope. The defense seemed to imply that perhaps they had been misplaced intentionally, but no real impact was made since Fuller never made it clear why the number of sequins was significant.

Kuzmik also was asked whether photographs were taken from the end of the bed where the alleged victim sat. Apparently, the defense must have felt that such photographs would have shown a view from the end of the bed which confirmed that the TV could be seen from there. This would be in direct contradiction to Washington's testimony that no T.V. could be seen.

Kuzmik was also asked whether Washington "had time to review her statement that she had given to Kuzmik." His reply was a stern "Yes," which meant apparently that she could have made changes in her statement if she had wanted to.

Forensic expert Mohammed Ahir was then called to the stand to provide details concerning the fluid specimen detected in Washington's panties. He testified that there were semen and blood samples on the panties, but could not say that he could separate what would be regular blood from menstrual blood.

The next prosecution witness was forensic expert Dirk Shaw, who was called to testify about the sequin found in the hotel room. Comparing it to sequins found on the garment of the alleged victim, he testified that they were identical.

In a light moment, when Garrison attempted to introduce the sequin into evidence, somehow the tiny sequin had become dislodged from the brown container, and could not be found. Embarrassed, Garrison moved ahead, but was saved when he located the sequin on the cuff of Dirk Shaw's sport coat.

Virginia Foster's testimony, in tandem with the sound technical and medical evidence, presented the jury with facts that Greg Garrison and Barb Trathen hoped would substantiate the story told by Desiree Washington. Outside of Washington herself, Greg Garrison had known that Virginia Foster would be his strongest witness. With seemingly no grudge to bear, at least that the jury would ever know about, Foster corroborated most of what Washington had testified to.

Vincent Fuller apparently miscalculated the major impact that this witness had on the jury. Perhaps he brushed off her testimony as unimportant. For whatever reason, he was completely unable on cross-examination to discredit the emotional Foster in any way.

Fuller did not have the same success with Foster as Roy Black had with a witness called by Prosecutor Moira Lasch in the Kennedy Smith trial. Like Foster, Ann Mercer was called to corroborate Patty Bowman's testimony by what she and her boyfriend observed when they picked up Bowman at the Kennedy estate shortly after the event. Mercer presented an interesting story on direct examination, but Black was able to cleverly carve up her story on cross-examination and ended up casting an additional doubt on whether Bowman had in fact told the truth as well.

Prosecutor Terry White also had trouble with one of his main corroborating witnesses in the Rodney King state case. California Highway Patrol Officer Melanie Singer was called to corroborate the fact that Sergeant Stacey Koon had taken over the arrest of King from her without cause, and that Officer Lawrence Powell had repeatedly struck King with head shots, causing severe injury to his face.

On cross-examination, however, defense lawyers were able to make clear that some of the procedures advocated by Singer demonstrated her lack of experience in dealing with such matters. Later, her account of the injuries she believed King suffered did not match photos taken at the scene, reducing her to less than an effective witness for the State.

Fuller's problems with Foster may have resulted from his impersonal federal courtroom style that put him at odds with her from the get-go. Due to Foster's unpleasant encounter with Tyson regarding his sexual advances toward her (the jury was not allowed to hear her discuss Tyson's behavior), it was plain that Virginia Foster had a grudge to bear. Fuller, however, never seemed to recognize his need to discredit this testimony, and his inability to listen well to the answers given by Foster to his questions proved fatal. In fact, instead of probing deeply into the inconsistencies of Foster's testimony, he ended up antagonizing her instead.

Never was this fact more apparent than in dealing with Foster's account of Tyson and Washington's behavior in the back seat of the limousine. Foster's blanket answer that she saw little or nothing left her wide open to follow-up, but Fuller's inability to ever get more than "yes" or "no" answers kept him from ever pinning her down.

Fuller, in fact, never tried to give the jury any reason why Foster would be biased against Tyson. Perhaps he was frightened away from the alleged incident with Tyson and Foster. Maybe he should have permitted Foster to tell the jury that Tyson had tried to come on to her, since many of the jurors might have felt that this allegation was absurd based on Foster's age and appearance. He nevertheless failed to give the jury some basis for confusion on the part of this witness. Instead, Virginia Foster was let go without a scratch and her revealing testimony may have very well been the   point at which some of the jurors began to change their minds about the innocence of Mike Tyson.

As for Dr. Richardson's testimony, Fuller and crew may have underestimated the testimony that the emergency room physician would provide. They may have thought that their medical testimony would balance out Dr. Richardson's medical testimony, but if so, it was a poor assumption. Dr. Richardson, in fact, turned out to be a great witness, while the defense physician was a complete and utter disaster.

The defense also made a cardinal error in dealing with Richardson's cross-examination. Apparently either through statements of his testimony provided by the State, or through a pretrial deposition (if there was one), Fuller should have known better than to ask whether the doctor had ever seen injuries such as those sustained by Washington. Instead, he apparently asked Richardson a question he didn't know the answer to, and got burned when the doctor said that he had only seen "injuries like that in two of 20,000 cases."

The medical evidence for the State did seem to meet their objective of providing the jury with impartial, basic evidence to back up the fact that Washington's version of the story could very well have happened the way she said it did. Most jurors tend to believe medical testimony because they believe the doctors have no reason to fabricate it, and the defense was unable to discredit that crucial evidence.

The performances of the respective attorneys during the presentation of this evidence were indicative of their differing points of view toward the evidence. Garrison seemed almost cocky, certain that the testimonies of the doctor and the detective were impressive to the jury.

He apparently felt confident that matters were indeed going his way. His propensity to object to somewhat trivial matters was clearly unnecessary in view of the points he seemed to be scoring with the jury.

While he was not making many points for Tyson, defense counsel Fuller displayed for the first time a sense of fight. His voice rising and falling, he seemed more comfortable and actually began moving around the courtroom with his arms folded. His focus on the alterations in the garment also seemed to be a preview of things to come. In fact, when Fuller misplaced his note pad, he seemed almost human and perhaps a bit more friendly to the jurors.

What impression the jury gathered from all of this evidence was difficult to assess. Washington's story had now been embellished by Virginia Foster's testimony and that of medical experts. For the prosecution, it was time to turn to other beauty pageant contestants to back up further the story presented by Washington.

10

◆

MORE BEAUTIES

In an attempt to bolster Washington's claims about the "rude and sex-driven" side of Mike Tyson, the State called several beauty contestants from the Miss Black America Pageant.

First to testify was pageant contestant Stacy Murphy from Chicago, who was a senior at Chicago State University working on a degree in microbiology. A pleasant lady with a light-up smile, she stated that she was one of Washington's better friends while at the pageant. Avoiding any discussion of the events before the alleged rape, she said that she and Washington were together the morning of July 19, the day after the alleged attack.

The event was a rehearsal in front of Union Station in downtown Indianapolis. "All of the contestants were sluggish," she testified, but she and Desiree Washington got a chance to talk together during a rest stop.

Describing their relationship, Ms. Murphy said that the two had kidded one another that "they neither one had rhythm." In fact, she joked that they were "sisters under one rhythmless motion." Murphy said Washington "wasn't enthusiastic that morning," but that she thought it was because of the late evening the night before. When she kidded Washington, she didn't kid back, and Murphy said she didn't know what was wrong.

Finally, Murphy said, Washington spoke up. "I feel so stupid," she said, "he raped me." She then said Washington started talking nonstop and said the following:

"He asked me to a party, a rooftop party. When we got in the limousine, he said he had to go to the hotel to pick up his bodyguards." Murphy said Washington next told her that "she felt stupid, went to the bathroom; he was all over me." When others began listening, Murphy said she started talking about "the story being a nice movie," so as to divert their attention away from Desiree's story. Later, after a producer told the girls to get back in line and continue to practice, Murphy advised Desiree not "to tell any of the girls—but to tell officials, tell her parents."

Ms. Murphy said she tried to keep Washington's mind off of the incident the rest of the day, but that Desiree wouldn't crack jokes. "It wasn't like it was before," she said. Murphy also testified that "looks tell so much," and "her look said it all . . . She was talking to me, but her soul was gone," she didn't look like herself, "she was a zombie. . . I tried to comfort her," Murphy said, "but she just kept talking."

While Tyson doodled on a note pad, defense lawyer Lane Heard took over for cross-examination. Heard proved to be the most effective of the defense team, with an easy manner and congenial personality. He also seemed to be a more formidable foe for Garrison, who appeared somewhat agitated by Heard's strong manner and unwillingness to back down when Garrison confronted him with objections to the court.

Kidding with Murphy, Heard elicited from her facts about the pageant itself. She said the "tension began to build," and that some of the contestants became "upset" and got "nasty" with each other.

According to Murphy, Desiree Washington told her that she saw Tyson while backstage at the Gill concert, and talked to Tyson after Alita Anderson had reprimanded her for being a groupie. Washington allegedly said that Tyson asked her out to a party, "a rooftop reception," where all the other contestants would be.

Skipping to the time when Washington went in the limousine with Tyson, Murphy testified that Washington told her that Tyson said "he had to go pick up a bodyguard," and that after they got to the hotel, "he raped me."

Heard hit the witness hard about the fact that Washington had not said anything to Murphy about certain portions of her own testimony, including:

1) Any hotel room phone call;
2) The kiss in the limousine;
3) The fact that she went in, and sat on the bed in the bedroom;
4) Any kiss on the bed;
5) Any removal of her panty shield in the bathroom.

Murphy was also asked whether Desiree Washington told her that she had been crying when she left the hotel room. Murphy said Washington told her she "gathered her things and left the room crying," and that she just had kept saying to Tyson "Stop. Stop." She also said Washington told her about going to the bathroom. On cross-examination, Murphy admitted she had never brought forth any of this information in prior statements.

(During this time, juror #6, a young T-shirt printer seemed to be mesmerized by Tyson. Either he didn't believe what he was hearing, or was insulted with what the witness was saying about Tyson. Other jurors, including the ex-Marine and the black lady next to him, continued to watch Tyson as well. It seemed as if they were watching the ex-champ for a reaction, but Tyson continued to show virtually no expression.)

Defense lawyer Heard then took Murphy back to the opening ceremonies held outside the Hoosier Dome. She remembered gaining Tyson's attention, and seeing Jesse Jackson reprimand Tyson for his behavior with the contestants. She also remembered Tyson making an "oh-shit" remark about Jackson, giving her a feeling that Tyson didn't want to be bothered with Jackson.

Murphy then described again the scene at the rehearsal hall. "Everyone flocked to Tyson," she said, and Tyson "was an octopus, with his arms around waists and touching the behinds and breasts of any girl he could find." She admitted that "if a girl didn't want to be touched," she shouldn't have been there and that she didn't like the fact that Tyson told everyone, "If you want your picture taken, you have to sit on my lap." Offended by the remark, she said she didn't have her picture taken.

On re-direct examination, Murphy testified that there were a lot of "backbiters" among the contestants. Some she said, "felt Desiree was too perky, and that her perkiness was just a game."

Murphy testified that everyone could see Tyson touching all the girls. "Tyson," she said, was "grabbing girls and feeling on them."

After this controversial witness testified, Miss Black America beauty contestant Charise Nelson was next to take the witness stand. Charise said she had met Tyson at the Apollo Theatre in New York some years before. The witness testified that Tyson had put his hand around her waist, but when she said "stop, he did."

Prosecutor Garrison took this witness directly to the 20th of July when she encountered Desiree Washington in the lobby of the Omni Hotel. She said Desiree had "no makeup on" and that she was waiting for her mother. "I'll wait too," Nelson said. "I'm going to the hospital," Washington replied, "I have cramps."

Moments later, Nelson said, Desiree asked her to "promise not to say anything." When Charise said she wouldn't, Washington told her, "I was with Mike last night." "Mike who?" Nelson asked. Desiree replied, "Mike Tyson—I was with him, he raped me."

Miss Nelson said her first comment was "take him to jail." Nelson then said Desiree Washington told her that Tyson said "Come to the hotel, 'cause I'll get my bodyguard." In the room, Desiree Washington allegedly said "Tyson started to take advantage of her, saying 'I like girls who say no.'" She testified Washington said Tyson asked her, "Am I too big?" Indianapolis police officer Cindy Jenkins was next to testify. In the early hours of July 20th, she saw Desiree. "Washington," she said, "was fidgety," and "looked down." She was "bug-eyed," her eyes were "wide open," said Jenkins. The woman was in a "state of shock," she said, "and very confused." Jenkins went on to say that Tyson told Washington they "would go around town," and would go to the Canterbury Hotel to "get the bodyguards."

Washington told Jenkins she "tried to fight him off," and "begged him to stop." She said she "screamed," and that Tyson said "Don't fight me—you know you want me." Jenkins said Washington was "disoriented as to time, and would jump from one topic to the other." The officer said Washington's head dropped when she talked about the assault, and that the woman told her she had talked to the chaplain some 25 hours after the attack.

Sizing up the testimony of the beauty contestants was difficult. The jurors were receiving a poor report card on Tyson's behavior toward the contestants, and his propensity to use lewd and suggestive sexual remarks to them.

Apparently missed by both sides was the close inspection of what Stacy Murphy told the jury Washington said to her: "I feel so stupid, he raped me." Ironically, the statement supported both the defense and prosecution theories regarding the incident. The prosecution could point to the statement backing up its contention that Washington was duped ("I feel so stupid") when she went to hotel room with Tyson. The defense, however, could counter with: a) The comment meant that Washington knew she shouldn't have gotten involved with Tyson and that she felt so stupid for having had sex with Tyson, and thus b) that because she felt stupid, and embarrassed, Washington struck back at Tyson by filing charges of rape.

In addition, Charise Nelson's testimony to what Desiree Washington told her was inconsistent with what Washington had testified to on direct examination. The defense, however, didn't seem to believe that Nelson had much credibility and never followed up with questions about Washington's account of the story to her.

Prosecutor Moira Lasch never did attempt to portray William Kennedy Smith as quite the same type of sexual deviant that Mike Tyson was alleged to have been. She did allude to his being a swinging bachelor, and a rich one at that, but due to the judge's ruling Lasch could not delve deeply into Kennedy Smith's background, to either present testimony about similar incidents such as the one alleged by Bowman, or Smith's other activities with the opposite sex.

Similarly, no real evidence was allowed to be presented regarding the sexual history of Clarence Thomas during his Senate confirmation hearings. Allegations of impropriety surfaced after Anita Hill's allegations, but for the most part they were swept under the table and disregarded by the Senate panel.

In this case, however, the jury now had clearly been presented with the "sexual animal" picture of Mike Tyson that the prosecution hoped was consistent with that provided by

Desiree Washington. Ironically, even though he could have successfully objected to much of the women's testimony as hearsay, Fuller seemed to purposely not challenge the accounts of Tyson's crude behavior, apparently believing that it added support to his contention that Washington should have known what she was in for with the ex-champ.

Whether the beauty contestants' testimony posed more questions than answers was pure conjecture, but the prosecution believed they were painting a portrait of a Mike Tyson who was indeed capable of committing rape.

11

---◆---

THE 911 TAPE

Just as in the Rodney King state case, tape recordings played an important part in the outcome of the Tyson trial. There was not, of course, a videotape with the same explosive impact as that which showed the beating of King. However, two audiotapes would be critical to the State's case, and for two completely different reasons.

Toward the end of the trial, the State would play for the jury an audiotape of Mike Tyson's testimony before the grand jury. Such would be offered to show the apparent discrepancy between Tyson's statements to Washington regarding his sexual intentions, which were given under oath to the six jurors at the grand jury hearing, and those that he testified to at trial.

The other audiotape would be offered by the State for a different purpose, and it was only by chance that this important piece of evidence finally saw the light of day.

If Desiree Washington had not mentioned the emergency 911 tape in the course of a deposition four weeks before trial, no one would have known of its existence. Amazingly enough, somehow the tape had slipped through the cracks of the police department when the call from Desiree Washington came in on July 20, 1991.

Although the tape was not played for the jury until the close of the prosecution's case, it went as follows:

DISPATCH TAPE

This tape is a copy of the Indianapolis police department 911 center for the date of July 20, 1991, being recorded from recorder number 2, line number 3, reference rape investigation beginning time 01.22.08.

Dispatcher: 9ll police emergency.
Washington: Yes, may I please speak with Corporal Goldman?
D. Who?
W. Corporal Goldman.
D. What sector?
W. Excuse me?
D. What sector? This is the Indianapolis Police Dept.
W. That's what I was told to ask for when I called.
D. What's the problem? Do you have a problem?
W. Yes, I'm calling to report a rape.
D. A rape?
W. Uh huh.
D. When were you raped?
W. Well, can I speak to this person?
D. OK, ma'am?
A   Yes.
D. OK, you were the person who was raped.
W. Uh huh.
D. OK, now I can find Corporal Goldman, or whoever it is, for you, I can try and find him, uh, you want to make a police report?
W. Well, I don't know.
D. OK.
W. I want someone, I don't know. Is this being recorded?
D. It is being recorded but you can still talk to me. I mean I am a human being and I can sympathize with you. I'm here to help you. I'm not here to condemn you or anything.
W. OK.
D. So obviously you need some type of help and that's what my job is and that's what I'm here to do.
W. OK.
D. So

W. I can just tell you what happened and you can determine, I . . .

D. OK, why don't you tell us what happened and then we'll see, we'll tell you what you can do. Your options and then we'll let you make the decision, OK?

W. OK.

D. OK.

W. OK, uh, I met this person during the day and uh, I went out with this person in a limousine that night and the person told me that he had to go to get his bodyguards and asked me if I wanted to come in for a second and I said oh, OK. Fine. You know, thinking this was a nice person. And we went in and the person started attacking.

D. Uh huh.

W. By attacking me, he became very aggressive.

D. Uh huh.

W. Trying to take my clothes off and I was like, well I have to leave. See, I'm not like that and so the person agreed, OK, fine, it is OK, then, you know, you don't have to do anything, you are a nice girl, you are a Christian girl, and things like that. And so, uh, I was like, well, you know, I just want to get that straight that I don't want to do anything and I kept saying that over and over again, and this person went on to say that that's what made him want me more because I didn't want to do anything basically. He kissed me and oh, you are turning me on because you are not like the rest of these girls. You are not a city girl. And then uh, person tried to take my clothes off again, and succeeded and then just basically forced himself upon me.

D. OK, you did tell him no when you said . . . ?

W. Yes, I said no, uh, I asked. . .

D. Do you know this person?

W. Yes.

D. Do you know him well or is this somebody you just now met?

W. It is someone that's like famous.

D. Somebody famous?

W. Uh huh.

D. Well, that's not, you know, keep them from being wrong. If you are wrong, you are wrong, I don't care who you are.

W. Yeah.

D. He forced himself upon you. He was wrong.

W. It is just that it will go so public, and it is, you know.

D. How old are you?

W. I'm 18.

D. You are 18. Nobody else knows?

W. Uh, my parents know. I told them. And uh . . .

D. Well hon, you know, you have to make this decision for yourself. You weren't the one that was wrong, right.

W. No. I just feel so disgusting.

D. Most rape victims feel that way.

W. I came out of the bathroom and this person was in his underwear and he just basically kind of did what he wanted to do and kept saying don't fight me. Don't fight me. And I was like saying, no no. Get off of me, get off of me please. Get off of me and he was like don't fight me. Don't fight me. And the person is a lot stronger than I was and he just did what he wanted and I was saying stop please stop. And he just didn't stop. And. . .

D. OK, now who is wrong?

W. Well, him.

D. You told him to stop, now who is wrong?

W. And he just kept saying, I'm not going to come in you. I'm not going to come in you and I kept saying, please stop, you are hurting me. Please stop. And then finally I go in, I said I have to leave and he was like well, you are welcome to stay, and I said well no, I said I liked you because I thought you were a nice person, this morning, not just because you were a star, and now I don't like you for either one. And I left and I was crying and uh, this person's limousine driver talked to me.

D. Do you think that you can be happy knowing that he did this and he is going to get away with it? What do you want to do about it? Your decision, what do you want to do about what he did to you?

W. I don't want, I'm afraid to go public, because, it is just, I have a title and everything and I'm so afraid.

D. But you need to talk to somebody about it, right.

W. Uh huh.

D. Well there are a few suggestions that I have for you. And I can tell you.

W. Uh huh.

D. Well you are 18, you are considered an adult now. You can make your own decisions, I can't make them for you. Your parents can't make it for you. You'll have to find these decisions within yourself.

W. Yeah. I just feel that people think it is my fault for going in his room, but I was just naive to believe that he was, you know, a nice person.

D. Irregardless to that, irregardless, you said no.

W. Uh huh.

D. Right?

W. Uh huh.

D. And that's where it should have ended.

W. OK.

D. A lot of people go on dates and there are people. See people in privacy or whatever, they, everybody has the right to say no and that should be respected.

W. Uh huh.

D. When you say no, it means no. It doesn't mean maybe, and it doesn't mean yes.

W. OK, I didn't go to the doctor right away. I came home, and I took, and I came back to my room and I took a shower and . . .

D. When did this happen to you?

W. It happened, uh, around this time last night.

D. OK, it is still not too late to do something about it.

W. And I got my period, so . . .

D. Have you had any kind of medical attention, have yourself looked at?

W. No, I haven't. Uh, my period had began to start yesterday, and when he started to do that to me.

D. Uh huh.

W. And I was trying to get out and then it just continued on today, so I'm afraid that, like if there is any evidence of what he did to me, it would be out now.

D. Uh huh, well, not necessarily see there are a lot of different things involved in a rape.

W. Uh huh.

D. You have to consider, I'm not trying to scare you, ok.

W. Uh huh.

D. Venereal disease, and things like that.

W. Uh huh.

D. So you have to decide within yourself if you want to pursue this if somebody has done you wrong if you want to do something about it or if you just want to forget it.

W. Every time I've seen this on television, I've always said I did want, I would do something about it, but, I just feel so scared. It is just so different when it . . .

D. You know television is not like real life.

W. To me, yeah, I know.

D. You don't know all the circumstances involved and things that you hear on TV or in the news.

W. Uh huh.

D. You have to decide for yourself who you are and what you want to do about it when somebody has violated you.

W. Uh huh.

D. And if you want, these are your options, I'm not trying to scare you. You could speak to a police officer.

W. Uh huh.

D. Or, you know, I can give you the number to victim's assistance.

W. Uh huh.

D. I could send somebody to talk to you or either you can call them.

W. Uh huh.

D. I mean nobody is going to force you to press charges.

W. Uh huh.

D. And it never hurts to talk to somebody about it.

W. OK.

D. After you talk to somebody about it, well, what are your options, if you want to pursue it, you can pursue it. If you don't, you don't have to.

W. OK.

D. So you know, we're at the position now, where you need to tell me what you want to do. And then I can help you whatever you want to do, I can help you from here.

W. I want to go to a doctor and see if there is anything wrong with me.

D. Uh huh.

W. Really.

D. Well if you want to go to a doctor and I feel that you need to. You have to listen to yourself.

W. Uh huh, and then I would have to take it from there.

D. Right. Well it is up to you. You know. If you want to talk to somebody, I can have somebody call you either if they have to be at your house or be at somebody else's house . . .

W. I don't live in Indiana.

D. Doesn't matter. This happened in Indiana. Right?

W. Uh huh.

D. Well, so if the crime has been committed within the state. . .

W. OK.

D. You are the victim. You are not the criminal.

W. OK.

D. You're the victim.

W. But I feel like one.

D. Well you are . . .

W. I mean.

D. So you need to let me know, you know, what you want to do.

W. Uh,

D. The only options that I have.

W. Uh huh.

D. To offer you.

W. Uh huh, uh . . .

D. Hello. Hello.

W. Hello.

D. Yeah, there are two of us sitting here ma'am. I'm training, there is two of us sitting here, she works . . .

D2. What's your name?

W. Do I have to tell my name?

D2. No, that's fine, but I was just listening to the conversation and personally, I'm not trying to tell you what to do. But first of all, you need to go to the doctor and get yourself checked out.

W. Uh huh.

D2. And I know you said that you saw it on TV that if something like this happened to you, that you would do something about it.

W. Uh huh.

D2. If you follow your heart, you follow your first instinct. If your heart is telling you to do something about it, then do it. Don't let this just slide by because this could scar you for the rest of your life.

W. Uh huh.

D2. Now just because he is a star and all this, that don't mean nothing. He's a person.

W. Yeah. That's what I said to him.

D2. So it doesn't matter now. He has done it.

W. Uh huh.

D2. And now it is up to you to do something about it.

W. Uh huh. How do you prove something like that though?

D2. Really now, it is your word against his.

W. Exactly.

D2. But see the fact of the matter is you, like someone told me, you tried.

W. Uh huh.

D2. Don't, all I can, I'm not trying to tell you what to do, but don't be scared.

W. But someone nationally known against someone just like me, a regular person, I mean, people like just kind of naturally think that I'm going for the money or something.

D2. You don't know that. Cause you don't know what might happen.

W. Uh. . .

D2. You don't know that. The only way you are going to find out is if you try.

W. Yeah.

D2. You are just as much a person as he is.

W. Yeah.

D2. If your heart is telling you to go ahead and do something about it, then you do something about it whether he is famous. If he was the president of the United States, if you feel like he should, if something should be done, then you do it.

W. Uh huh.

D2. Is it what you want to do?

W. Part of me wants to do something, and part of me is just scared.

D2. You want to talk to somebody?

W. Yeah.

D2. OK. Let me . . . do you want to leave a number or do you want somebody to come out to you?

W. Uh, I'm at a hotel right now.

D2. That doesn't matter.

W. And it is like for a pageant, so, if someone were to come talk to me, then it wouldn't look good for me.

D2. I understand.

W. Uh . . .

D2. Do you want to talk to somebody on the phone?

W. Yeah.

D2. OK. Let me give you, OK, what's your phone number?

W. OK.

D2. What's the phone number where you can be reached at?

W. OK, I'm at the Omni Biltmore, I'm at the Omni Biltmore and the number is 317-634- and I'm in room 2, I'm in room 443, but it says 2443.

D2. So you are in room 243.

W. Uh huh. And I think the number to the Omni is 6666. Or 6661. But . . .

D2. Are you the only one there in your room?

W. No, there are my two roommates. But I told them about it already.

D2. Do you feel comfortable leaving your first name?

W. Desiree.

D2. Or, them to ask for you, or just, you don't really have to leave your name as long as they need to talk to. You can make up a name.

W. My name is Desiree.

D2. You-Desiree?

W. Uh huh.

D2. OK. I'm going to have somebody call you from victim's assistance.

W. OK.

D2. OK.

W. Alright thank you.

D2. Uh huh. Bye.

W. Bye Bye.

Ending time is 01.35.41. This tape was recorded by Gail Larsen, Tape Research Analyst, IPD.

Admissibility of the tape became the subject of a strong debate between the lawyers. Kathleen Beggs argued for the defense that the tape should have been entered into evidence while Washington was on the witness stand so that cross-examination could have been held. The defense also argued that: a) The tape wasn't relevant because of the gap in time between when the alleged rape attack occurred and when the call came; b) the witness was no longer available for cross-examination; c) the strong responses from the dispatcher on the tape were highly prejudicial, and d) by no stretch of the imagination could the tape be an "excited utterance, and thus admissible under an exception to the hearsay rule," due to the time gap. This argument was in reference to the fact that situations occur where a statement made directly after or in association with the alleged act itself is allowed into evidence. Beggs's argument was that because a significant amount of time had gone by between when the act had occurred and when the statement was made, Washington's statement was inadmissible.

Prosecutor Garrison stated that to leave out the contents of the tape "takes a piece out of our case." Calling Beggs's argument "silly," he countered that the tape portrayed Washington's state of mind (another exception to the hearsay rule) and therefore was highly relevant.

To this point in the trial, Judge Patricia Gifford had been very careful not to allow any evidence in that was peripheral to the actual facts involving the attack in the hotel room. However, here the judge ruled that the contents of the tape went to motive, and since the defense had portrayed the accuser as a greedy, money-motivated woman, the tape would be allowed into evidence in order to show an alternative motive. Some parts of the tape would be cut out (due to their inadmissibility) but the rest of the tape was played for the jury as a prior consistent statement by Washington, and not as an "excited utterance" by her.

Most important, however, was whether or not the Judge's ruling allowing the tape into evidence was a correct one. Most certainly the tape was clearly hearsay, since it was an out-of-court statement offered for the truth of the matters therein. The tape also had the character of a prior consistent statement (a statement that is consistent with the witness's in-court testimony), and as such, would be considered cumulative and inadmissible, since the tape for all practical purposes allowed Washington to testify twice.

When asked about this matter, Indiana University Law Professor Thomas Schornhorst, an expert on Indiana law, concluded, "The rules of evidence require that the jury base its decision [by and large] upon the testimony it hears in person from a witness, and which is subject to contemporaneous cross-examination by the opposing party. Hence, for this reason also, prior *consistent* statements of the type represented by the 911 tape are generally inadmissible. There is an exception to this rule of exclusion that would apply, for example if the thrust of the defense cross-examination of Desiree Washington was to suggest that her in-court testimony was the product of recent fabrication. In such instances, her prior consistent statements which were made *before* the purported motive for fabrication arose are admissible to rebut that claim. However, as I understand the defense strategy, their position was that Ms. Washington's motive to fabricate what occurred arose contemporaneously with her leaving Tyson's hotel room. Hence, a call made to the police department the following day would not satisfy the conditions for admissibility upon the grounds described above."

Prior to trial, both the prosecution and defense had made a big deal out of the 911 tape. When it was discovered by accident, it was thought that its contents corroborated the victim's allegation that she had called the police for help. Perhaps it did, but there were inconsistencies within Washington's testimony that made it subject to differing interpretations. In the final analysis, the 911 tape appeared not to be the explosive bit of evidence some experts speculated it would be, although the strong references by the dispatcher regarding Washington being a "victim" and so forth obviously influenced the jurors.

The playing of the tape did serve two other purposes for the prosecution. It allowed the jury to hear the tone of voice of Desiree Washington shortly after the alleged incident, and judge for themselves whether she seemed legitimate in her discussions with the telephone dispatcher.

Second, the fact that Washington even made the call gave the jurors some evidence to consider concerning her state of mind. They were left to ponder her intentions as to other motives for finally filing the charges against Tyson, but the fact that Washington genuinely sought out information concerning the alleged incident must have impressed even the most doubtful juror.

12

◆

THREE WHO NEVER APPEARED

For the most part, the trial had been easy sailing for Judge Patricia Gifford. The high-powered lawyers had behaved themselves, and even the crazed media had abided by the court rules.

The judge was put to the test, however, when defense lawyer Fuller filed a motion requesting permission to add three material witnesses to the defense witness list. The point of their testimony was to describe that they observed "two people all over each other in the back of the limousine when it came to the Canterbury Hotel."

The witnesses names were Carla J. Martin, Pamela Lawrence, and Renee Neal.

The motion filed in behalf of the request read, in part, as follows:

> Comes now defendant Michael G. Tyson and moves the Court for an order permitting the defense to add three newly-discovered witnesses to its witness list. The names and addresses of these witnesses, which have already been provided to the State, are being filed under seal with the Court.
>
> These persons were present near the front entrance of the Canterbury Hotel in the early morning of July 19, 1991, and witnessed a limousine pull up in the driveway. One of the witnesses observed two people in the back seat of the limousine hugging and kissing and pointed that fact out to the second

witness. One of two persons that emerged from the back of the limousine was a young black woman with prominent hair; the first witness recognized the other person to emerge as Mike Tyson, and she pointed him out to the second witness. The third witness, who was on the telephone in the hotel parlor and was looking out the window, noticed the two people holding hands after they exited the limousine and entered the hotel. The witnesses also described a heavy-set black man with gold glasses who emerged from the limousine's front passenger seat and a woman who emerged from the driver's seat.

Defense counsel apparently first learned of these witnesses on Thursday, January 30, when a secretary at Black Expo contacted Mr. James Voyles's office. (Uncertain who to approach, one of the witnesses had contacted Black Expo because she knew Rev. Charles Williams from an aerobics class.) A representative of Mr. Voyles's office (not a member of the trial team) spoke to two of the witnesses by telephone that night and arranged to interview them at greater length the next day. Based on that interview, he concluded that the witnesses should be taken seriously and so advised defense counsel Friday night. At first cautious of these new witnesses, defense counsel sought an order from the Court on Saturday, February 1, to inspect the limousine driven by Virginia Foster on the night in question, in order to verify that one could see through the tinted windows, as the witnesses said they had done.

Trial counsel met with the first two witnesses for the first time (and spoke with the third on the telephone for the first time) on Sunday, February 2. Counsel then also called the aunt of one of the witnesses, who is an attorney with whom the witnesses stated they had discussed their observations in late summer.

Because of the large number of persons who have come forward erroneously claiming to have relevant information, defense counsel deemed it necessary to take all these precautionary steps before deciding to seek to add the witnesses. Having taken these steps and concluded that the witnesses appeared to be telling the truth, counsel immediately notified counsel for the State, Mr. Garrison, and provided full information concerning all three witnesses.

Due Process requires that the Court to grant leave to add these new witnesses to the defense's witness list despite the fact that the deadline for naming witnesses had expired. The Indiana Supreme Court has stated that "the most extreme sanction of witness exclusion should not be employed unless

defendant's breach of a discovery deadline has been purposeful or intentional or unless substantial and irreparable prejudice would result to the State." Wisehart v. State, 491 N.E. 2nd
985, 991 (Ind. l986). The Wisehart court further held that "[i]n
order to reach a just decision which fully assesses the right of
both parties to a fair trial and the criminal defendant's Sixth
Amendment right to present witnesses on his behalf," a court
considering late addition of defense witnesses should consider
questions such as when the witnesses first became known to
defense counsel; how vital the potential testimony is to the
defendant's case; the nature of the prejudice to the State; and
whether the State may be afforded an opportunity to interview
the new witnesses and conduct further investigation if necessary.

The Wisehart standard, in accordance with the Sixth
Amendment and the requirements of due process of law,
compels the addition of the three new witnesses. The delay in
adding the witnesses was not intentional or purposeful. Before yesterday, trial counsel had no confirmed information
that these witnesses existed. The witnesses only became known
to defense counsel after trial had begun; there was no lack of
diligence on our part, nor any way that we could have learned
of them earlier. The testimony of all three witnesses is critically
important, because it significantly contradicts the complainant's testimony and indicates that she was engaged in consensual romantic activity with the defendant as they entered the
Canterbury Hotel on the night in question. Any prejudice to
the State is remediable; the prosecution has been given full
information concerning the witnesses, and they are a v a i l -
able to be interviewed or deposed by the State immediately. If
further time for investigation is necessary, a recess or continuance may be granted.

Defense lawyers Fuller and Voyles also filed an "Offer of
Proof," which stated:

Comes now defendant Michael G. Tyson and presents the
following offer of proof specifying the testimony that could be
given by Carla J. Martin, Pamela Lawrence, and Renee Neal.
If called to testify, it is anticipated that Carla J. Martin
would testify as follows:
Ms. Martin, along with Ms. Lawrence and Ms. Neal, attended the Johnny Gill concert at the Hoosier Dome on the

night of July 18, 1991. Ms. Martin did so because she was the girlfriend of a man who was playing the drums in Mr. Gill's band on this particular tour. Because Mr. Gill's band was staying in the Canterbury Hotel, Ms. Martin had changed her clothes on the day of the concert in a room in the Canterbury Hotel and left a bag with her belongings at the front desk.

After the concert ended sometime after 12:30 a.m. on July 19, Ms. Martin and her two companions went to the backstage area of the Hoosier Dome in which Mr. Gill's bus was parked. When Mr. Gill's band was fully packed onto the bus, Ms. Martin said good-bye to her boyfriend and she and her companions left the Hoosier Dome.   They went to Ms. Lawrence's Nissan 300ZX.

With Ms. Lawrence driving, the three women proceeded to the Canterbury Hotel, in order to pick up Ms. Martin's belongings. Ms. Martin sat crammed behind her two friends in the two-seat sports car. They arrived at the hotel at approximately 1:30 to 1:40 a.m. They pulled their car up next to the curb, just beyond the entrance to the semicircular driveway of the hotel. Ms. Martin went inside to retrieve her bag, and Ms. Neal also entered the hotel in order to make a phone call.

Ms. Martin got her bag, exited the hotel, and sat down in the front passenger seat (since Ms. Neal had not yet emerged from the hotel). As Ms. Martin sat there, a limousine pulled slowly into the semicircular driveway. Ms. Martin looked at the limousine, was able to see through the tinted side windows into the back seat, and noticed a man and a woman hugging and kissing. Ms. Martin exclaimed to Ms. Lawrence that the two people were all over each other.

Ms. Martin then observed that people began to exit the limousine. The woman exited first, from the passenger door facing the hotel, and stepped back so that her upper body was visible to Ms. Martin above the trunk portion of the limousine. Ms. Martin noticed that she was a black woman with shoulder-length curly hair.   The second person to emerge from the limousine was a husky black man with large glasses; he exited from the front passenger seat of the limousine. Then, the driver of the limousine, who was a black female with tinted hair, exited; she began to walk around to the passenger side of the limousine. The man who had been kissing in the back seat then exited the limousine, and Ms. Martin immediately recognized him as Mike Tyson. She noted that fact to Ms. Lawrence. Ms. Martin observed the woman moved toward Mr. Tyson until their upper bodies appeared to be touching, and she appeared to put her arm in Mr. Tyson's.

Ms. Martin then observed Mr. Tyson and the woman enter the Canterbury Hotel, at about the same time that her third friend was leaving the hotel. Ms. Martin observed that Ms. Neal bumped into Mr. Tyson and the young woman.

****

If called to testify, it is anticipated that Pamela Lawrence would testify as follows:

Ms. Lawrence attended the Johnny Gill concert on July 18, 1991, at the Hoosier Dome with Ms. Martin and Ms. Neal. After the concert ended at approximately 1 a.m. on July 19, Ms. Lawrence accompanied Ms. Martin and Ms. Neal to the back-stage area of the Hoosier Dome where Mr. Gill's tour bus was parked. Ms. Lawrence watched Ms. Martin say good-bye to her boyfriend, who played the drums in Mr. Gill's band, and then she, Ms. Martin, and Ms. Neal walked to Ms. Lawrence's red Nissan 300ZX, which was in an adjacent parking lot.

Ms. Lawrence then drove her car, with Ms. Martin sitting behind the two seats and Ms. Neal sitting in the passenger seat, to the Canterbury Hotel. Ms. Lawrence pulled her car up to the curb in front of the Canterbury Hotel, just beyond the entrance to the hotel's semicircular driveway. Ms. Martin entered the hotel to pick something up, and Ms. Neal went into the hotel to make a telephone call.

As Ms. Martin exited the hotel and returned to the car, a large limousine pulled into the hotel's driveway. Ms. Lawrence heard Ms. Martin remark that the two people in the limousine were all over one another; Ms. Lawrence looked over and saw two persons sitting in the back seat of the limousine in close proximity to one another. One of the persons appeared to be a female with prominent hair.

Ms. Lawrence then observed a young black female emerge from the rear passenger-side door of the limousine. Ms. Lawrence observed that the woman had a prominent hair style of a kind not commonly seen among black women in Indiana. Then Ms. Lawrence observed a black male exit from the rear passenger-side door of the limousine. Ms. Lawrence heard Ms. Martin say that the black male was Mike Tyson. Ms. Lawrence further observed a heavy-set black man in the vicinity of the limousine. Ms. Lawrence observed Mr. Tyson and the young black woman entered the hotel together.

****

If called to testify, it is anticipated that Renee Neal would testify as follows:

Ms. Neal accompanied Ms. Martin and Ms. Lawrence to the Johnny Gill concert at the Hoosier Dome on July 18, 1991. The three women left the Hoosier Dome at approximately 1:30 to 1:45 a.m. on July 19. They drove to the Canterbury Hotel in Ms. Lawrence's red sports car, and Ms. Neal entered the hotel to make a phone call.

As Ms. Neal stood in the hotel parlor and made her call, she looked out the window and observed a gold limousine pull into the hotel's driveway. Ms. Neal observed that the limousine pulled up so close to the hotel that it appeared that it might come through the parlor window.

Ms. Neal then observed a black man and a thin black woman exit the limousine. As she was leaving the Canterbury Hotel, Ms. Neal observed the man and woman holding hands as they entered the hotel. Ms. Neal also observed a heavy-set black man with gold glasses standing near the limousine as she left the hotel and returned to Ms. Lawrence's car.

The defense's forgotten man, attorney James Voyles, argued that these witnesses were only discovered the previous Thursday and Friday (this being a Tuesday). He stated that many people had called his office since the trial had begun suggesting information, but that many of them were crank calls that were disregarded.

However, when one of his office attorneys talked to these three people they seemed legitimate, and so he suggested that Voyles talk to them. This meeting was held on Sunday, and after it, Voyles immediately called Garrison to inform him of the newly discovered witnesses.

The clash with the prosecutor over this point became a heated battle over reputation and bruised egos when it was suggested by the prosecution that the defense, especially Voyles, was being less than candid with the court. Voyles shouted back, "You've jumped on the wrong bull's back," when confronted with allegations of improper conduct on his part. Voyles also pointed out that he disclosed the witnesses at the very first opportunity, and that Garrison and the other prosecutors had a chance to interview the witnesses on Sunday evening.

Garrison told the court that, not only had his star witness testified already, but most of his critical witnesses as well. "Must the prosecution start over?" he said, citing the unfairness of the late disclosure of these witnesses.

No issue involving a motion to add witnesses was heard in the William Kennedy Smith case, the Rodney King state case, or the Bensonhurst trial. However, three witnesses who could have testified to Kennedy's apparent involvement in sex assaults not unlike the one he was charged with were excluded from his trial, and their exclusion was a tremendous victory for the defense because it precluded the prosecution from parading these witnesses up to the witness stand and showing a pattern of behavior on Smith's part.

In the Tyson trial, the defense knew that these three witnesses could very likely testify to facts that would put in question a critical piece of testimony from Desiree Washington. If the jury were allowed to hear them, and if their statements were believed about the activities in the back of the limousine just prior to the alleged sex attack by Tyson, then Washington's credibility would be severely diminished.

Before ruling on the question, Judge Gifford made it clear that she did not appreciate being put in her current position. She told the lawyers that strict guidelines for discovery were set up, and that the personality conflicts between the lawyers would not enter into her decision.

The judge ruled that the three witnesses would be excluded, due to her belief that to allow testimony from the witnesses would cause "substantial prejudice to the State's case." The "prejudice," she said, could not be cured by a recess or a continuance since the State's witnesses had already testified. Judge Gifford cited the case of Wisehart as the precedent for her decision.

Throughout the trial, Judge Gifford had taken great pains to carefully evaluate every decision she was asked to make. Usually she consulted with her court commissioner, David McNamer, before rendering a decision so that every decision would be based on solid ground.

With the decision on the admissibility of the three witnesses, however, Gifford seemed determined to deny the motion. She seemed to turn a deaf ear to the well-conceived arguments made by the defense to the effect that the State had, in fact, already talked to the witnesses, and thus its case would not be prejudiced to any great extent. The judge clearly was not going to let Fuller run her courtroom, and seemed to take personal offense that he and Voyles had put her in such a tough situation.

While legal precedent may prove her decision to be a correct one, the judge seemed unwilling to allow the testimony no matter how strong the argument was by the defense. In fact, she seemed to indicate that she was uneasy with the decision when she, almost as an afterthought, labelled the evidence "cumulative" when there appeared to be no reason for her to do so.

In retrospect, the decision by Judge Gifford to exclude the three witnesses was definitely her most important legal ruling in the case. The jury would now never hear from these three witnesses and be able to judge for themselves whether they were telling the truth.

Judge Gifford had given the prosecution the exact kind of decision that Jeff Modisett had hoped for by having the case heard by the ex-prosecutor. The defense had lost a major battle, and the momentum of the trial continued to roll in the direction of the prosecution.

Most courtroom observers were shocked by the decision, and the "personal" manner with which Gifford handled this important question of law. By ruling for the prosecution, Gifford had added support to those legal experts who believed she should have disqualified herself from hearing the case in the first place.

Once the hearing regarding the three witnesses ended, Washington's mother, Mary Washington, took the stand. Her highly emotional testimony was brief but very important. Mrs. Washington said she was the one who, after learning from her daughter of the alleged rape, told her to call 911.

When she saw Desiree in the lobby of the hotel, Mrs. Washington said her daughter "looked terrible." She said, with tears running down her face, "She's not the same daughter I sent here."

As to her daughter making a formal complaint, Mrs. Washington said she told Desiree that "this was a decision she must make, but whatever decision she made, I'll be behind her one hundred percent. I encouraged her to do whatever is right."

During this testimony, Nancy, Juror #7 in the back row, began to cry. Whatever credibility the jurors were giving to Desiree and her mother's testimony was still unclear, but there was no doubt that the jury felt sympathy for the alleged victim and her mother.

Such emotion should have triggered an alarm in the defense that the "greed" and "money hungry" motive defense would certainly backfire. Instead, Fuller and company continued to pound away at this point, and did not concentrate enough on the "consent" issue.

For some illogical reason, Vincent Fuller asked the emotional mother just two questions:

1)   Do you consider your daughter an intelligent woman?
2)   Do you love your daughter?

To both questions, Mrs. Washington replied, "Yes."

After the playing of the 911 tape, the State rested. Garrison and company never called Pasha Oliver, the roommate of Desiree Washington, or other beauty contestants who could further verify the accuser's version of the story. Obviously, Garrison and Trathen were basing their case on the credibility of their main witness, on the corroborative evidence provided by Virginia Foster, and on the medical testimony of Dr. Stephen Richardson.

Was the evidence presented by the State enough to prove Mike Tyson guilty beyond a reasonable doubt? If the defense had rested at that point, many observers felt that the State would have come up short. Tyson still seemed to wear an aura of invincibility, and opinions were mixed as to whether Desiree Washington had proved to be such a believable witness as to erase any reasonable doubt of Tyson's guilt.

The decision of whether to rest a case following the completion of the State's case is always a difficult one. Most trial experts believe that the jury "expects" to hear from the defense, and usually from the defendants themselves. However, an experienced trial lawyer will always attempt to place his or her line of defense in the questioning of the State's witnesses. That way the jury already has the defense theory in mind, regardless of whether the defense chooses to present testimony.

In the William Kennedy Smith case, defense lawyer Roy Black had never committed Smith to testify. In fact, he had wisely never had Smith make any comment other than a terse response of "not guilty" to the charges. The prosecution was left then to wonder whether Smith would ever take the witness stand in his own defense, and, in turn, wonder what he would say if he did so.

Based on their assessment of the testimony of Patty Bowman, Black and his associates eventually decided that Smith should testify. Apparently they believed that her testimony had given the jury enough reason to convict Smith, and thus it was necessary for Smith to answer Bowman's charges before the jury.

Placing the defendant on the stand is not without heavy risk. Even though much pretrial preparation is involved with preparing the witness, each defendant reacts differently to the pressure of having to refute serious charges against him or her. In the Kennedy Smith case, Smith was able to handle the pressure and to persuade the jury that he was innocent of the charges.

In the Clarence Thomas/Anita Hill confrontation, the two squared off in a bizarre no-rules situation with United States senators firing questions at them left and right. Neither had the benefit of counsel to defend them or to object, and the "jury" of senators was able to see both combatants basically in the raw.

The Rodney King state case was a most interesting one in that the star witness never appeared. Apparently the Los Angeles District Attorney, Ira Reiner, and lead counsel Terry White made the decision to keep King off the witness stand, based both on conflicting postarrest statements he made and on the fact that defense lawyers would have been able to cross-examine him regarding his criminal record.

Hindsight proved that this decision was in fact a disaster. Instead of seeing King on the witness stand and hearing him testify about his terrible ordeal, the jury was left to decide the case based on the image it perceived from the videotape.

In the King case, all four defense lawyers did decide to have their defendants testify, and with the pro-law enforcement jury were able to convince the jurors to acquit the men.

Lemrick Nelson did not take the stand in the Bensonhurst trial. Defense lawyer Arthur Lewis made that decision based on the existence of postarrest statements that were in effect confessions of guilt. Even though the judge had disallowed their admissibility at trial, Lewis could not take the chance of putting Nelson on the stand.

Instead, Lewis was able to turn the attention of the trial toward the veracity of the police officers who handled the investigation. By putting their believability on trial, he shifted the burden of proof for the prosecution to defending their own witnesses' accounts of what occurred on the night of the murder of Yankel Rosenbaum.

Vincent Fuller must have believed that there was never any question that Mike Tyson would need to testify, and so he had boxed himself into a corner and thus restricted his options. Assessing whether Fuller had weaved into the case his line of defense through questions and answers to the prosecution's witnesses was indeed difficult. By choosing to defend on so many fronts, Fuller had probably provided the jury with insufficient evidence on the most critical defense theory—that of consent.

Regardless, Fuller now faced that most critical decision for Tyson. Did the jury absolutely need to hear Tyson's version of the incident with Washington, and other testimony as well, or could the defense bet that the State had not sustained its burden of proof, and merely rest its case?

13

♦

THE DEFENSE
ATTACKS

Rest they did not, however.

In line with the strategies outlined in Vincent Fuller's opening statement, the defense began to call witnesses designed to: a) indicate that Desiree Washington gave inconsistent statements concerning what happened during the alleged rape attack; b) show that, because of Tyson's bad behavior and lewd language, Washington knew of his sexual intentions; c) point out that her appearance in his hotel at 2:00 a.m. indicated her intention to have sex with Tyson; d) suggest that while in the hotel room she engaged in consensual sex with Tyson; and e) demonstrate that Desiree Washington's motivation for filing the charges against Tyson was that she anticipated suing the ex-champ for millions if he was convicted.

If Fuller and company had simply concentrated on the consent issue, and abandoned the others, the outcome of the trial might have been different.

Tyson's close friend and confidant John Horne was the first to testify for the defense. In order to counter the claim by the prosecution that Tyson unlocked the door to the hotel room, Horne testified that "Tyson never carried any credit cards or keys. He holds on to nothing. He has trouble holding on to things."

Horne also testified that he drove from Albany, New York, to Cleveland in order to be there when Tyson arrived on

July 19. Such testimony was meant to show that Tyson always intended to be in Cleveland on the 19th (the day of the attack), and thus did not leave Indianapolis suddenly after the alleged rape attack as the prosecution had alleged.

Mrs. Joan Bates, a hostess at St. Vincent Hospital in Indianapolis and the aunt of B Angie B, the rapper girlfriend of Tyson, testified next for the defense.

Bates said that her niece told her that Tyson would be joining her in Indianapolis during Black Expo. After the concert they would go back to Cleveland for another concert there.

Mrs. Bates testified that she saw Tyson at her home on the 17th of July, when B Angie B and Tyson walked around their neighborhood with a bodyguard. Mrs. Bates also said she saw B Angie B the next morning, and then took her to the airport to meet Tyson on the 19th for their Cleveland flight. No questions were asked of Bates regarding the demeanor of Tyson at the airport. The jury was thus left with the impressions of the hotel personnel who had testified about Tyson's "bad" attitude when he left the hotel.

Sgt. Eugene Boyd of the Indianapolis Police Department testified that he saw Desiree Washington at approximately 1:15-1:30 a.m. on July 20 in the lobby of the Omni Hotel.

This incident occurred when the parents of Desiree came to the hotel and asked permission to double-park in the entryway. When Sgt. Boyd asked why they needed to do so, Mrs. Washington replied, "My daughter has been raped." "Where?" he asked.

"At another hotel," Mrs. Washington replied.

Sgt. Boyd said he then saw two young black females in the lobby. He wasn't introduced, but inquired whether police assistance was going to be forthcoming.

"Yes, we've called 911, and a police officer is going to assist us," was the reply from the older lady.

At the car before the parents and Desiree left, the Sergeant remembered that there was a comment made from Mrs. Washington. While the Court sustained the objection as to what the comment was, Sgt. Boyd could testify that Desiree replied to that comment, "Oh Mom."

Desiree's father, Donald Washington, was next called to the stand.

"Haven't you hired civil lawyers?," Fuller bellowed.

"Could you bring a civil suit?," he added.

"What about the garment Desiree wore and the sequins?" Fuller went on.

To these questions Donald Washington was vague and somewhat evasive. However, his demeanor gave no impression that Desiree's motive was greed, and the jury was left to wonder why he was called in the first place.

Perhaps the strongest testimony given among all the defense witnesses was that of Reverend Kathryn Newlin.

The resident chaplain at Methodist Hospital, where Washington was treated, Rev. Newlin came off as a witness that more likely would have been called by the prosecution to soften the blow of any potentially damaging testimony.

But it was the defense that called Rev. Newlin and questioned her about her dealings with Desiree Washington when she came to the hospital to report the rape.

"Was the victim in pain? In physical discomfort?" "No," the chaplain replied, "she looked tired; she was quiet."

Listening to the conversation between Desiree and Dr. Richardson (the mother may also have been present), the chaplain said that Desiree told her that "Tyson was touching some of the girls."

Regarding the physical attack itself, Desiree said Tyson "was touching her breasts and panties." When Desiree said "No more," the chaplain recalled, "Desiree said Tyson continued on."

"Did you get a read on what Desiree's involvement was," the defense asked.

"Yes, I had a feeling there was some sense of participation."

The chaplain had thus provided two key pieces of evidence for the defense: 1) The victim saw Tyson fondling other contestants, and 2) there was a feeling by her that Desiree had "some sort of participation" with Tyson. Whether that meant "foreplay" or not was pure speculation, but clearly this totally impartial witness provided testimony that was very strong for the defense.

Vincent Fuller's intentions by calling Sgt. Boyd and, especially, Chaplain Newlin seemed clear. Apparently, Fuller chose to permit the jury, through Boyd's testimony, to consider the fact that Desiree Washington may have been influenced heavily by her mother to file charges against Tyson. Chaplain

Newlin, on the other hand, brought forth the allegation that Washington had some sort of "foreplay" with Tyson, lending credence to the defense theory that Washington consented to have sex with Tyson.

While both of these witnesses contributed to the defense position, Fuller's attempt to show, through Washington's father, that she was motivated to file charges of rape against Tyson because of greed seemed to fail. Coming on the tail end of the strong evidence given by Boyd and Newlin, Fuller's decision to present evidence of a "greed" motive may very well have diminished the effect of their testimony.

The testimony that sets the stage for the presentation of the defendant to the jury must be carefully orchestrated to provide the jurors with information that will then be enhanced by the defendant's testimony. With the knowledge that Tyson was about to take the stand, Fuller instead produced witnesses whose testimony had no common theme or purpose. By alternating evidence regarding Washington's ulterior motives, the consent theory, and the claim that Tyson's bad behavior warned her of his intentions, the jury seemed confused about where Fuller was headed.

In spite of all of the pretrial praise of Vincent Fuller as a great organizer of trial matters, the defense appeared disorganized as it approached the big day when Tyson would take the witness stand. The prosecution clearly had the upper hand, and it appeared more and more likely that Mike Tyson himself would now be forced to save the day.

14

---◆---

HOTEL FIRE KILLS THREE

On February 5th, a three-alarm fire raged through the third floor of the downtown Indianapolis Athletic Club, killing two firefighters and one guest at the hotel where jurors in the trial were sequestered.

Twenty-six people in all were evacuated from the seven-story building. Killed in the early morning blaze were Captain Ellwood Gelenius, 47, and Private John J. Lorenzano, 29, of the Indianapolis Fire Department. A third victim, businessman Thomas Mutz, was found dead in a sixth floor stairwell, apparently overcome by smoke. At least 12 people were also injured in the blaze.

All of the jurors were escorted from their sixth floor rooms through a Meridian Street exit to Vermont Street by Marion County Sheriff's Deputy Donald Marshall and two Court bailiffs.

About 10 minutes later the jurors were taken to the City-County Building in a jail bus before moving to other locations. Jurors had to flee in their nightclothes, leaving behind the rest of their clothes.

Joe Champion, the chief clerk for Judge Patricia Gifford, said, "The jurors were in good spirits under the circumstances."

Cause of the fire was not determined, but an official report finally concluded that the fire was accidental. Prosecutor

Jeffrey Modisett ordered the grand jury to look into the matter, but their report backed up the findings of the official report.

Accident or arson? No one of course knew for sure, and perhaps no one will ever know the real truth. Some suspected that Don King or another of Tyson's supporters had a hand in the fire, but no direct link has been found to date.

More important, perhaps, was the estimate of whether the fire would affect the jurors, the trial itself, and the ultimate verdict.

The first question that arose was whether the jurors would even connect the fire with the trial. Speculation among the reporters and court personnel was that it would, of course, but how and with what result was still a question. Would they feel that perhaps the fire was an intentional warning to them that even worse could happen if they brought back the wrong verdict, i.e., a guilty verdict against Tyson? Could they put two and two together and decide that the real message was to give them notice that they better resign from the jury right away, thus causing a mistrial?

Judge Gifford's dilemma was to try to obtain answers to these questions without planting any seeds in the jurors' minds that she in any way felt there was a connection. To accomplish this, the Judge had each juror brought individually to the Court chambers to meet with her and the respective attorneys. Although the questions were never revealed to the media, the jurors were apparently asked about their own personal well-being and whether they could or wanted to continue as a juror. With the exception of juror member #11, the black ex-employee of a law firm, who was excused because of his "state of mind," all remained on the jury.

Several unknowns resulted from the fire. First, would the jury be influenced by their own personal speculation about what had happened? Secondly, would the exclusion of one of the three blacks from the jury influence the eventual outcome? And, finally, did the fact that the defense did not ask for a mistrial mean they felt there was no basis for a mistrial? Or did the defense feel there was a possibility of a motion for mistrial being granted, and choose not to ask because they were pleased with the make-up of the jury, and/or felt they had the upper hand at that point in the trial and wished to go forward?

After the trial, there would be reports that the jurors had been less than candid with the judge when asked about their feelings concerning the fire. At least two admitted that they had observed flags flying at half-staff, and thus knew that perhaps someone had died in the fire.

Was the fire a coincidence, or arson? No one can ever be certain, but there is no question that the timing of the fire and the resulting unfortunate deaths most certainly had an important impact on the outcome of the trial.

Perhaps most important of all, the jury now had one less black member than before. Ten whites and but two blacks would now decide Tyson's fate.

15

♦

BEAUTIES AND THE BEAST

After the fire, security on the second floor outside the courtroom in the City-County Building changed dramatically. New metal detectors were set up, and dogs were brought in to sniff for any bombs. Security officers said beefed-up security was merely a coincidence, but everyone knew better.

Rumors abounded about the cause of the fire. Some reporters familiar with Don King and Tyson's former trainer, Richie "The Torch" Giachetti, were certain King was behind it. Most reporters wondered more about whether the fire would cause a mistrial, and if so, what would happen then? Some asked whether the fire would present a ready opportunity for the defense to gain a mistrial and thus a new start.

Apparently that sort of defense motion never was filed. After questioning the jurors individually, Judge Gifford's law clerk announced that the trial would resume, absent one juror who asked to be excused. When it did, 11 original jurors and one of the alternates began to hear evidence on the eighth day of testimony.

Madelyn Whittington, a 20-year-old beauty pageant contestant from Washington, D.C., took the stand for the defense after a delay of one day.

Whittington testified that Washington told her that "she wanted money, wanted to be like Robin Givens." She also told of Mike Tyson and Washington hugging after she had danced at the rehearsal like she "wanted someone to notice her."

Whittington testified that Tyson talked to her and the other contestants at the opening ceremonies, saying, "Do you want to come to my room? I know I'm not gonna get nothin', but I'll ask anyway." When Tyson made advances on her, Whittington rebuffed him, saying she wanted nothing to do with him. When he heard her comments, Tyson apparently withdrew saying, "'Who does she think she is, that little Catholic school motherf . . . ?'" she said.

Did she notice any difference in Desiree's behavior from the start of the pageant to the end?   "No." Was Desiree absent from any of the competition? "No," said Whittington.

In answer to Prosecutor Garrison's fishing-expedition cross-examination, Whittington testified that she overheard Washington talking after the swimsuit competition was over.   In response to her not being named one of the 10 finalists, Desiree allegedly said, "I'm a 10, all the boys want to know my name at the beach."

Whittington's testimony bolstered the defense's notion that the Desiree Washington portrayed by the prosecution as being a "goody two-shoes" instead used foul language and made sexual innuendoes herself. The testimony also indicated that Desiree heard the sexually suggestive comments made by Tyson and thus knew what she was in for when she went out with Tyson.   Important as it was, the defense never emphasized Whittington's testimony in their arguments.

Cecilia Alexander then took the stand for the defense. From Charleston, South Carolina, this beauty pageant contestant told the jury that she intended to become a dentist upon graduation from college.

Turning to the rehearsal at the Omni on July 18, Cecilia said that she noticed "Desiree Washington's arm hit Mike. They hugged, and she hugged back," Cecilia said. "He asked her to go out," the witness told the jury, and then she heard Desiree say, "Sure." Cecilia also said she and Tyson talked back and forth. "Tyson," she said, "asked where I was from." I told him, "Georgia, and we kidded about Holyfield being from Georgia."

Later, while she was in a bathroom stall, Cecilia said she overheard Desiree and "Madelyn" talking about "Tyson and his intelligence." "He's not intelligent," Desiree allegedly said, "he's dumb, ignorant; look at the money Robin Givens got!"

Later, at the Opening Ceremonies, Cecilia said she heard Desiree and another contestant talking. According to the witness, the other contestant said, "Here comes your husband! He doesn't speak very well." Desiree then supposedly said, "Mike doesn't have to speak. He'll make the money, and I'll do the talking." This comment seemed to have an impact on the jury, and juror #2 looked squarely at Tyson, who showed a slight smile.

Ms. Alexander also saw Desiree Washington show a picture to Tyson of her in a swimsuit. His comment, "Boy—I have the advantage; I've seen you in a swimsuit."

Cecilia also testified "Desiree competed in all the activities Friday, Saturday, and Sunday and I saw no change in her demeanor." However, later at Fitzgerald's, she saw Desiree sitting on a chair by herself. Desiree told her "she was feeling bad, had menstrual cramps." Cecilia was told that Desiree's mom and dad were coming, and she waited with her.

At the swimsuit competition, Cecilia said Desiree was upset that she wasn't a Top 10 finisher. "I don't understand why others won, I'm no loser," she quoted Desiree.

When the FBI called later to ask her if she knew anything about the rape, Cecilia said she asked them who the woman was? When they wouldn't tell her, she asked them if she could guess by calling out a name. When they said that would be all right, Cecilia apparently said the name Desiree Washington. The judge sustained the prosecution's objection before her answer was uttered, but in all likelihood the jury knew who Cecilia had in mind.

Greg Garrison's cross-examination seemed to only reinforce Alexander's testimony. A seemingly impartial witness with little or no axe to grind, Cecilia was quizzed by Garrison about mostly insignificant and incidental matters. In total, Alexander proved to be a very strong witness for the defense. Her name, however, never really surfaced again, and again Vincent Fuller did not emphasize her strong testimony in final argument.

The housekeeper at the Canterbury Hotel, Iva Rogers, was called next to testify. Extremely hard of hearing, this witness was asked about the bed, the covers, and the sheets that she found in room 606. A member of the defense team patiently questioned the lady in order to gain some testimony that would show inconsistencies with Desiree Washington's testimony as to what happened on the bed, but it was extremely hard for anyone to estimate what the testimony was really worth.

In the end, Rogers apparently confirmed that it looked like the woman in the room had sat on the bed, and that there were spots of blood like the witness had seen when "girls get married."

Most important, neither this witness nor any other were asked about the discarded panty shield left by Desiree Washington in the bathroom. Either no one ever found it, or nobody was interested in where it was. No explanation was given, and the jury was left to speculate about this important fact.

If Judge Pat Gifford had not called a recess about halfway through Dr. Margaret Watanobe's duller than dull testimony, everyone in the courtroom would have been asleep. Juror #6 and Juror #2 actually had their eyes closed for much of the testimony. (In fact, Juror #6 sat sideways and used his full-length hair to hide his sleepiness.)

Called to counteract the testimony of prosecution witnesses Richardson and Aiken, Indiana University Professor Watanobe was an unadulterated disaster for the defense. Questioned in a similarly dull and academic manner by Kathleen Beggs, the good doctor took the jury through an unwanted sexual lesson concerning everything you never wanted to know about pelvic examinations.

Beggs finally reached the main reason why Watanobe was called when she tried to elicit one main fact from the professor: Was it possible, from the abrasions in the vagina of Desiree Washington, to say that they were caused by forced sex? To this question, the doctor answered emphatically: "I don't know!"

Parquita Nassau, another Miss Black America pageant contestant, testified next for the defense. Her main testimony produced the fact that Tyson and the woman embraced and "cuddled" shortly after they met at a July 18 dance rehearsal. "I saw them talking," she said. "I saw them cuddling up to each other. They were more intimate as far as their contact and conversation. It looked like they were involved with each other."

During cross-examination, Greg Garrison accused Nassau of altering her story after being contacted by defense lawyers "eleven times." During interviews with police, Garrison argued, Nassau never said Tyson and Washington cuddled. "You just forgot they were cuddling all these minutes behind the post?" Garrison asked. "I said they were cuddling," she replied, "hugging and cuddling are the same thing to me." Ms. Nassau also testified that Tyson said to the group in general, "If you don't want to go out, I can go on. I can have any one of you bitches," and "I know you want me. I know you want me."

Apparently Washington also overheard the discussion and asked what Tyson said. When Nassau said "He's asking us all out," Washington said, "Yeah, I know."

Dressed in a blue suit coat and white blouse, 31-year-old Tanya Traylor testified next for the defense. From Miami, Florida, she presented a sharp contrast (in age and experience) from the other, much younger beauty pageant contestants.

Asked what are the keys to participation in beauty pageants, Miss Traylor said that a contestant needs to be "focused, needs to practice a great deal," and needs to be "physically fit."

Because of her age and experience, Miss Traylor's testimony about Tyson's behavior at the rehearsal seemed to leave quite an impression on the jury. The woman said Tyson's actions made him out as "not a nice person, and that everything he said had sexual overtones." He asked "everybody to go out," she said, and "if he got a no, he moved on to the next girl." He talked about taking girls "back to the room, and that a kiss will do, but sex is better."

He was "rude," she said, and his insisting that "the girls sit on his lap if they want their pictures taken" bothered her enough that she didn't have her picture taken. "I didn't want to have my picture taken that badly," she said.

At the opening ceremonies Tyson's irreverent conduct continued. When "Carlina," another contestant, asked him about the size of his hands and how big they were, Tyson made a very suggestive remark about what the "hands could be used for." When Traylor asked Tyson why he was like that, he said, "People expect it, and next time you'll know me."

Later, at the Johnny Gill concert, Traylor said she saw Tyson again. Backstage with "Norma, another contestant,"

Traylor said she again got to talk to Tyson, and this time it was a different story. Based on perhaps an "hour" of conversation, she went ahead and had her picture taken with him. He was "polite," she said, "a nicer person, more down to earth."

Defense lawyer Lane Heard unsuccessfully tried to discuss the fact that pageant official Alita Anderson had reprimanded Washington for being a "groupie" backstage, and thus told her to leave. When the witness was asked what Anderson said to Washington a hearsay objection was sustained, (over no argument from the defense), and no answer was allowed.

Traylor did tell the jury that her husband videotaped all of the competition. That video would be shown to the jury later on in the trial, and Desiree could be seen singing, dancing, and smiling all over the television screen.

Finally, Tanya testified that she saw no change in the demeanor of Washington in the two days after the alleged incident. "Her spirits seemed the same," Traylor said.

Cross-examination brought home the fact that Traylor thought Desiree Washington was a nice person, and that the woman had invited Desiree to her home in Miami.

Traylor then again brought up the lewd remarks and distasteful behavior of Tyson and the fact that Washington saw all of this take place. When asked whether Tyson "grabbed her buttocks when she was backstage," the witness said, "No, that did not happen." Controversy arose as to whether the witness had used the word "affectionate" to describe Tyson's conduct before, but the judge moved to let the jury decide that for itself.

More important than Traylor's testimony, however, was what was observed among the jury while she was testifying. About halfway through her time on the stand, juror #9, the ex-Marine, began to pass out breath mints to the other jurors as they watched a sidebar conference between the judge and the attorneys. Such conduct confirmed what most believed before, that the minister-like, IBM salesman would end up becoming foreman of the jury. As the only note-taking member, he would become *the* most important decision-maker as to where Mike Tyson would spend his time after the trial.

Tanya Traylor's testimony again portrayed a different side of Washington. Although prosecutor Garrison showed, through a later prosecution witness, some potential variation from Tanya's story about what happened backstage at the Gill concert, Traylor still was an impressive witness.

Thus, the testimony, even if not totally believable, could be interpreted to show that perhaps Washington had dual personality traits as well as Tyson. If the jury had been reminded of Traylor's words about Desiree more emphatically, perhaps her testimony (along with that of the other contestants) would have had more impact.

Of all of the beauty pageant contestants, Jacklyn Boatwright was perhaps the most stunning. Dressed in a beautiful red outfit, this native of Georgia said she was a communications major who "tells it like it is."

Unlike the other contestants, Boatwright told the jury that she never saw Tyson at the rehearsal. Instead, she ran into the ex-champ outside the Omni Hotel in downtown Indianapolis. Because she wanted to meet him, Boatwright went across the street and introduced herself. Boatwright said Tyson told her, "You're pretty, give me a kiss on the cheek, and a hug."

At the opening ceremonies, she again saw Tyson, this time with his "Together in Christ" badge on. At that time, she testified that another contestant had her arm around Tyson, and that "he patted her on the rear." He got a "look that could kill" from Washington. Boatwright also testified that when she met Desiree Washington on Friday she was "happy and smiling," and that the woman "was the same when she last saw her." During cross-examination, Garrison asked whether this witness had heard of Tyson's bad behavior. "Yes," she said, "I heard he was a creep."

What an impressive figure singer Johnny Gill made as he walked to the witness stand. The son of a minister, he testified that he had been performing since the age of five. A good-looking man of 25, he stated that he had first signed a recording contract with Atlantic Records in 1983. Five albums and five million records later, some solo and some with the group New Edition, he was still shy to admit the number of awards he had won during a brief but sensational career.

He testified that he had come to Indianapolis in July as a part of his commitment to "Prom Promises," a tour concept that involved gaining "prom promises" where kids would promise not to drink alcohol or do drugs at high school proms.

Gill said that he got to Indianapolis on Thursday, July 17, and stayed at the Canterbury Hotel. The morning of the 18th, he testified, Mike Tyson came to his hotel room. Although Gill said the two were friends, they "didn't see each other too much." Tyson, he said, "had been to several of my concerts." After the two men had lunch at a local restaurant, Rev. Charles Williams, the head of the Black Expo event, suggested they go over to the Omni Hotel to say hi to the contestants.

At the rehearsal, Gill said, "All of the girls got very excited when we came into the hall." Pictures and autographs were requested, and then he watched Tyson do a promotional video spot with several contestants.

Tyson, he said, "put the moves on the contestants," and his hands were "on their bottoms."

(Gill's testimony was split into two parts during the trial. He was allowed to testify to the above information, but was excused when he began to discuss certain comments that he heard from Tyson at the Omni Hotel during the rehearsal. The judge ruled that Gill could not testify to these comments unless or until Tyson testified because otherwise the testimony would involve hearsay, as well as facts that were not yet in evidence. The fact that Gill's testimony was interrupted severely diminished its effectiveness, and put into question the defense strategy of putting him on the witness stand before Tyson testified.)

"There's twenty million dollars!" That's what Prairie View, A & M Grad School student/beauty pageant contestant Caroline Jones told the jury Desiree Washington said about Mike Tyson at the rehearsal.

Ms. Jones also testified that at the opening ceremonies, she saw Tyson and said something to him about his hands being "pretty." She remembered Tyson's return comment, something about using the hands a "little horizontal, a little vertical."

On Friday the 19th, the morning after the alleged rape, Jones said Washington told her, "I think I've been raped."

"Either you're raped or you're not," the witness said she replied. Then Desiree began to tell her the facts, most of which conformed to versions told to other contestants. However, Washington said that "Tyson snapped, ripped my clothes off," and after it was over, allegedly said, "You're nothing, get out of here." "No, you're nothing," Washington allegedly told Tyson, "You're supposed to be a positive influence, a role model." "What have I done?" was the response from Tyson, Washington told Jones.

"I was in shock," said Jones. Washington told her "not to tell," and Jones said she wouldn't. Then Jones made a very shocking statement. "I had my doubts about her story," the witness said. Left with this answer from a witness who expressed no profound like for Tyson, the jury might have inferred some real question about the credibility of Desiree Washington. However, instead of merely leaving the evidence to speak for itself, the defense's next question allowed Jones to answer that she felt this way because Desiree seemed "confused." This answer took the punch out of her testimony, since it gave an explanation for Washington's confusing comment.

Jones then said that she told her mother that "Desiree thought she'd been raped," a comment that would later be embellished upon by Ms. Jones. Cross-examination revealed that Ms. Jones did see Tyson and Jesse Jackson praying together outside the Convention Center at the opening ceremonies.

Prosecutor Barb Trathen got an answer to a question she didn't anticipate about the taping outside Union Station. Asking about Desiree's conduct, Jones said, "Miss Washington was mocking the way the defendant talked."

Trathen was able to bring out inconsistencies in the woman's testimony. In her deposition, the prosecutor said, "didn't you use the word 'shocked and confused' when describing the demeanor of Washington?" "Confused" she remembered, "Shocked" she did not.

The witness had also told prosecutors in the deposition that Washington told her that Tyson said "you can't hurt me," when she was "trying to get away." Also, Washington told her "she was crying" when the attack occurred. Desiree Washington told Jones that, "she didn't know what to do."

Caroline Jones's mother, Ethel, an elementary school principal from Texarkana, Texas, verified much of her daughter's story.

During the competition, Mrs. Jones met and got to know eight or nine of the girls very well. Of Desiree Washington, she said the girl was "intelligent, very nice, friendly, and athletic." Mrs. Jones also described her as "very aggressive" and at photo sessions, she always managed to "get to the front."

On Friday the 19th, as a result of a conversation with her daughter, Mrs. Jones said she became very upset, gave her daughter some advice, and then went to the hotel.

At about 11:00 a.m., Mrs. Jones saw Desiree in the foyer at the hotel. She was "acting the way she always acted—no different from the past." She "was smiling, seemed happy. I saw nothing on her hands or body, no bruises—nothing."

Later, at the swimsuit competition, Mrs. Jones again said she saw no bruises. On Sunday, Desiree seemed "in a very happy mood," said Mrs. Jones; "she placed [overall] in the Top 10."

Frank Valentine, a 22-year-old Moorhouse College student, testified that he was asked to work with the pageant by his aunt, Alita Anderson, with whom he lived in Washington, D.C.

At the rehearsal, Valentine testified that Desiree Washington was "jocking on Mike," meaning she was trying to get Mike's attention. Later, Valentine saw Washington backstage at the Gill concert. He witnessed Anderson reprimand Pasha Oliver and Desiree by saying "Stop acting like groupies." He also testified that Desiree was never absent from any part of the competition, and that she never appeared to act any differently to him from the way she acted at the beginning of the competition.

On Sunday, Valentine disclosed that he saw Washington at about 10:00 a.m. on the second floor of the Omni.

"Did you go out with Mike Tyson?" he asked. "She looked at me strange," Valentine testified, saying that Washington responded, "Why ask me that?"

Later in the conversation, Valentine said, Washington said she "went out with him and got raped."

"Are you sure?" he asked her. "She didn't seem sure," he testified. "She told me she screamed; nobody came; there was a bodyguard outside the door."

After he returned home from the pageant, Valentine called Washington, he testified, "to see what had happened."

"She wasn't sure," he said, there was a lot of pressure for both people. "She was hesitant," he said, "she didn't say much."

Garrison's cross-examination was as unnecessary as Trathen's with the previous witness. Instead of leaving well enough alone—(since the evidence wasn't all that strong)—Garrison attempted to discredit the man by showing that he had certain days mixed up and other trivialities. It was all needless confrontation.

It is difficult to ascertain what impact all of this evidence had on the jury. Certainly the testimony from Cecilia Alexander, Jacklyn Boatwright, and especially Tanya Traylor proved that Washington not only had told differing versions of what happened to her, but also was completely aware of the dark, dangerous, sex-obsessed side of Mike Tyson.

Unfortunately, for the defense, Dr. Watanobe proved to be a windbag who left nothing certain with the jury. While Dr. Richardson gave the jury some layman facts to consider, Dr. Watanobe produced a physics lesson on sexual intercourse, including the comment "one patient I examined had to be chased around the room when I began the pelvic exam."

With all the resources available to the Tyson defense, one wonders why they couldn't search out a better, more credible witness to offset Dr. Richardson. Greg Garrison and company must have gotten out the champagne after Dr. Watanobe testified. In fact, Garrison used her testimony more in final argument than Fuller did, and based his plea for the guilt of Tyson on the medical testimony of two prosecution medical witnesses *and* one defense medical witness.

Tanya Traylor was an impressive witness for the defense. Greg Garrison must have thought so because he tried to bring out the "Jekyll and Hyde" personality of Tyson through this lady's testimony. By attempting to show that Tyson was a good guy one moment and distasteful the next, he followed up the accuser's point that Tyson indeed had two personalities.

However, Garrison's questions again seemed to be part of a very dangerous fishing expedition. Asking questions that he obviously didn't know the answer to, his approach unveiled information that in fact bolstered the defense's contention that Desiree Washington knew exactly what kind of person Tyson was when she went up to his hotel room.

Johnny Gill was thought to be the bombshell witness for the defense who would blast the prosecution's case to smithereens. Somehow he was not as effective as predicted, and came off as a person who would do anything to save Tyson.

Caroline Jones was a witness whose testimony was less effective than it seemed to the prosecution. In fact, prosecutor

Barb Trathen did not measure the impact of this witness very well. While Jones did make some points for the defense, they were balanced with other evidence she presented that favored the State. All in all, this witness was probably a draw, but Trathen's personal attack on the witness told the jury that perhaps the prosecution felt the witness had been damaging to its case.

Tyson's case was hurt severely by the complete ineffectiveness of his own medical testimony. The other witnesses may have strengthened his chances somewhat, but Margaret Watanobe was an utter and unnecessary disaster.

The defense, in total, had provided the jury with testimony on many different subjects. Due to this strategy, it was difficult to separate the significant points being pursued by Fuller, because as soon as one issue was addressed, another was then thrown into the mix. With the knowledge that Tyson was about to testify, it would have seemed more prudent to slowly but surely ease the testimony along, so that when Tyson rose to take the witness stand, a practical foundation had been laid to enhance whatever testimony the ex-champ would give.

Many times during the trial, when either his attorneys were in the judge's chambers, or away from the counsel table, Mike Tyson would sit all alone with a look of abandonment on his face. Now, though, the time had come for the ex-champ to take the witness stand and after Fuller's direct examination of him, face a boxing match with the formidable Greg Garrison that would be the most important fight of his life.

16

♦

MIKE'S STORY

In Vincent Fuller's mind, there was apparently never any question of whether Mike Tyson would testify.

Many felt prior to trial that the most important issue would be whether the State could present a strong enough case to force the defense to put Mike Tyson on the witness stand. If they could, then the defense would have no choice. Iron Mike would have to stand the test. Winner take all, a trial moment for all of history.

Fuller, however, never allowed the drama to unfold. To the surprise of everyone, especially those legal experts covering the trial, Fuller had announced in opening argument that "he will tell you," meaning of course that his client, Mr. Tyson, would testify. Some observers even wondered whether Fuller had mistakenly used those unfortunate words, but whatever the reason, he had painted himself into a corner with the jury.

Tyson would now take his place on the hot seat where only a few months earlier William Kennedy Smith had saved himself from the gallows. In that case, Roy Black had carefully prepared his client to testify, and they had been over and over a scripted program that Black would use to take Smith through his testimony. Without any advance notice that Smith would even testify, and no knowledge of what he would say about the incident, Kennedy Smith enjoyed a great advantage over the prosecution when he stepped from behind the counsel table, and began to tell the jury what he thought happened at the Kennedy estate on the night in question.

Because of Fuller's unwise proclamation during his opening argument, and also Tyson's disastrous performance with the grand jury, the ex-champ did not enjoy the same advantages that Kennedy Smith had at his trial. The prosecution knew that Iron Mike would have his say, and they were chomping at the bit to hear the story.

On February 7, at 4:02 p.m., the former heavyweight boxing champion of the world unceremoniously took the stand. When Judge Patricia Gifford said, "Next witness" and Vincent Fuller called out the name "Michael Tyson," the courtroom came alive. Main event time was here. The famous boxer would now tell his side of the story to the jury.

Positioned in the middle of the defense witnesses—not the last witness, as one might expect— Iron Mike still looked formidable as he left the seat he had occupied at counsel table for the entire trial.

Whether he had to testify or not now would be questioned only in hindsight. When Mike Tyson took the oath to "tell the truth the whole truth, and nothing but the truth," the game was on.

The first portion of Tyson's testimony gave the jury a brief glimpse into his early life. The ex-champ testified that he was born in the Brownsville section of Brooklyn, June 30, 1966; he was 25 years old. He said he had been a professional prize fighter for seven to eight years, was a high school dropout (10th grade), and had been befriended by the legendary trainer Cus D'Amato (Floyd Patterson, Jose Torres) just after a stint at reform school.

"D'Amato," he said, "died in 1985." In 1986, at age 20, Tyson said he was the youngest man ever to become heavyweight champion of the world. Tyson seemed almost embarrassed to talk about his achievements, but testified he was the champion for four years until he lost unexpectedly to James "Buster" Douglas in Tokyo in February 1990.

Tyson said his professional record was 41-1, with 38 knockouts, and that after defeating Donovan "Razor" Ruddock, he had been scheduled to fight current champion Evander Holyfield for the championship on June 28, 1991. Tyson said he was forced to postpone the bout due to a rib injury.

While this background was important, Fuller didn't give Tyson much opportunity to elaborate on his answers. Perhaps the jury felt they'd gotten only a thumbnail sketch of the man, left without vital facts which could have given them insight into Tyson's early years. Did they get to know more about Tyson the man from this line of questioning? Probably not.

Fuller may have worried that if he got too close to home, Tyson could later be questioned about the reform school years, petty theft charges, and his other problems with the law. However, Fuller seemed to skirt vital parts of Tyson's upbringing and his rise from the slums of Brownsville to being heavyweight champion of the world.

Nevertheless, Fuller left this questioning for other territory. Answering politely, saying "excuse me" several times, Tyson said that he had come from Washington, D.C., to Indianapolis to attend the Black Expo where his girlfriend was performing. He told the jury he arrived at 4:00 a.m. on July 17, accompanied by Dale Edwards, his bodyguard, and B Angie B, his rapper girlfriend whose aunt lived in Indianapolis. Upon arrival they had gone to B Angie B's Aunt Bates' house and then to the nightclub Seville for two hours, where Tyson said he signed autographs and he and B Angie B kissed and hugged.

Facial reaction from jurors #3 and #8 seemed to indicate that they were hoping to hear from Tyson a believable story that would allow them to acquit him of all charges. They expected Tyson to live up to their expectations and to tell them what really happened. Were they believing Iron Mike?

Tyson said that, after visiting the club, the three returned to the Canterbury Hotel where Edwards, B Angie B and he checked in. Skipping any details as to the process of checking in, or who was seen and what was said (so as to rebut any of the testimony of hotel employees), Fuller diverted the testimony to the morning of the 18th of July.

Confirming Johnny Gill's testimony, Tyson said that he and Gill got together in Gill's room at about 10:00 a.m. After lunch, they returned to the hotel lobby with Rev. Charles Williams, who suggested they go over to the Omni to say hello to the contestants.

When they arrived at the rehearsal hall, Tyson testified that the girls got very excited, and started hugging and kissing him and asking for autographs. When Tyson was asked to "participate in a promo," he said, he agreed to do so, and proceeded to do a rap number having to do with all the beautiful women around him. "I'm not much of a rapper," Tyson said, and so he had to do quite a few takes of the rap songs because he kept "messing up."

He said that when he came in contact with a girl who later turned out to be Desiree Washington, Tyson asked her if she wanted to go out, to which she replied, "yeah, sure."

Tyson then said he wanted to get "more familiar with the girls," so he said, "Want a picture, sit on my lap?" "Yes," he testified," my arms were about them," but he didn't remember if Desiree Washington sat on his lap or not. Tyson admitted that he used "explicit sexual language" and that some girls rebuffed him.

After doing a promotional tape with three of the contestants, one of whom was Desiree Washington, Tyson said he entered into a discussion with Desiree and her roommate behind a pillar. "Would you be upset if I ask out your roommate?" he said he asked Pasha, and she said no. Again he asked the question, Tyson said, this time to Desiree. Her reply was yes. "Well, Johnny can come then," Tyson said he said. "Are you happy now?" Desiree, Tyson said, told him yes.

When some discussion came up as to a "movie or dinner" or something, Tyson said he told Washington, "I just want to be with you; I want you."

Tyson then said perhaps the 11 most important and most pivotal words in the trial. "I explained to her that I just wanted to f . . . her," Tyson said.

Her reply was "That's kinda bold," and moments later, "Sure, just give me a call." To Fuller's question of why he would use such vulgar language, Tyson testified, "That's the way I am, I just want to know what I'm getting into before I'm getting into it."

Prior to his use of the "I want to f . . . you" comment, Tyson told his counsel he would only use the words "if your honor (meaning Judge Gifford) allowed me to do so." When the judge gave her okay, Tyson then spoke the strong words.

It is of course one thing to say to someone what someone else has said, and another to hear it straight from that person. To hear Johnny Gill say later that Mike Tyson said, "I want to f . . .

you" certainly made an impression, but when Tyson himself spoke the words, he may very well have driven the nails into his own coffin.

When Mike Tyson said the infamous "f . . ." word, it was as if a bolt of lightning struck the jurors' faces. They had heard of his lewd behavior and disgusting language, but that was secondhand. This was Iron Mike saying it, and any aura of invincibility he had to that point in the trial was swept away with that fatal word.

Tyson also erred because either he wasn't well coached by his counsel as a witness or he exaggerated his previous testimony on his own. In his unfortunate grand jury testimony, Tyson had said he used the words "I want you." Now he was saying that he used the more direct "I want to f . . . you." Worse, Tyson said the woman's response, "That's kinda bold" and "Sure, just give me a call," never changed. While the jurors might have bought what both Washington and Tyson said her response was to "I want you," that response seemed absurd following the much stronger sexual statement by Tyson. Nevertheless, Tyson testified that after this exchange of words, Washington gave him her room telephone number.

Regarding the alleged "You're a nice Christian girl" comment, Tyson said it came from a conversation he had with Charlie Neal, a sportscaster for Black Entertainment News. Tyson said he didn't mean anything "holy" by the comment, he only used the phrase because Neal did.

Later, Tyson said he "tried to reach Desiree at the Omni, but couldn't." At the opening ceremonies, he said one of the military men on guard gave him the Christian badge he wore. Politicians spoke; "I didn't listen," he said, and "I walked up and down and around through the lines of the contestants." When he came to Desiree Washington, he walked around her, and said it's "Too bad you've got dresses on; I can't see what you got."

At some point, Tyson said, Desiree Washington got his attention. She showed him "two pictures of her in a bathing suit" and he said he replied, "Good, now I know what you've got."

He did, Tyson said, "have prayer with Jesse Jackson." Jackson asked him to dinner, and they ate together that evening.

Tyson then said he went to the Johnny Gill concert. He said he didn't remember seeing Desiree Washington backstage, but that he did see B Angie B and asked her, "You gonna make that flight [to Cleveland] or not?" and she said, "Yeah."

After the concert, Tyson said he went to the Canterbury with Dale Edwards ("Edwards always sits in the front seat") to pick up messages. Then the limousine headed for the Omni, where Edwards placed the call to the hotel room. Tyson said he spoke to Desiree Washington for about 10 minutes, telling her to put on something "loose." When she came to the limousine, Washington got in on the driver's side. "I kissed her," he said, "and she kissed me."

Little detail was given as to how the limousine then ended up at the Canterbury. Virginia Foster was never asked who told her to drive there; the bodyguard Edwards was never called as a witness; and neither Tyson nor Washington was asked who gave the order. Such a fact could have been important, since the State alleged that the seduction of Washington was preplanned.

Tyson testified that he and Washington were "kissing and hugging," in the limousine on the way to the hotel. "Me and Desiree and Dale went into the hotel," he said, and then Dale opened the door to room 606 with a key because "I don't carry keys."

The ex-champ then said that Desiree Washington went into the bedroom when he did. When asked where Dale Edwards was, Tyson said, "I believe he was supposed to be in the whatchamacallit, the parlor. That's where he was supposed to have been, the parlor." Tyson then admitted the door was closed, and that he really didn't know where Edwards was.

In the bedroom, Tyson said, "We started talking about what . . . talking about Rhode Island, where I'm from; where she's from, she had a scholarship. I asked her about a fighter from Rhode Island, does she know him? She didn't know him."

Concerning their respective positions on the bed, Tyson pointed to his place at the top right-hand corner of the bed and to her position down on the right corner of the bed. She was sitting like a "Buddha, with her legs crossed," Tyson said.

At this point, Fuller asked Tyson about what Ms. Washington was wearing.

"She had on the outfit you had showed me [Washington's yellow sequined dress], it was like that. I wasn't sure, then I saw the pants outfit. I wasn't sure if it was the same pants she had on. The pants matched the jacket, but it didn't look like—it looked pink to me."

They talked for about "10 minutes maybe," Tyson testified, and "when we were talking, my hand was on her leg." Were you kissing her, he was asked? "Yes, I was kissing her." Was she kissing you? "Yes."

As to his memory concerning Washington going to the bathroom, Tyson said, "I don't remember that."

Fuller asked if there was a time when Tyson moved Washington physically? "Just to bring her down back...we were kissing up . . . her back was more facing the head of the bed, so I had to slide her down some."

When Fuller asked "Did you undress her?" Garrison objected, and in sustaining the objection, Judge Gifford scolded Fuller, saying "He [Garrison] wants you to quit asking leading questions." The jury, always respectful of Judge Gifford's opinion, looked at Fuller as if they hoped he would quit too. It was almost as if they were saying "Let the man testify," quit putting words in his mouth.

Tyson then began to give the details of the incident. "As I'm kissing her, she was moving fast. She was dropping her jacket, you know, getting her jacket off quick. And I'm just kissing on the neck, and around the ears, back of the neck and chest and nipples, the stomach.

"I believe she had a white shirt on as well. She was trying to get that off, so I came back while she was taking that off. She had taken off those shorts, she had. . . . I'm sure she took off the shorts.

"I took my shirt off at the time she had took off her underwear. She had underwear, and she took off her underwear, and the underwear dropped to her knees, and I pulled them all the way off. And then I took off . . . I had short pants on, and I continued kissing on the body.

"We were having oral sex for a while, and she had told me to stop and told me to come up, come up, she said no, she, no, come up."

Tyson then said they enjoyed sexual intercourse for "probably 15-20 minutes."

When he was about to come to a climax, he said, "She told me not to come in her, 'don't come in me, don't come in me. I'm not on the pill, and I pulled back, and oh, I ejaculated on her stomach and her legs." He said, "She went to the bathroom, I guess, to clean herself off or something."

Tyson said, "I was watching her. She had underwear on, they were polka dot. I thought they were flowers. They looked like flowers then, but they were polka dots. She was in the mirror doing her hair, a little dance, like shoo, shoo, shoo, doing her hair.

"And I offered her to stay the night with me, because she had said, her and some other girls I had spoke to earlier, they had a 5:00 wake up call. And I said I had to get up early as well, so perhaps she could stay with me. She didn't want to stay.

"So I informed her that my limousine was downstairs and would take her where she wanted to go. And she wanted me to walk her downstairs. I said I was too tired. I was only going to have a few hours of sleep.

"She said, 'You're not going to walk me downstairs?' 'Listen, trust me, I'm tired, I'm sorry, I can't walk you downstairs. If you would like to stay, you're welcome to stay, I would love for you to stay. I would love for you to stay, I really would love for you to stay. If you don't want to, you can take the limousine downstairs or you can walk.'"

To Fuller's question, "Did she express irritation toward you?" Tyson replied, "She was irritated because I didn't walk her downstairs."

Tyson then was questioned by Fuller about his leaving the hotel with Edwards, going to try to find B Angie B, and then the drive ultimately to the airport to catch the plane to Cleveland.

How effective was the direct examination of Tyson by Fuller? Courtroom observers seemed split down the middle. Some felt Fuller had led the ex-champ so much that what testimony he gave was highly ineffective. Others felt that Tyson's politeness was a huge plus for him, and that he gave a plausible story of what happened in the hotel suite.

One thing was for certain. The jury was unable to get better acquainted with Tyson's version of what had occurred between him and Desiree Washington. Fuller's strategy was to lead Tyson along with the hope that he could avoid a disastrous remark that would convince the jury of Tyson's guilt.

Perhaps it wasn't so much what Fuller did as what he did not do. He obviously was aware of Tyson's grand jury testimony (or his version of the facts from private discussions with him about the incident) which had made him aware that Tyson had only said, "I want you" and not "I want to f . . . you" to Washington at the rehearsal. Two problems thus arose. The first problem was: since he knew of the difference in testimony, why did he not try to soften the blow, knowing Garrison would make a big deal by asking Tyson why he didn't say "I want to f . . . you" at the grand jury? By checking the exact questions and answers given, he could have brought out Tyson's answer and explained away the discrepancies. Instead, he had Tyson answer with a different version of what he said, and left it for Tyson to suffer the damage when his testimony at the grand jury was played on tape.

The second problem was that the addition of the strong language used by Tyson made Washington's "That's pretty bold" and "Call me" answers appear absolutely absurd. Later, in argument, Garrison would point out to the jury the virtual impossibility of that happening, and there is no question that must have been an important point with the jury.

There were two other implausible points that Fuller let stand with regard to Tyson's testimony: 1) the statement that he watched Washington "do her hair" in the bathroom, and 2) that Washington was only upset because Tyson had refused to walk her downstairs.

Tyson's version of Washington "doing her hair" was in direct contradiction to the testimony of limousine driver Virginia Foster (especially since Washington's having long hair would make it difficult for her to fix it in a short time), who noticed how messed up Washington's hair was when she came down from the hotel after the alleged attack. If the jury believed Foster, Tyson's version was a lie.

As to the testimony about the refusal by Tyson to walk Washington down to the limousine, Tyson's version also went against the grain of the bellhop and Virginia Foster, who clearly saw the accuser in a state of shock when she came out to the limo. As it was, the jury was left to wonder whether Tyson's mere refusal to walk Washington downstairs would trigger the filing of rape charges.

Looking at the testimony from the jury's viewpoint, Tyson's story, when matched up against that of Washington and Foster, was very tough to believe, if the jury believed the two women. In the "who's telling the truth" match-up, Tyson was falling behind.

At the end of Tyson's direct testimony, Fuller asked the usual questions.

"Mr. Tyson, at any time did you force Desiree Washington to engage in sexual intercourse with you?"

"No, I didn't. I didn't violate her in any way, sir."

"Did she at any time tell you to stop what you were doing?"

"Never, she never told me to stop, and she never said I was hurting her. She never said no, nothing."

"At anytime, did you place your fingers in her vagina?"

"No, I didn't."

"Did you touch her private parts?"

"Yes, I did."

"What did you do?"

"I just stroked her with my finger around her clitoris area."

Vincent Fuller had two alternative plans in his questioning of Tyson. One was to put the champ through a vigorous, almost prosecution-like examination designed not only to elicit as many details as possible, but to prepare him for a similar rigorous cross-examination as well. This alternative had some risk to it, because even though Tyson had been put through a pretrial sample cross-examination by members of the defense team, he might still have been unable to handle tough questioning designed to catch him off guard.

Fuller's other tactic was to provide the ex-champ with an opportunity, through simple questions, to give his side of the story in his own words. No yes or no questions here, just questions that would allow the jury to see for themselves that Tyson was telling the truth.

The defense lawyers in the Kennedy Smith and Rodney King cases had to make similar decisions. Roy Black chose to allow William Kennedy Smith to carefully answer each question posed in the beginning of his testimony, and then seemed to give Smith more latitude to answer questions as the defendant became more comfortable with testifying.

Black also chose to not in any way "put words in Smith's mouth," but instead allowed his client to tell his story as he saw fit. This strategy permitted the jury to see Smith as a strong witness, and Black as a confident lawyer who was not afraid to allow his client to testify on his own.

The most impressive attorney in the Rodney King case was Darryl Mounger, the lawyer for Sergeant Stacy Koon, who was in charge of the police officers who were charged with beating King. Mounger and his colleagues all determined early on a potent strategy. By slowing down the action in the explosive videotape, they had been able to show that perhaps the first perception that "excessive force" had been used was not an accurate one.

Believing this to have been successful, the lawyers, and Mounger in particular, knew that their clients needed to testify to refute the "excessive force" claims against them. Therefore, Mounger mounted a concerted effort for a common strategy to the effect that King had continued to resist arrest and therefore was deserving of any force used to subdue him.

In deciding how they wanted their clients to testify, the lawyers all took the approach that the jury needed to hear the accused men, to learn about their personal lives and their life-threatening careers as police officers. Realizing they were in friendly territory, with the positive attitude displayed by most of the jurors toward police officers in general, the attorneys carefully avoided restricting their clients and what they would say on the witness stand, for fear the jury would believe the men were hiding some important piece of information.

Mounger was especially effective in directing the testimony of Koon. He promoted the assets that his client had—good policeman, family man, career law enforcement officer, etc.,— while de-emphasizing his intent to in any way deliberately seek to hurt King when the arrest took place. Koon thus came off as a caring, family man who was merely doing his job when the unfortunate event took place with King.

In the Bensonhurst case, attorney Arthur Lewis, knowing that the evidence against Lemrick Nelson was strong, chose to divert the jurors' minds from his client by placing the creditability of the police in issue. By employing this strategy, Lewis successfully changed the focus of the trial and put the police on the defensive.

Vincent Fuller confronted these same sort of decisions as he approached the game plan to be utilized with Tyson's testimony.

Unfortunately, and perhaps for valid reasons known only to him, Fuller decided that the "I will testify for him" manner of questioning would be best suited to Tyson's testimony.

Vincent Fuller thus had asked many questions that were so leading that Judge Gifford ended up scolding him for his blatant behavior. Tyson was left to provide a "yes" or "no" here and there, or to provide incomplete facts that left the jury with only part of the story. Such questioning produced more of Fuller's thoughts than Tyson's, and also provided Tyson with no preparation for the anticipated cross-examination confrontation with Garrison. This strategy gave the impression to the jury that Fuller was not confident about having Tyson testify freely, and earmarked Tyson as a weak witness who had to be led along by his attorney.

If Fuller was looking for a big finish to Tyson's testimony, it never came. His somewhat confused termination provided no opportunity for Tyson to give any emotional plea of his innocence to the jury. Tyson only barked out the answers he perhaps had been coached to give. In retrospect, the mistake of allowing Tyson to appear before the grand jury was obvious, and Tyson's preparation for rigorous cross-examination was thwarted by ineffective direct examination. Fuller sat down looking somehow pleased with himself, and Mike Tyson readied himself for the combative Garrison.

The anticipated confrontation would not take place that day, however, as Judge Gifford, with no explanation, surprisingly postponed the resumption of testimony until the next morning, even though Tyson's testimony ended in mid-afternoon. Instead of just a few minutes to gather their thoughts, the judge's decision assisted the prosecution by permitting them a full evening to prepare.

Greg Garrison could now review Tyson's grand jury testimony and his direct-examination answers, and decide for himself the most potent way to knock out Mike Tyson once and for all.

17

♦

ATTACKING IRON MIKE

At 9:00 a.m. on February 8, armed and ready, Prosecutor Greg Garrison stood to confront Mike Tyson. The big moment of the trial was here and it was time for the high noon confrontation between Iron Mike Tyson, 41-1-0 with 38 knockouts, and Garrison, who boasted that he hadn't lost a case since 1973.

Taking on the famous Tyson was not without its risks for Garrison. In the Thomas/Hill confrontation, the senators' personal questions to Thomas had absolutely infuriated him to the point that he threatened to stalk out of the proceedings. Personal questions to Professor Hill also went perhaps beyond the bounds of good taste, and angered her so much that the viewing audience was embarrassed for her.

In the Kennedy Smith case, prosecutor Moira Lasch performed what famed lawyer F. Lee Bailey called "the worst cross-examination I've ever seen in a courtroom" in confronting Smith. Trial experts said Lasch made almost every mistake possible by angering the judge (at one point, Lupo warned Lasch that "this is not a course in trial practice," when the prosecutor continued to ask improper questions), and giving Smith questions that let him repeat his version of the story almost unchallenged. Lasch also did not take the opportunity to probe Smith on the inconsistencies in his story, and instead focused on too many issues, especially ones that did not involve a clear contradiction or go to the heart of the case.

Prosecutor Terry White encountered problems with the four police officers charged in the Rodney King state case when he sought to underplay their feeling that they were acting as they did because of the "threat to life" situation that they face every day.

White could not crack the officers' story that King was resisting arrest, and that he may very well have had a gun, another weapon, or would somehow physically strike back at the officers who were trying to arrest him. The more White tried to question the motives of the officers, the more he seemed to sense that he was pounding home just the opposite theory to the jury, who seemed to buy the "threat to life" argument.

For the confrontation with the dreaded Garrison, Tyson chose a blue suit with a white shirt and red paisley tie. He stalked to the witness stand and prepared to defend himself against the prosecutor who wanted to send him to prison for 60 years. Quickly, Garrison rose to meet him, coming within about five feet of the ex-champ and squarely in front of the jury as if to say, "I'm not scared of you, Mike Tyson; in fact, you should be scared of me."

As with Fuller's alternative strategies concerning direct examination of Tyson, Garrison had numerous possibilities as to how to cross-examine Tyson. He could use the rapid-fire, machine-gun approach, designed to surprise the ex-champ, throw him off-guard, and then secure a disastrous answer that would lock the prison door behind him.

Garrison could also utilize the "he-said, she-said" approach where he could take critical portions of Tyson's direct examination, confront him with Washington's version, and ask Tyson to explain the obvious discrepancies. Such a strategy would put Tyson on the defensive and leave the jury with Garrison's belief that his client easily won the "who do you believe" sweepstakes.

Unfortunately for the jury, Garrison chose neither. Hungry for more facts about the incident in the hotel room, the jury instead watched Garrison avoid the rape incident almost entirely and give them a picture book look at the 25-year-old ex-champ.

Garrison began with Tyson's past. Careful to avoid the boxer's confrontations with the law as a juvenile, the prosecutor chose to discuss Tyson's training with the legendary trainer Cus

D'Amato. After some early observation of Tyson's skills D'Amato got right to the point. "If you listen to me," he told Tyson, "you will be the next champion of the world." Tyson was less than 15 years old at the time.

Asked about D'Amato's approach to boxing, Tyson said Cus was an advocate of being "very elusive," and "having a great deal of anticipation." Garrison then asked, "How do you accomplish being elusive in the ring?" Tyson thought a minute, and then said, "Avoid the punches. . . . Your head is so big. Some people's heads are bigger than others, and punches come in. You anticipate the punch, and put your head inside the punch."

As for elusiveness in the ring, Tyson said that there were numerous types. "What do you do?" asked Garrison. "I go forward" replied Tyson, "you go forward. You watch his shoulders, both shoulders. You can't watch his hands. You watch the shoulders, and watch if the shoulders move. And you anticipate, and you must be very relaxed."

Not having elicited the word he was looking for from Tyson, "deceptive," Garrison finally used it himself in talking with Tyson about the way he avoids punches in the ring. "He [D'Amato] didn't want the guy to be able to see. He always wants you to be where he wasn't able to see the punch."

Feeling that either he had gotten his point about deception being a part of Tyson's background, or that it was simply time to move on, Garrison then began to hit his key target, Tyson's grand jury testimony.

He began by talking about Tyson's approach to women, pointing out that he had said to the grand jury that "You don't just go right up to a girl and say, quote, want to screw?" Garrison then turned to Tyson's previous testimony to the grand jury concerning his conversations with Desiree Washington.

The prosecutor pointed out that on page 76, Tyson apparently had said, "I want it to be me and you. I want to be with you alone. I said, I want you." Then Tyson said Desiree Washington said, "Okay. Just call me."

Garrison then confronted Tyson with his infamous "I want to f . . . you" quote of the day before. "How come you didn't tell that to the grand jury?" Tyson tried to explain that deputy prosecutor David Dreyer "cut me off," because there was more to say.

The prosecutor, however, told Tyson that he was asked, "Did you say anything else?" to which Tyson replied, "No, I had to leave."

As to why the "f . . . " word wasn't used, Tyson testified, "You know, I didn't feel comfortable using the word at that particular time in the grand jury because there were no younger kids in there my age or anything." Garrison then asked Tyson, "You were more comfortable saying it in here yesterday." Tyson said, "No. I'm pretty much under pressure to say it. I felt very uncomfortable saying it in front of the jury, in front of the judge and my mother."

Johnny Gill's testimony was then brought up. Garrison admitted that Gill had previously told investigators that Tyson "had said those words to somebody," but that he was shown pictures of all the girls and couldn't pick anybody out. Tyson said he couldn't explain that. "I don't know Johnny Gill's memory functions," Tyson told the jury.

After a somewhat strained back and forth discussion of whether Garrison's memory was good or not (Garrison: "Mine's [memory] not so hot sometimes—that's what my kids tell me." Tyson: "Fooled me"), the prosecutor turned his attention to the missing witness, bodyguard Dale Edwards. Garrison's point was to show that Edwards had never been called to testify, a point that would be brought up again in final argument. Garrison also wanted the jury to know how much money Tyson carried. "About how much cash do you think you had on you when you were in Indianapolis?" Tyson's reply was "$30,000." Perhaps more than some of the jurors made in a year.

Rev. Jesse Jackson's name was then bantered about. Garrison emphasized that Jackson baptized Tyson in 1988, and that Tyson considered him to be "a friend." The prosecutor also honed in on Tyson's lie to Jackson about going to visit the Marion County Jail the next day. Tyson explained "As he [Jackson] continued to pressure me . . . he said, 'Can you make it?' I said, 'No, I've got to be somewhere.' Jackson then said, 'No, you got to be there.' Finally I said, 'All right.'"

Garrison asked, "When you said, 'Okay, I'll be there,' you didn't intend to go, did you?" "No way I could make it," Tyson said. "He wouldn't take no for an answer, and he didn't understand; he didn't respect me."

Garrison then found an area that he felt could be pivotal. His main credible witness, Virginia Foster, the limousine driver, had told the jury that Tyson "begged" Washington to come down to the limousine. The prosecutor sought to exploit Tyson's inconsistencies with that testimony.

Tyson's version of the 1:36 a.m. call to Desiree's room was, "She had told me, I believe, that she was in bed. She was sleeping. She looked horrible. And I said, 'Well, that doesn't matter. Throw some water on your face, and wear some loose clothes.' She said, 'I'll see you tomorrow,' and then I told her, 'Well, I'm leaving tonight.'" Finally, Tyson said, Washington told him, "I'm coming down."

Foster's testimony, Garrison reiterated, was that Tyson had said, "I just want to talk. Come on down. We'll see the sights."

Garrison then brought up Tyson's testimony about wanting Washington to "wear something loose." "How come?" asked Garrison.

"Because I had intentions of doing it in the limousine. I just asked her to put something on loose so I could easily get to her."

Garrison: "You figured she was coming down to have sex with you?"

Tyson: "Yes."

Garrison: "How come?"

Tyson: "I believe from our conversation we had earlier indicated that."

The prosecutor and Tyson then went round and round with the description of the clothing Desiree had on. Tyson's description of the clothing was that it was "pink." Tyson also said the shorts in evidence "didn't seem like the same shorts she was wearing." From the grand jury testimony, Garrison read Tyson's testimony: "She had on very short hot pants. I believe they were very short pants. Her thighs were showing. They were tight. They were very short. She had a little cut-off blouse. It was cut off to her stomach, I believe."

Whether the blouse "was open or not" was debated, and Tyson explained, "I'm not a professional at women's attire. I just saw what she had on. She had the jacket open."

Tyson then was asked about his grand jury testimony where he talked about what he and Desiree did while in the limousine on the way to the Canterbury. "We started hugging and kissing," was what Tyson had said, and Garrison got him to admit to the inference that "You are touching all over her body, and you are kissing her real passionately and they were long kisses."

"But," Garrison said, "when you go to the Canterbury, you sit down on the bed, and you talk for 15 minutes?" Tyson answered, "I believe we both made it clear earlier that day what was going to happen when she came to my room at 2:00 in the morning. I'm sure we made it clear."

As to the conversation itself, Tyson testified, "It was just a conversation. I never came to say, 'well, let's do it right now.' It wasn't that kind of climate where we were going to make passionate love as soon as we walk in the door on the floor or something!"

It appeared that Garrison was not pleased with where Tyson was going with all of this, so he returned to Tyson's buddy, Dale Edwards.

"Did you know that Dale Edwards said [at the grand jury] that while you were in the back in the bedroom with Desiree he was in the living room of your suite?" Tyson's reply was simple, "I didn't know he said it that way." Garrison continued on, "And you know three different people who worked at the hotel testified at the hearing that that's not true? Edwards was all over that hotel. He made calls from 604. He placed a room service order at the front desk. He took telephone calls in the parlor. He talked to the limousine driver out front all the while you were upstairs in 606. You know that to be a fact, don't you?"

Tyson: "Well, no. I know he should have been in that parlor room. That's where he was supposed to be."

Garrison then hit home with the fact that Tyson told the grand jury that Edwards was in the parlor and now he was saying he wasn't sure.

Garrison: "So when you answered the questions in the grand jury, you were supposing where he was, but you didn't really know."

Tyson: "I didn't know, really know. I was to believe that he was in the parlor."

Garrison: "Kind of like supposing somebody wants to have sex with you, but you don't really know, isn't it?"

Vincent J. Fuller (left), Don King's $5,000-a-day hired gun, surprised the prosecution and courtroom observers with his confused arguments and misguided defense of Tyson.

Indianapolis attorney James Voyles (right) was hired as local defense counsel, but Fuller's failure to take advantage of Voyles's county courtroom experience, his familiarity with Judge Gifford, and his knowledge of Indiana juries was another of the defense's miscalculations.

Defense attorney Kathleen Beggs had an unfriendly relationship with fiery prosecutor Greg Garrison, resulting in several heated exchanges during the trial.

Mary Ann Carter

Defense lawyer F. Lane Heard III (left) was thought by many to be the most effective member of the defense team. He was a formidable foe for Garrison, who appeared agitated by Heard's strong manner and unwillingness to back down when Garrison confronted him with objections to the Court.

Mary Ann Carter

Chief Prosecutor Jeffrey Modisett (right) spoke for the prosecution at Tyson's sentencing, claiming "Tyson still doesn't get it. . . . Heal this sick man. Mike Tyson, the rapist, needs to be off the streets."

Mary Ann Carter

Prosecutor Greg Garrison made many damaging and normally inadmissible remarks during the trial that were never objected to by Fuller.

Mary Ann Carter

During deliberations, the first vote taken by Tim, the ex-marine jury foreman (fifth from left), was six votes for "guilty" and six votes for "not guilty" on the charge of rape. Two votes and several hours later, all twelve jurors voted to convict Tyson on all three counts.

Prosecutors Greg Garrison and Barb Trathen were surprised throughout the trial by the lack of competition they received from the defense team.

Tyson's smirking face and remorseless attitude throughout the trial led jurors and many courtroom observers to believe that he was indifferent to Washington's accusations and the seriousness of his situation.

Protesters outside the courthouse in Indianapolis mirrored the intense public interest in the Tyson rape trial.

Mary Ann Carter

*Prosecution-friendly Judge
Patricia Gifford initiated legislation leading to the passage of a
strict rape shield law that protects
women from embarrassing
questions about their sexual
histories in rape cases. Her
selection as judge weighed heavily
in the prosecution's favor.*

*Even though promoter Don King
has come under fire for his
handling of Tyson's affairs, the
ex-champion remains fiercely
loyal to King.*

Mary Ann Carter

Contestant Claudia Jordan testified that Washington's description of the rape included "sex on the floor" and that "she was screaming" when Tyson attacked her.

Strong defense witness Cecilia Alexander (left) told the Court she overheard Washington say "He's [Tyson's] not intelligent . . . he's dumb, ignorant . . . Look at the money Robin Givens got," and "Mike doesn't have to speak. He'll make the money and I'll do the talking."

Defense witness Parquita Nassau (right) testified that Tyson said to the contestants "If you don't want to go out, I can go on. I can have any one of you bitches, and I know you want me."

Mary Ann Carter

Mary Ann Carter

Mary Ann Carter

LaShauna Fitzpatrick jolted the defense when she said during cross-examination that Washington "looked like death" the day following the alleged attack.

Mary Ann Carter

Beauty contestant Tanya St. Clair Gilles testified that at the rehearsal Washington said Tyson had "a butt to hold on to" and Washington wanted "a man with money."

R & B singer Johnny Gill corroborated Tyson's testimony word for word, but he did not turn out to be the bombshell witness the defense had hoped for.

Dale Edwards, Tyson's bodyguard, was supposed to be outside the bedroom at the time of the alleged rape, but was reportedly seen by several witnesses in the lobby making phone calls and ordering room service.

In a letter read by Jeffrey Modisett to the Court on the day of Tyson's sentencing, Washington said "In the place of what has been me for 18 years is now a cold and empty feeling. I can only say that each day after being raped has been a struggle to learn to trust again, to smile the way I did, and to find the Desiree Lynn Washington who was stolen from me and those who love me, on July 19, 1991. Although some days I cry when I see the pain in my own eyes, I am also able to pity my attacker. It has been and still is my wish that he be rehabilitated."

Tyson's flamboyant appellate counsel Alan Dershowitz, defender of famous clients Leona Helmsley, Michael Milken, and Jim Bakker, is thought by many to have stretched the boundaries of judicial ethics in his appeal for Tyson.

Mary Ann Carter

◆

Tyson told Dershowitz what he misses most in prison is "the privacy, the ability to do what I want, to eat healthy food, to hug my mother, to joke around with my friends, to feed my pigeons, to sleep in my own bed."

Mary Ann Carter

Mary Ann Carter

Tyson continues to receive support from
his many fans in over 100 letters a day
sent to the Indiana Youth Correctional
Facility. With parole possible in 1995,
boxing fans around the world wonder,
"Will Tyson fight again?"

Camille Ewald, Tyson's
surrogate mother, who
lived with trainer Cus
D'Amato for nearly forty
years, was devastated by
Tyson's sentence.

Mary Ann Carter

Tyson never had to answer that question because Garrison withdrew it. Perhaps more important, he withdrew it even though Vincent Fuller never objected to it, or ask that it be stricken.

This was perhaps a small point, but Garrison got away with asking many improper questions and making cute remarks during the trial that damaged Tyson. Either Fuller didn't care or they somehow went right over his head. Either way, Garrison's inadmissible remarks made points with the jury.

In fact, Fuller never did give Garrison a hard fight. His failure to do so gave the jury the impression that Fuller either didn't want to provoke a confrontation, or simply was not up to the task.

Fuller's smooth, almost formal demeanor, also never allowed the jury to see the smart-alec side of Garrison, or a quick temper that the prosecutor tried to hide. The jury was thus left to see Fuller as the much weaker of the two men, which in turn reflected negatively on Tyson.

After discussing the fact that 10 minutes (according to Tyson's testimony) of oral sex by Tyson would make "things pretty wet down there," Garrison asked Tyson whether he began sexual intercourse after the oral sex.

Garrison: "When you injected or inserted yourself in her, did you have any trouble getting inside?"

Tyson: "I don't remember if I had problems getting inside or not."

Leaving this area without a followup, Garrison then talked about Tyson's sexual relationship with B Angie B.

Garrison: "Did you know that she told Ms. Trathen [prosecutor] in her deposition that when you went to the Holiday Inn [before the incident with Washington] you engaged in sex for a long time?"

Tyson: "Could have been. I'm not really sure of the situation of being long. I'm not really sure."

Garrison: "You have forgotten whether you had sex with B Angie B at the hotel? . . . Is it an event that was not of particular interest to you?"

Tyson: "That's not necessarily true at all, no."

Garrison: "You remember having sex once with Desiree Washington, but you forgot having a couple of hours worth with B Angie B the day before."

Tyson was then asked whether he had sex twice with B Angie B. Again, he was a bit evasive, but for a reason.

Tyson (to the judge): "May I use gross, crude language for a moment, ma'am?"

The court: "Help yourself."

Tyson (to Garrison): "What do you mean? Do you mean every time I climaxed, that's one time. If I do it again, that's another time. What do you mean?"

Garrison: "Yes, that will do."

Tyson: "Then I don't know."

Garrison: "Would you be surprised to know that Miss Boyd has a specific recollection of all those things?"

Tyson: "Well, she must have enjoyed it a lot."

Garrison probably didn't obtain exactly the answers he wanted, but he drew some blood. Tyson's selective memory was the target, and he implied that Iron Mike remembered what he wanted to remember and forgot what he wanted to forget (i.e., couldn't remember sex with his girlfriend, but could with a school girl). Garrison closed off the topic by pointing out that Tyson's relationship with B Angie B apparently had deteriorated recently, implying that B Angie B wasn't too happy with Tyson's sexual prowess as well.

Garrison next attacked Tyson's relationship with religion, again as much by innuendo as by proof of fact. He mentioned Tyson calling Washington "a nice Christian girl," his wearing of the "Together in Christ" button, and his prayer with Jesse Jackson.

Garrison: "Those were not spiritual events in your life?"

Tyson: "I don't understand what you're trying to get at."

To finish up, Garrison again returned to what he felt was the most unbelievable part of Tyson's testimony.

Garrison: "You said to Desiree Washington, 18 years and one month, just graduated from high school, 'I want to f . . . you,' and she said 'That's bold, call me?' Is that the conversation?"

Tyson: "No. She said, 'That's pretty bold.' I said, 'Well, that's the way I am. I want what I want.' I said 'I just want to know where we stand.' She said, 'Sure. Call me.'"

Garrison: "So this 18-year-old incoming freshman from Coventry, Rhode Island, says basically, You want to f . . . me? Fine, call me."

Tyson: "Well, she told me to call her."

Redirect and recross-examination merely hammered home the points that had been fought for with previous testimony. Fuller could not clear up Tyson's problems with forgetting the "I want to f . . . you" comment at the grand jury; in fact, his disorganized redirect may have made the matter worse.

As with Fuller's cross-examination of Desiree Washington, Garrison's inability to successfully implement his well-planned and cohesive cross-examination of Tyson again left the jury without enough facts about the incident in the hotel room. Garrison, later, rather amazingly admitted he left out some important points, but while he never could produce the "dark side" of Mike Tyson as promised, he did mix the ex-champ up on important points. More important, Garrison did not fall on his face, as had Moira Lasch with her abominable performance in the Kennedy Smith case, or Terry White had done when he had actually driven home the defense point of view with his ill-conceived questions to the four police officers charged with using excessive force to subdue Rodney King.

Many wondered why Garrison did not go for the jugular when he cross-examined Tyson. Garrison was aware that he could not afford to make the ex-champ look stupid or dumb and risk him becoming a sympathetic figure in the eyes of the jurors. Also, it appeared that Garrison was pleasantly surprised by Tyson's at-odds testimony with the grand jury record regarding the "I want to f . . . you" comment, and believed that this strong discrepancy would in the end doom Tyson. Garrison seemed to believe that the tall tale that Tyson was telling wouldn't sell with the jury, and so there was no reason to bombard the ex-champ and attack his dignity.

Whether Tyson's appearance on the stand was more positive than negative will long be debated (most jurors said later that they didn't believe him). Few new facts were uncovered about the actual rape attack, and no questions were asked about the unusual nature of a rape that included oral sex and Miss Washington having been on top of Tyson during the sex act.

Most important though, Fuller had permitted Tyson himself to utter the distasteful "I want to f . . . you" words, and in doing so allowed Garrison to show the jury that Mike Tyson, the celebrity, was just a foul-mouthed belligerent man capable of rape after all.

18

♦

IN SUPPORT OF TYSON

With the testimony of the two main stars in the trial, Washington and Tyson, now completed, the defense returned to its game plan of bringing witness after witness to appear in the courtroom, in support of its scattershot approach to defending the ex-champ.

To that end, singer Johnny Gill returned to the witness stand. Gill began by discussing the rehearsal and the conversations with Pasha and Desiree by the pillar.

Now that Tyson had testified, the famed R & B singer then confirmed Tyson's testimony about the "I want to f . . . you" comment made to Washington. "She never flinched," he said. The comment "shocked him," Gill said, "it was from out in left field."

The corroboration by Gill that Tyson had used such blatant words seemed unfortunately to have little effect on the jury. Maybe the jurors were still full of Tyson's testimony, but somehow Gill did not make as strong a supporting witness as the defense had hoped for.

Beauty contestant Tanya St. Claire Gilles from Illinois was then called to the stand. Defense lawyer Lane Heard guided her straight to the rehearsal, where she testified that Desiree Washington said that Tyson "was really built," and that he had a "butt to hold on to." Further, Gilles said, Desiree told her that "she wanted a man with money." St. Claire Gilles then said Desiree Washington compared Tyson with his bodyguard, saying that the bodyguard was "chubby," while Tyson was "just right."

St. Claire Gilles' final bit of testimony was a shocker. She stated that on Sunday, Desiree became very upset about another contestant's performance, called her "a bitch and a whore," and then sat down on the floor "beating and stomping."

From the first question on cross-examination, it was apparent that this witness was not one of prosecutor Barb Trathen's favorite people. Emphasizing that "the pageant didn't go well for you [Gilles]," Trathen sought to portray St. Claire Gilles as an unhappy contestant.

Pageant contestant Claudia Jordon followed Gilles to the stand. She testified that Desiree Washington told her there was "sex on the floor" and that "she was screaming" while Tyson attacked her.

La Shauna Fitzpatrick's version of what Desiree Washington told her differed from any other. Called by the defense, this contestant ended up providing the State with one of its best descriptions of Washington after the alleged rape.

Why the defense called this lady was a real question mark. While she did reveal some inconsistencies in Desiree Washington's version of the story, they were not so important as to discount the story's veracity. Her tale that Washington said, "Well, he kinda, sorta, yeah, he raped me" gave emphasis to Washington's uncertainty, but most of the other facts she provided verified elements in Washington's testimony. Her statements to Fitzpatrick that Tyson "restrained her" and "pushed her to the floor" gave the jury something to think about, and the other testimony seemed only to enhance the State's claim that, while Desiree Washington may have told somewhat different stories, she was indeed raped.

The disastrous statement for the defense came during cross-examination when Garrison asked about how Desiree Washington appeared when Fitzpatrick saw her on July 20. The witness jolted the defense when she recalled that she (Desiree Washington) "looked like death!" Both jurors #2 and #5 turned and looked squarely at Tyson for his reaction. There was none.

(Shocking statements that come about in a trial are normally few and far between, and normally occur when lawyers

ask questions they don't know the answers to.) Defense lawyer
Michael Stone allowed this to happen in the Rodney King trial
when he inadvertently allowed prosecutors to ask his client,
Lawrence Powell, about statements he made over the radio just
before the King beating. Powell, who apparently stalled his
answer waiting for the proper objection, then was forced to say
that he said on the radio that he had intervened in a domestic
disturbance involving a group of African-Americans that was
right out of *Gorillas in the Mist*, a reference to the movie about
African wildlife.

After the Fitzpatrick revelation, and in a surprise move,
the defense then called Pasha Oliver to the stand. As one of
Desiree Washington's roommates during the pageant, she was
with Washington when the fateful conversations took place with
Tyson and Johnny Gill at the rehearsal. Pasha was also there
when the 1:36 a.m. phone call came from Tyson in the limousine
to Washington, and she was present when Desiree Washington
came back from the alleged rape attack on Friday morning.

The State had decided not to call Oliver as a witness
because she was also interested in Tyson and apparently his
money as well. She had retained civil lawyers to sue Tyson for
inflammatory comments made to her by him. Answers to
preliminary questions by the defense indicated that Oliver's
lawyers had recently sent a demand letter to Tyson's attorneys
seeking compensation on a sexual harassment charge. Such was
enough to convince Judge Gifford that the lady could be labeled
a "hostile witness."

Gifford's designation of Oliver as a "hostile witness"
meant that the defense could examine her much as if they were
cross-examining her. This leeway is permitted if the witness is
antagonistic toward the questioning party, and would simply
provide meaningless "yes" or "no" answers to direct questions.

As to the important conversation with Tyson, Gill, and
Desiree Washington at the rehearsal, Oliver said that Tyson's
comments made it "clear that's [sex] what he's looking for."

As for the early morning phone call, Pasha testified that
she asked Desiree Washington to see if Johnny Gill is there and
"can I go out with him?"

Regarding what Washington told her about the rape
incident, Oliver said that in the room Desiree "agreed to kiss

him" and "then he ripped her clothes off." Oliver testified Desiree said that Tyson's "hand was over her mouth," and that "Tyson refused to take her home."

Such questions, which would normally be "hearsay" since they are out-of-court statements made by a third person, were allowed because the questions pertained to the potential inconsistent statements made by Tyson's accuser. In effect, use of these questions and answers were the only way to discredit the statements made by Washington as to what occurred between she and Tyson.

Greg Garrison seemed to not know what to do with Pasha Oliver. Perhaps he would have been better to leave her alone, but instead he reviewed her testimony, and especially focused on her inconsistent statements as to whether Tyson ever made lewd comments to her, or actually touched her in a suggestive way, or both.

Reading inconsistencies from her grand jury testimony, Garrison finally became exasperated and asked, "Do you know what perjury is?"

On February 9, the videotape of certain portions of the beauty pageant that was recorded by Tanya Traylor's husband was played. The tape, which was all recorded after the rape, included dance footage of the pageant and statements by Desiree Washington to the effect that her ideal date "would be athletic" and that she "would reach for the highest star." With the playing of the tape, the defense rested.

It is of course pure speculation to evaluate how effective the defense really was. There certainly had been no "knock them out of the water" testimony as was given by Kennedy Smith at his trial, or testimony to compare with the impressive performances of the four police officers in the Rodney King case.

Unfortunately, it appeared that in total the defense testimony, including that of Tyson, proved if anything to enhance the State's chances for conviction. It appeared that Fuller's defense team had in fact helped the State along, and given the jury a better perspective of the critical facts in the case than the State had done on its own.

In addition to problems with the evidence the defense did produce, they also erred in not calling Tyson's bodyguard or singer B Angie B to back up Tyson's story. This unfortunate decision by the defense allowed Garrison to continually remind the jury of their absence, and ask them to question why the two witnesses were not called to testify.

Tyson's disjointed testimony, though, was of course the telling blow. The ex-champ's attempt to defend himself in front of 12 jurors served unfortunately to further incriminate him. Tyson had begun the trial with an aura of invincibility, but step by step he had fallen from grace.

At the beginning of the trial, Fuller and company obviously felt that Tyson's testimony would be not only valuable, but absolutely critical to his defense. Apparently, they believed Tyson would make a credible witness who could withstand not only the discrepancies between his courtroom testimony and his grand jury testimony, but a rigorous cross-examination by Garrison as well.

Tyson, too, appeared confident that he was equal to the task, and that his testimony would permit the jury to learn the truth about the unfortunate incident with Washington. Whether he or his counsel felt that they achieved their goals by having him testify is unknown, but by the time Tyson stepped down from the witness stand, his fate had been all but decided.

19

♦

THE STATE
STRIKES BACK

Once the defense has rested its case, the State may not
bring forth new evidence to bolster its allegations against the
defendant. However, the prosecution can call witnesses to rebut
(challenge, contradict) the testimony offered by the defense.

Once that has taken place, the defense then has an opportunity to bring forth additional rebuttal witnesses to rebut the
State's rebuttal testimony, and so on and so forth. Judges,
however, will not provide either side with much latitude in
continuing the process over and over unless there is an excellent
reason to do so.

Most times, rebuttal and surrebuttal testimony is aimed
squarely at a critical piece of evidence that will weigh heavily in
the outcome of the trial. To that end, the prosecution must have
been greatly concerned about the impact of the testimony of
beauty contestant Tanya Traylor, since Indianapolis Fire Department Deputy Fire Marshal Teresa Harris was their first rebuttal
witness.

Called to rebut Traylor's testimony about seeing the
"friendly, gentlemanlike" Tyson backstage at the Gill concert,
Harris testified that "the contestant in white" (meant to be
Traylor), was "gripped from behind more than four times by
Tyson." Harris said she "was appalled at the behavior, it was
disrespectful to women."

Indianapolis Police Department Detective Charles Briley was then called to counter the testimony of Tanya St. Claire Gilles. Present at the witness's statement to Prosecutor Trathen, he said that Gilles used the words "big dick" to describe a comment by Desiree Washington. Detective Briley also said that St. Claire Gilles's father said something about his daughter's testimony "sounding like a green monster," whatever that meant.

Yet another contestant, the reigning Miss Black America, Charmell Sullivan, was then called to discuss the fact that she never saw Desiree Washington throw a tantrum or "beat on the floor" while watching other contestants perform. Sullivan also didn't hear other disparaging remarks allegedly said by Washington, countering previous testimony by defense witnesses.

Nineteen-year-old pageant contestants Tasha Jarrett and Kycia Johnson were also brought to testify concerning the behavior they saw from Desiree Washington. Both women remembered none of the tantrums portrayed by defense witnesses, and neither felt that Desiree would use the dirty language supposedly attributed to her by other witnesses.

The final piece of evidence for the State came in the form of an audiotape of Mike Tyson's testimony before the grand jury. During cross-examination at trial, Tyson had tried to explain the discrepancy between what he testified to at the grand jury ("I want you" to Desiree Washington), and what he testified to at trial ("I want to f . . . you" to Washington). While the tape was a bit difficult to hear, the State did show that Tyson's explanation that he was cut off by Grand Jury Deputy Prosecutor David Dreyer, as he had said he was during direct examination, was simply not the case.

While not a highly critical piece of evidence on its own, the tape and even just the words "grand jury" implied that Tyson had appeared before a group of law-abiding citizens, not mentioned the "I want to f . . . you" statement, and had been indicted to stand trial. The perception of what all this meant may have outweighed its actual value, but the jury was again left with a less than truthful view of the ex-heavyweight champion of the world.

In surrebuttal, the defense called one witness, the stepfather of Tanya St.Claire Gilles, Anthony Rogers. Since Rogers was present during his stepdaughter's interview with prosecutor Trathen, he remembered that Gilles didn't use the words "dick" or "penis," but instead had said one of the most unusual expressions at trial, "thumb thumb." He also talked about the "green-eyed monster" quote, but his explanation wasn't clear as to who had said what and what was meant.

Basically this highly unusual testimony made no point at all except for calling Deputy Prosecutor Trathen a liar. On that peculiar note, the testimony in the Mike Tyson rape trial ended at 2:01 p.m. on February 10, 1992.

Sometimes a trial becomes known more for what evidence was not presented by either side than for the evidence that was presented. Based on the content of the testimony at trial, history would show that the Mike Tyson trial produced very little testimony about the actual rape incident itself. Instead of learning in detail the specific facts about the rape incident, the jury would need to determine the outcome of *Washington* v. *Tyson* based more on their impressions of the evidence than the actual facts themselves. When this is the case, both sides take an enormous risk, because many times a jury will consider inadmissible evidence or irrelevant factors when they finally decide the case. Whether this would occur in the Tyson case or not was still an unknown, but neither the prosecution nor the defense had adequately done their job in outlining the critical facts about the rape incident to prevent possible improper speculation by the jury.

In comparison with the Kennedy Smith trial, the Rodney King state case, and the Bensonhurst trial, the evidence presented in the Tyson trial fell far short of providing the jury with the necessary evidence upon which to base a verdict. Due to the less than compelling performances of the attorneys, the jurors in the Tyson trial would be left to speculate about the evidence, much as the senators and the American viewing public were in the Thomas/Hill confirmation hearing confrontation.

20

♦

THE LAWYERS SPEAK

In view of the lack of critical evidence about the actual incident of alleged rape that was the basis for the charges against Tyson, the final arguments by the respective attorneys took on great importance.

For Garrison and Trathen, who seemed ahead on points, but perhaps still shy of convincing the jury that Tyson was guilty beyond a reasonable doubt, sound final arguments were necessary to pound home salient points to the jury.

For Vincent Fuller, the opportunity for final argument would provide a chance to redeem himself in the last round of a bout that he was clearly losing. Regardless of his poor performance during the trial, all could be saved if the famous barrister could rise to the occasion and give the speech of his life.

Roy Black had certainly done so in the William Kennedy Smith trial. In his two-hour closing argument, Black methodically recounted all of the evidence. He argued that the accuser was not bruised enough to have been raped, her clothes were not torn enough to have undergone an assault.

Most importantly, Black pointed out the fact that it was preposterous to believe Smith would attack a screaming woman within earshot of relatives, including his mother. This argument was intended to give the jurors the reason they could use to justify to their family and friends why they voted to acquit the nephew of the famous Kennedy brothers.

Prosecutor Lasch countered these arguments by telling the jury that the guilt of Kennedy Smith was clear-cut, saying "Bowman said no, and he [Kennedy Smith] didn't care."

In the Rodney King case, Prosecutor Terry White argued that "excessive force" was used by the police officers, and their claims that they were simply defending themselves against a madman were ridiculous. Defense lawyers continued to press the fact that King was the instigator of the fracas, and that the officers simply responded with equal force as they were trained to do.

Arthur Lewis made the believability of the police the main issue in his plea to the jury in the Bensonhurst trial, and tried to convince the jurors that the police's inconsistent statements regarding Lemrick Nelson left reasonable doubt as to his guilt.

In the Tyson trial, the first attorney to gain center stage was Garrison's sidekick, the very capable Barb Trathen.

At 9:25 a.m. on February 11, 1992, the deputy prosecutor began to address the jury. Throughout the trial, she and Garrison had shared prosecutorial duties, and the plan seemed to work quite well. Like Garrison a controversial choice to prosecute the case in light of the banishment of veteran sex crimes prosecutor Carol Orbison to the sidelines, Trathen nevertheless had put on a very credible performance.

Known to go overboard at times with her meticulous detail, Trathen had only lost her composure two or three times in the case when she became too involved with a witness's testimony and took the witness's remarks personally. Otherwise, she was thorough and professional, and presented the State's case in a methodical, low-key manner.

Trathen began her final argument by stating that Tyson used his fame and reputation like a thug in an alley would use a gun or knife. She stated that forcible rape, "date rape," is serious, and must not be considered "half a crime. Rape is rape," Trathen shouted, when there is "force or the threat of force."

Tyson's "tools" that he used to seduce Washington, Trathen argued, were the religious, not the sexual innuendoes.

Tyson's use of "You're a nice Christian girl," and the wearing of the "Together in Christ" badge made him out to be a "wolf in sheep's clothing."

Beginning her speech three feet in front of the jury, Trathen then pointed to the first row of spectator seats where Desiree Washington sat with her mother.

"Tyson," Trathen said, was a "role model" for Washington's father, and when she saw Tyson praying with the famous Jesse Jackson, "What was this 18 year old supposed to think? Tyson," she told the jury, "had taken on the cloak of Christianity."

To Washington, Trathen argued, "Tyson was not a real person." She "knows how to handle young boys" back in Rhode Island. Tyson was a different story, she said "It would be special to be with him."

Turning to the important medical testimony, Trathen brought up Dr. Richardson's testimony that the injuries sustained by Washington were "consistent with forced sex. In 20,000 cases," the prosecutor argued, he had only seen "twice these types of injuries with consensual sex."

Trathen then asked the jury to focus in on the "quality" testimony, and asked them to discount beauty pageant contestant testimony motivated by jealousy or mistake. Instead, Trathen argued, remember that the defendant's motivation was that he found an "impressionable young woman" (Washington) whose date with Tyson would be a "big moment" for her.

Trathen then told the jury about "The Big Lie." Could they imagine, she said, that after Tyson said, "I want to f . . . you," this 18 year old from Coventry, Rhode Island, would merely go 'ha, ha,' and say, 'yeah, sure, give me a call?' That's what the defendant wants you to believe," Trathen said.

"Tyson also has a selective memory," Trathen said, "especially with what he remembers about sex with B Angie B." He never mentioned the "I want to f . . . you" statement to the grand jury, and Johnny Gill's "same verse and chapter" account is too pat to consider valid, said Trathen.

The defense, Trathen argued, brought you Pasha Oliver, a witness who clearly had committed perjury; Frank Valentine, another defense witness, who was "mixed up;" and St. Claire Gilles, whose disappointing pageant results made the woman who studied at the Little Princess Modeling School an unreliable witness.

Tanya Traylor, according to Teresa Harris of the Indiana Fire Department, had not told the truth about Tyson's behavior backstage at the concert.

"Evaluate the defense witnesses," Trathen said.

As for the 1:36 a.m. phone call, Trathen asked the jury to remember that the important issue was how "Washington wanted to spend time with Tyson. She asked Mike to come up." Trathen argued, "She was innocent and naive."

"Virginia Foster was a key witness," Trathen said. "She told you Tyson was begging and pleading for Desiree Washington to come down and talk. Washington even brought her camera," Trathen argued, perhaps not realizing that later the jurors would see that point as being highly pivotal in the eventual outcome of the case.

"Tyson and bodyguard Dale Edwards were working together," Trathen said, insinuating that Edwards "even waited a few minutes before getting into the front of the limousine while it was parked at the Omni."

At the hotel, "what happened to Dale Edwards?" Trathen speculated. Night clerk McCoy Wagers remembered him being there, and at 2:02 Edwards made calls in the lobby.

Tyson's testimony about Desiree's behavior in the bathroom after the sex had taken place was then brought up. Tyson said that Washington "straightened her hair, as if to say I've bedded the champ." Does Washington's demeanor after she left the hotel room "coincide with the champ's testimony?" Trathen argued. "Virginia Foster," Trathen continued, "told us what Desiree Washington was like," and Virginia had years of training to help her determine that "the child had been raped."

According to Trathen, Tyson and Edward's plan was clear and Washington's "fate was sealed" when she left the Omni with Tyson. In closing, she reminded the jury that "rape is not a half crime," once again, and pleaded for conviction of Tyson on all counts.

"Your role as a juror is the most important component of the judicial system," Vincent Fuller began.

Back to his professional position behind the safety of the podium, the booming voice of the Washington D.C. attorney told the jury that the "core issue" of the case was "consent."

Reminding the jury of presumption of innocence, burden of proof, doubt based on reason, and the need for unanimous verdict (Fuller seemed to sound as if he were pleading for a hung jury), he said the need for a "12-0 verdict is because we are terrorized by the thought of convicting an innocent man."

Of Tyson, he said, "He's not a trained student, he's a trained fighter." In sharp contrast to Washington, Tyson is a "high school drop-out," Fuller argued.

Talking about Washington, Fuller said that she had an "ability to interact with national people" citing Vice President Dan Quayle and Elizabeth Dole, among others.

"She's poised, mature for her age, one of 34 out of thousands chosen to go to the Soviet Union. She's young in years," Fuller argued, "but not young in experience."

The State, Fuller countered, says that Washington was "oblivious to Tyson's conduct. Even the 1:36 a.m. telephone call was an act of rudeness."

In the limousine, Tyson moves over and "kisses and hugs her." It "insults your intelligence," Fuller argued, "to believe this woman didn't know of Tyson's intention.

"The State would have you believe that Tyson lures her to the suite, lures her to the bedroom, lures her to the T.V."

When Tyson said "you're turning me on," Desiree Washington says she went to the bathroom. "If she was unnerved," Fuller said (making his most important point) "there was a quick exit route right out the door."

There were plenty of other signs of Tyson's intentions as well, said Fuller. Desiree was on Tyson's lap at the rehearsal; the remarks by Tyson at the rehearsal were "raunchy," and Desiree heard them, he argued.

He also cited Frank Valentine, who said Desiree Washington was "jocking" Tyson with sexual overtones; Kycia Johnson, who said she heard Desiree talk about "Mike Tyson's body"; and Johnny Gill, the son of a minister, who said he heard Tyson say "I want to f . . . you."

Fuller then attacked the prosecution's claim that Tyson's failure to mention those words to the grand jury was a red herring. He argued that simply the admitted use by Tyson of the words "I want you" was indeed sufficient to give Washington notice of his sexual intentions.

Tyson's defense lawyer went on to say that Washington made her intentions clear at the opening ceremonies when she said, "I'm going out with Mike Tyson. He's got a lot of money. He's dumb. Look what Robin Givens got."

Fuller then made a strong argument for Tyson's innocence when he told the jury that they should disregard Washington's claim that Tyson said he was going to pick up a bodyguard at the Canterbury Hotel. "It's naive to believe he would fabricate such a story," Fuller said, "when the bodyguard was not only there, but went into the hotel with Washington and Tyson."

But during his argument, Fuller again seemed a bit confused. He misstated a date, was unable to find an exhibit, mistakenly thought another exhibit was in evidence when it was not, and kept calling "the State," "the Government."

In fact, the restlessness of the jury was broken when juror #5 surprised everyone by raising his hand asking permission to go to the bathroom.

After the break, Fuller actually became more animated and finally reached the real point of his defense when he said, "What woman who didn't have sex on her mind would go to a bedroom at 2:00 a.m.?"

Fuller then turned his attention to the dress that Washington was wearing the night of the attack. "She told you that the dress she was wearing was very important to her since it had been given to her by a pageant official in Rhode Island," Fuller explained. "Why then," Fuller argued, "would she remove a panty liner and risk destruction of the garment?"

As to the attack itself, Fuller said, "Rape is not a considerate crime." Washington said Tyson used his fingers. "Would a rapist do that?" Fuller countered. How about her allegation that Tyson was on top and withdrew before ejaculation? "Why would a rapist do such a thing?"

"Tyson weighed 220, Washington 105," Fuller argued, "Dr. Richardson said there wasn't a bruise on her body."

Washington gave different versions of the crime as well, Fuller stated, trying to raise doubt about her version of the incident. To some contestants, she said "she was on the floor." To some "she said she screamed." To others, "that she didn't [scream]," because "Tyson's elbow was in her mouth." To Kycia Johnson, "she said she thought she'd been raped."

Fuller next referred briefly to the testimony of Chaplain Kathryn Newlin of Methodist Hospital. This witness, he said, "noted some sense of participation between Washington and Tyson."

As for the garment Washington wore on the evening of the attack, Fuller argued that no mention of the dress being damaged was ever brought up before Washington's father told the police about it in a phone conversation. "We don't know what it looked like before it left here," Fuller argued. "The State is asking you to speculate."

Jumping back and forth again, Fuller argued that Washington was "comparing herself to Robin Givens." When a contestant said, "Here comes your husband," Washington replied, "He'll make the money, and I'll do the talking."

Fuller also stated that Washington obviously had future plans with Tyson. When Tyson said, "Does your family like me?" Washington replied, "They haven't met you yet."

As for the events that followed the sexual act, Fuller argued that Desiree Washington became offended when "Tyson rolled over, and wanted to go to sleep."

"She was treated like a one-night stand," Fuller pleaded. "Her dignity was offended. 'Get out, you're nothing,'" was the implication to a woman of great pride and achievement, Fuller told the jury.

As to her conduct after the incident, Fuller pointed to the many witnesses who saw no change in her demeanor. The videotapes show the "manner of Desiree Washington in the next few days. She was jumping and leaping," Fuller said.

In summary, Fuller told the jury, "The panty shield removal and the chaplain's statement leave more than reasonable doubt." With that, he politely thanked the jury, and sat down beside his client.

Greg Garrison may have thought twice about even getting up to rebut the final argument by Vincent Fuller. After all, Fuller had for the most part discussed only the obvious, and it seemed clear that the jury had not been all that impressed with his presentation.

However, Garrison had to live up to his promise in opening argument that the jury would find "in their hearts and in their heads" that Michael Tyson was guilty beyond any reasonable doubt.

This final argument, before not only the jury, but the hundreds of media organizations set to cover the speech, would be the coup de grace to Garrison's performance during trial. It would be the prosecutor's chance to become a politician, defender of the rights of society, and the last advocate for the pursuit of truth, justice, and the American way.

Obviously, Garrison must have felt confident about his case as he had prepared for the most important day of his life. Prior to argument, he had gone over to Washington, sitting with her mother in the front row, and said, "The fight's over for you; just loosen up. We kicked his ass."

For Garrison this would be a last chance to plead the case of his tiny, innocent victim, and so he launched into his speech by talking about the injustice done to Desiree Washington.

"The innocence of the defendant has become secondary to the guilt of the victim," he began. This "law platoon from Washington [D.C.] has sought to massacre the victim, and denigrate a courageous young person. Let's bring a fan in here and blow away Fuller's smoke," Garrison yelled, mocking the defense tactics of Fuller.

Garrison then quickly scrambled for the blackboard, pointing to the medical testimony of the three physicians in the case. "Dr. Richardson," Garrison said, "told you in 20,000 exams that injuries such as Washington's involving consensual sex are as 'rare as hen's teeth.' Even the defense witness, Dr. Watanobe," he went on, "told of the extreme rarity of such injuries where consensual sex occurred." All three doctors agree, Garrison argued, that the chances are very small, around .03 percent.

Calling the defense tactics, "a week-long barbecue of the victim," Garrison said that sure his client's testimony had been inconsistent. "Coach Knight," he said, referring to the legendary Indiana University basketball coach, "calls his players, kids. One minute they're great, and the next they can't find the gymnasium." Garrison said.

"Corroboration is the key," Garrison told the jury. The phone call to the limousine and the "C'mon, I just want to talk" comment by Tyson were corroborated by Virginia Foster. "These are like a fingerprint," Garrison argued.

"A woman of the world doesn't go out on a date like this in her pajamas," Garrison pointed out, referring to the underclothing that Washington had worn.

Garrison also referred to the absence of Dale Edwards, Tyson's bodyguard, who could have testified about important details in the case. "Where is he?" Garrison asked.

Garrison then asked the jury, "Does it make sense to talk about pigeons for 15 minutes after supposedly hugging and kissing in the car?"

A fatal blow to Tyson's story, he said, was his testimony that he asked Washington to stay the night. "How is she rejected if he's asked her to spend the night?" Garrison asked. "She's hit a home run," he said, implying that if Washington was really after Tyson she would have been thrilled to spend the night with him.

Garrison also mocked the defense's contention that Washington was a "golddigger." It's "a ridiculous fairy tale," he said, pointing out that if the woman had truly been after Tyson's wealth, she would have accepted his invitation to spend the night as a prelude to a more enduring relationship.

"If she really wants money . . . she's won the ball game," Garrison told the jury, "when she can sleep with him."

Garrison also asked the jury if Desiree would have messed up her own hair, and faked being frightened and scared after the alleged attack? "'Anxiety and fear,' that's what Virginia Foster told you Desiree Washington was like when she came down to the limousine," Garrison reminded the jury.

"Vincent Fuller keeps saying how smart Desiree Washington is," Garrison asserted, "but next time you [pointing to Washington] frame someone for money, Desiree, do a better job."

Garrison then talked to the jury about what he considered the three measurements the jury should use in making its decision: corroboration, character, and the persona of those who take the witness stand.

Garrison then went over in detail his evaluation of each of these "measurements" in lieu of the evidence presented at trial. He began with discussing the character issue.

Concerning the defendant, Garrison said Tyson "practices being deceptive by profession. He's aggressively deceptive," the prosecutor told the jury.

"Is he honest?" asked the prosecutor. "He even lied to Jesse Jackson, the man who baptized him."

Finally, Garrison drew to a close. "The world's eyes want to know if the citizens of Marion County have the courage to convict Tyson. A beautiful, honest kid came to town and got deceived by a professional deceiver who isolated, defeated, and raped her," Garrison told the jury.

Did any of the final arguments make a difference in the eventual outcome? Of the three who spoke, Trathen was probably the most successful with her methodical, no-nonsense approach. Fuller's scatter-shot methods certainly didn't influence any of the jurors' minds, and Garrison, while somewhat more dynamic, presented no real new points for the jury to consider.

After all was said and done, the jury was again left to decide Tyson's fate more on their perceptions than on the sketchy evidence presented at trial. Observers who watched the closing arguments sensed that the jury was tired of hearing talk about the case, and instead seemed ready to decide in their own minds whether Tyson was guilty or innocent of the charges against him.

21

◆

INSTRUCTIONS TO THE JURY

Prior to final argument, the defense proposed an important final instruction dealing with "implied consent." The memorandum in support of the proposed instruction read as follows:

Defendant has proposed a jury instruction making clear that he cannot be guilty of rape (or any other crime of which lack of consent is an element) if the conduct of the complainant under all the circumstances should reasonably be viewed as indicating consent to the acts in question. For the reasons stated herein, the Court should read the defendant's proposed instruction to the jury.

BACKGROUND
The defense in this case is consent. In accordance with that defense, defendant has presented considerable evidence that Washington manifested her consent to the sexual acts in question through a consistent course of conduct leading up to and including the acts themselves. A number of witnesses have testified that the defendant's sexual intentions were made plain while he was in the complainant's presence, that she accepted an explicit sexual invitation from him, that her conduct toward the defendant was at all times consistent with a desire to engage in consensual sex with him, and that she herself described consensual physical contact prior to the alleged rape.

ARGUMENT

The crimes of rape and criminal deviate conduct under Indiana law are "specific intent" crimes—their statutory definitions require that a defendant "knowingly or intentionally" force another person to submit to the sexual acts in question. See Wells v. State, 554 A.2d 713, 717 (Conn. 1989). "[A] defendant is not chargeable with knowledge of the internal workings of the minds of others except to the extent that he should reasonably have gained such knowledge from his observations of their conduct." Id.

The Smith court concluded that where applicable under the facts, a defendant is entitled to an instruction "that the state must prove beyond a reasonable doubt that the conduct of the complainant would not have justified a reasonable belief that she had consented." Id. Such an instruction is necessary to effectuate the principle that "[i]f the conduct of the complainant under all the circumstances should reasonably be viewed as indicating consent to the act of intercourse, a defendant should not be found guilty because of some undisclosed mental reservation on the part of the complainant." Id.

The courts of other jurisdictions have also recognized that a defendant's honest and reasonable mistake as to consent is a defense to rape. For example, in People v. Mayberry, 542 P.2d 1337 (Calif. 1975), the California Supreme Court ruled that the trial court had erred by refusing to give an instruction directing the jury to acquit the defendant of rape if the jury had a reasonable doubt as to whether the defendant reasonably and genuinely believed that the complainant consented to intercourse. Id. at 1345. See also Reynolds v. State, 664 P.2d 621, 622-26 (Alaska Ct. App. 1983); State v. Dizon, 390 P.2d 759 (Haw. 1964); State v. Foster, 631 S.W.2d 672, 675 (Mo.Ct.App. 1982); United States v. Short, 4 C.M.A. 437, 444-45 (1954).

The evidence developed in this case certainly creates the foundation for a jury finding that the complainant's conduct and all the surrounding circumstances gave rise to a reasonable belief on Mr. Tyson's part that the complainant consented. The jury should be instructed that it must find Mr. Tyson not guilty if it harbors reasonable doubt on this issue.

Prior to reading the final instructions, the judge summarily denied the motion to include the instruction. This decision was a significant setback for the defense. Even though they had not pounded hard enough at the "She knew what she was getting

into and she still came to Tyson's hotel room at 2:00 a.m."
defense, Tyson's lawyers needed to have the jury hear what
implied consent was all about.

Among the final instructions the judge did read to the
jury were the following:

INSTRUCTION NUMBER 19
Rape
The crime of rape is defined by statute as follows: A person
who knowingly has sexual intercourse with a member of the
opposite sex when the person is compelled by force or imminent threat of force commits a rape, a Class B Felony.

To convict the defendant the State must have proved each
of the following elements. The defendant Michael G. Tyson:
1. Knowingly or intentionally
2. Had sexual intercourse with Desiree L. Washington
    when
3. Desiree L. Washington was compelled by force or
    imminent threat of force.

If the State failed to prove each of these elements beyond a
reasonable doubt you should find the defendant not guilty.

If the State did prove each of these elements beyond a
reasonable doubt, you should find the defendant guilty of rape,
a Class B Felony.

INSTRUCTION NUMBER 20
It is not the law of this State that a person who is raped be
required to resist by all violent means within her power. The
law requires only that the case be one in which the complaining
witness did not consent. The complaining witness' resistance
must not be mere pretense, but in good faith. The law does not
require that the complaining witness do more than her age,
strength, and all attendant circumstances make it reasonable
for her to do in order to manifest opposition. The question of
resistance is a question of fact for you to determine and find,
and not a question this Court can decide.

INSTRUCTION NUMBER 21
Criminal Deviate conduct
The crime of criminal deviate conduct is defined by statute
as follows: A person who knowingly or intentionally causes
another person to perform or submit to deviate sexual conduct

when the other person is compelled by force or imminent threat of force, commits deviate sexual conduct, a Class B Felony.

To convict the defendant, the State must have proved each of the following elements:

The defendant Michael G. Tyson:

1. Knowingly or intentionally
2. Caused Desiree Washington to submit to deviate sexual conduct when
3. Desiree Washington was compelled by force or imminent threat of force

If the State to failed prove each of these elements beyond a reasonable doubt, you should find the defendant not guilty.

If the State did prove each of these elements beyond a reasonable doubt, you should find the defendant guilty of criminal deviate conduct, a Class B Felony.

INSTRUCTION NUMBER 22
Deviate Sexual Conduct

"Deviate sexual conduct" means an act involving:

(1) A sex organ of one person and the mouth or anus of another person; or
(2) The penetration of the sex organ or anus of a person by an object

INSTRUCTION NUMBER 23

A finger is considered an "object" for purposes of showing deviate sexual conduct.

INSTRUCTION NUMBER 24

It is not essential to a conviction that the testimony of the complaining witness be corroborated by other evidence. It is sufficient if, from all the evidence, you believe beyond a reasonable doubt that the crime of rape and/or criminal deviate conduct was committed by the defendant.

INSTRUCTION NUMBER 27

The defendant is a competent witness to testify in his own behalf. In this case, the defendant has testified as a witness. It is your duty to consider and weigh his testimony in the same manner as that of any other witness.

Of these instructions, numbers 20 and 27 were most important. Number 20 set out for the jury the parameters involved with "consent" of the victim, and number 27 dealt with criterion the jury would use to weigh the testimony of Tyson.

Again, though, the absence of the "implied consent" instruction threw yet another curve at the defense. Without the critical instruction, there was no question that the verdict would come down to a "whom do you believe?" decision on the part of the jurors.

22

♦

THE DOWNFALL
OF MIKE TYSON

The world may have been shocked, and vengeful riots may have occurred across the United States, when the four officers in the Rodney King case were acquitted, but there was a similar, if more subdued reaction when 12 jurors brought back a guilty verdict in the Mike Tyson trial on February 10, 1992.

William Kennedy Smith and Lemrick Nelson were able to walk out of the courtroom free men, as were the four officers in the King case. Only Tyson would now be a convicted felon for the rest of his life, and wear the label of "rapist" wherever he went.

When the jury finally returned its verdict of guilty against Tyson, many theories were proposed as to why the jurors acted as they did.

In celebrity trials, the jury is often more worried about what their friends, neighbors, and especially family will think of their verdict than about the verdict itself. So the lawyers must give the jurors compelling reason to justify why they decided for or against the accused, as Roy Black did successfully in the William Kennedy Smith case.

This case, however, would be different. Although Greg Garrison, Barb Trathen, and the prosecutor's office would get most of the credit (and they deserved much of it), the dismal performance of Tyson's attorneys, and their unfortunate strategy appeared to make the trial a mismatch from the beginning.

When all was said and done, Fuller and company had to take responsibility for the following miscalculations:

1) Vincent Fuller was brought into the case by Don King.

Fuller had acquired a celebrity status of his own, representing such notables as John Hinkley, junk bond crook Michael Milken, and Don King himself.

When King was indicted for tax evasion, he hired Vincent Fuller. Fuller in time produced a bit of a miracle, and in a "pencil-pushing, paperwork" trial, Fuller gained an acquittal for King.

What's good for King would be great for Tyson? Wrong! Fuller's reputation was gained mostly in federal court, and he had no experience in sex crimes cases. His stuffed shirt, impersonal manner became a distinct liability in Tyson's case.

Everyone kept waiting for the high-powered $5,000-a-day lawyer to come to Tyson's rescue. He never did. Instead of providing Tyson with a strong, well-planned defense, Fuller's mistake-prone, bumbling defense may have been more responsible for the guilty verdict than all of the following miscalculations combined.

2) Tyson's appearance at the Marion County Grand Jury.

In an ill-fated attempt to head off the indictment, Don King and Vincent Fuller reportedly told Tyson that by appearing at the grand jury, he could tell his story, the jury would believe him, and he could go home.

No way. A grand jury is impaneled to do one thing: indict people. Six people sit and hear evidence. There are no courtroom rules and regulations; they hear it all. If five of them vote to indict, so be it. It takes two votes to return a "no-bill," and in a case of Tyson's magnitude, the chance that would happen was small.

This decision to have Tyson testify at the grand jury came back to haunt the defense in three ways. First, the prosecution was able to learn of Tyson's version of the facts. Second, when Tyson was required by the defense to testify at trial, the grand jury testimony was used to impeach his testimony, especially about the "I want to f... you" comment. Third, prosecutors were able to bring up the words "grand jury" once Tyson had testified, with the implication that, since Tyson had been indicted by them, they must have felt he was guilty.

3) Vincent Fuller hired Jim Voyles as local counsel, and then never utilized his skills.

A highly respected criminal defense attorney in Indianapolis, Jim Voyles and his partner, Denny Zahn, have great trial skills, and, more importantly, are highly respected members of a somewhat closed legal community. If Mike Tyson wanted Vincent Fuller to represent him, that was his choice, but Fuller's failure to use Voyles and his intimate knowledge of local trial rules, not to mention his friendship with Judge Gifford, was a costly mistake.

4) The defense did not request a change of judge nor retain a jury selection expert, therefore they did not have a competent plan for selection of the jury.

Regarding jury selection, one deputy sheriff in the courtroom observed that there were "too many cooks," and other observers, including myself, watched as a helter-skelter, "who do you like, what do you think?," plan was utilized. Without adequate input from Jim Voyles, and with no jury selection expert, the ex-Marine and the auto parts manager were left on the jury.

5) Fuller's mistake in allowing juror #9 to be on the jury.

This error reminded most trial experts of F. Lee Bailey's critical mistake in the Patty Hearst case when he left an Air Force colonel to sit in her judgment.

Juror #9's appearance and background should have turned on a red light to the defense. An ex-Marine, with a rules-and-regulations/right-and-wrong background, the minister-like man in the suit and tie stuck out like a sore thumb. Questions in voir dire also indicated he was a political conservative, and the fact that his wife was a nurse might make him especially familiar with the medical evidence which proved so vital to the outcome of the case.

During the trial, this man was the only one who took notes. He passed out breath mints to the other jurors, and no one was surprised when he was named the foreman of the jury. When he made his thoughts about conviction known in the early hours of jury deliberation, the other jurors fell in line.

6) Vincent Fuller's opening statement contained a dangerous proclamation.

"He [Mike Tyson] will tell you," Fuller said, giving him no choice but to have Tyson testify. Why Fuller chose to back himself into a corner was a mystery to every lawyer who learned of this fundamental mistake. Regardless of whether he intended to call Tyson to the stand, the defense lawyer handbook prohibits such an unneeded statement, especially where such a decision ended up being so questionable.

7)   Vincent Fuller was highly ineffective in the cross-examination of Desiree Washington.

Obviously wary of upsetting the victim, and allowing sympathy for her with the jury, Fuller back-stepped from any vigorous cross-examination of the witness. Unlike Roy Black's extensive but still sensitive, cross-examination of the accuser in the William Kennedy Smith case, Fuller's questions were so soft as to not elicit any real details about the alleged attack.

8)   Vincent Fuller's impersonal, federal-courtroom style made the jury want to avoid him.

Speaking initially from behind a podium and later in an uncomfortable position by the prosecution table, Fuller never found any degree of comfort with the jury. By excluding Voyles, and not appearing to be "close" with Tyson, he emphasized his position as an outsider in the case, and allowed Garrison to make it an "us and them," State of Indiana v. Washington, D.C., power attorneys, battle.

Fuller also mixed up the facts in the case, couldn't find exhibits, fumbled in his delivery, didn't listen carefully to witnesses, and failed to object at critical times both to inadmissible evidence and to Garrison's damaging remarks.

9)   Tyson's defense lawyers portrayed him so extensively as an uncouth, bad boy sexual animal that the jury decided they were right.

In an effort to show that Desiree Washington must have known that Tyson was out for sex, Fuller and then witness after witness, pointed out lewd remarks and crude behavior by Tyson toward the beauty pageant contestants. At the beginning of the trial, Tyson enjoyed an untouchable celebrity status, but near the end the defense had helped knock him down to a size at which the jury could convict him.

10) From the opening statement, Fuller portrayed Washington as a money hungry bitch after Tyson's money and fame.

This move backfired because, regardless of whether the jury believed the woman and her mother, they felt some sympathy for them. The victim's demeanor on the witness stand didn't stack up with the greed motive, and Fuller's attempts to beat this dead horse were clearly ineffective.

11) With apparently no other real choice, the defense put Mike Tyson on the witness stand.

Greg Garrison said later that this decision was the turning point in the case. Whether Tyson ever had to take the stand was a real question, because the combination of the State's testimony and the defense witnesses to that point left many wondering whether the State had proven its case beyond a reasonable doubt. Nevertheless, Tyson was called to testify, and his exaggeration of his grand jury testimony ("I want you") to his courtroom testimony ("I want to f . . . you") was a disaster. Perhaps Fuller's preparation of Tyson was not thorough enough, but from the moment the jury, and especially juror #9, heard him say those vulgar words, the case was all but over.

12) Fuller's final argument was a disaster.

He seemed disoriented and unable to focus on critical points that would decide the case. He never presented the jury with any evidence to elicit feelings of closeness or sympathy with Tyson. Fuller's final plea to the jury sounded like a plea for a hung jury, not a proclamation of innocence for his client.

Besides producing competent medical testimony and a potent Virginia Foster to back up Washington's story, perhaps Garrison's and Trathen's best achievement at trial was their strategy in successfully presenting Desiree Washington as the shy, inexperienced, naive, prim and proper college student that they in fact knew her not to be. Utilizing the full protection of the rape shield law, and fully aware that Washington had in fact signed an agreement to sue Tyson and sell her movie and book rights, the prosecutors, who were also aware of Washington's questionable sexual past, and her need for therapy, made certain that the jury never saw any indication that Washington was anything other than a church-going goody-two shoes.

That the rape shield law was not intended to allow prosecutors to intentionally distort the image of a woman like Washington seems clear enough, and the decision to do so, and to apparently conceal the existence of the attorney fee agreement overshadows an otherwise competent performance by Garrison and Trathen.

With Gifford in the driver's seat, Fuller on the outside looking in, and Garrison and Trathen cozying up to a somewhat perplexed group of jurors, the only question at the end of the trial was how long it would take the jury to find Tyson guilty.

The defense, however, was somehow still optimistic, and at about 8:45 p.m. while the jury was deliberating, the defense team was having a lavish dinner at the top of the Hyatt Hotel in downtown Indianapolis. When I made an observation to Vincent Fuller that juror #9, the ex-Marine, would be a problem, he commented, "Oh, we're not worried about juror #9, maybe #5 and #6, but not #9." Obviously, the high-powered lawyers still had not seen the error of their ways.

Why, though, did this jury decide to convict Mike Tyson of rape? First, and foremost, the jurors said that they believed Tyson was not telling the truth when he testified at trial. Magnified perhaps by the fact that the jury initially wanted to believe that Tyson was not capable of such a distasteful act, his ill-conceived testimony swept away his aura of invincibility and for the first time made the jury feel that they COULD in fact find Tyson guilty.

Combined with the highly plausible story presented by Desiree Washington, the effective testimony of the State's medical experts, and the presence of the prosecution-friendly judge and the powerful prosecution-friendly jury foreman, Tyson's testimony served to seal his doom.

In the end, it is possible that the ex-champ still could have been saved, however, since much of the damage could have been avoided through better representation by defense counsel. If Tim, controversial juror #9, had been stricken, and Tyson had not taken the stand to utter the despicable "I want to f . . . you" words, the jury might have found that the State had not proved him guilty beyond a reasonable doubt.

Life is full of choices, however, and Mike Tyson decided that he wanted to have sex with Desiree Washington in the early morning hours of July 19, 1991. To this day, Tyson may still feel that he did nothing wrong, even if every single word that Washington has spoken about the rape incident is true.

That's because many celebrities like Tyson feel they play the game of life by different rules. Most of the time they are able to get by with actions even worse than Tyson's.

This time, though, Mike Tyson picked the wrong woman. Don King picked the wrong lawyer. Vincent Fuller picked the wrong defense strategy.

Don King and Vincent Fuller went home. Mike Tyson went to prison.

23

---◆---

JUDGMENT DAY

At 9:00 a.m. on March 26, 1992, 252 days after the rape of Desiree Washington, Mike Tyson stood before Judge Patricia Gifford to be sentenced.

That Tyson did in fact appear in court was somewhat of a surprise. Even the judge felt there was a likelihood that Tyson would board a late-night flight for some far-away corner of the earth, never to be seen in the United States again. Several potential countries were discussed by the media that had no extradition treaties with the United States, but in the end there proved to be no evidence that the Tyson "brain trust" ever considered such alternatives for the ex-champ, who almost certainly faced a lengthy prison sentence for his deed.

Instead, for much of his last few days of freedom, Tyson apparently holed up in his mansion outside Cleveland. No one knows for sure what was going through his mind, and the only time he made the morning papers was when police ticketed him for speeding.

Still in the company of his much-maligned defense lawyer Vincent Fuller (even Don King had questioned Fuller's trial tactics), Tyson arrived with about 25 supporters, including King and foster mother Camille Ewald.

Dressed in the same gray pin-striped suit he had worn the first day of the trial, Tyson took his place at the counsel table between Fuller and local attorney James Voyles. Seated a few rows behind them was newly acquired appellate counsel Alan Dershowitz, the famed Harvard law professor who represented such public celebrities as Leona Helmsley, Claus von Bulow, and Michael Milken.

Prior to the sentencing, there was speculation in the press about the pre-sentence investigation report that had been prepared on Tyson. The report was highly confidential, but sources close to the case reported that: 1) the probation department felt that Tyson, if not treated for his psychological problems, would "probably" commit the same crime again, and 2) that Tyson's net worth had dribbled down to a mere $5 to $8 million.

Prosecutor Greg Garrison told ESPN's Charley Steiner that Tyson's assets still totaled "eight figures." A source inside the probation department said, "Tyson has lots of assets, but they're all tied up with Don King."

Documents filed by the defense in Criminal Court 4 claimed Tyson's fortune had shrunk to about $5 million. "If the former champion is not allowed to fight, he would be forced to sell some of his assets," the report stated.

Listed among those assets were a fleet of 30 luxury cars, including a Ferrari and Lamborghini, a 30,000-square foot mansion complete with a movie theater, and a multimillion-dollar jewelry collection.

Tyson faced up to 60 years in prison (20 per count). Judge Gifford's average sentences for crimes similar to Tyson's were seven for the year 1991 and 10.7 for 1990.

Besides locking up Tyson, Judge Gifford could also suspend the sentences, since Tyson had no previous criminal record. She could also place Tyson in an alternative sentencing program involving a work release center or community service facility.

Tyson's victim, Desiree Washington, now 19, had apparently decided not to face her attacker at the hearing. Instead she sent a letter addressed to the court.

Defense counsel Vincent Fuller listed four potential witnesses for Tyson:

1)   Lloyd Bridges—head of the Riverside Community Corrections Center, a work release program in Indianapolis.

2)   Camille Ewald—Tyson's surrogate mother who, along with boxing trainer, Cus D'Amato, helped raise Tyson.

3)   Rita Akins and Steven Brock—owners of a private sentencing group in Indianapolis. They were hired to conduct a "private" pre-sentence report about Tyson.
4)   Jay Bright—a long-time friend of Tyson.

Don King was not listed.

Also prior to the hearing, appellate counsel Alan Dershowitz had filed a motion with the court setting out at least 10 reasons why the conviction should be overturned:

1)   Exclusion of a black potential juror from the special grand jury that indicted Tyson;
2)   Judge's refusal to dismiss indictment based on defense allegation that the indictment resulted from a system utilized to select a jury not representative of a cross section of the community;
3)   Denial of three motions for continuance;
4)   Denial of a defense motion to admit proof of domestic problems between Washington's parents. Such problems apparently involved domestic violence and the arrest of Washington's father;
5)   Improper selection of the trial judge;
6)   Jurors' inconsistent answers given concerning their feelings about the hotel fire;
7)   The exclusion of three witnesses who would have testified that Tyson and Washington were "all over each other" in the limousine prior to the attack;
8)   Refusal by the court to permit the defense to ask questions of witnesses about "conclusions drawn from firsthand observations;"
9)   The court's admission into evidence of the "altered" clothing worn by Washington the night of the attack;
10)   Prosecutor Garrison's improper rebuttal argument summation.

Of these issues, Dershowitz apparently felt the exclusion of witness error seemed most likely to be the best chance for reversal of Tyson's conviction.

Exclusion of the black juror from the grand jury, and the judge's refusal to dismiss the case based on improper representation of a cross section of the community with the jury, are age-old arguments that normally fall on deaf ears at the appellate court level. Allegations of error due to the denial of a motion to continue, the judge's refusal to permit evidence about domestic problems in Washington's household, improper selection of the trial judge, refusal of the court to permit the defense to ask questions of witnesses about "conclusions drawn from firsthand observations," and prosecutor Garrison's improper rebuttal argument summation all go to the matter of judicial discretion, or current court rules, and thus appeared on the surface to have little chance of success on appeal unless the court would decide to reverse and, in effect, make new law.

Allegations concerning improper admission of Washington's garment would certainly go to the weight of the evidence, and not to the admissibility, and thus, unless the appellate court would feel that the trial court truly abused its discretion, this argument's chances for success would be minimal.

Argument that the jurors gave inconsistent answers to questions about the fire at the hotel would depend on what the potential damage would be to Tyson's not having gotten a fair trial, and unless the defense could point to potential perjury instances, the appellate court would be left to decide how such answers would have affected the outcome of the trial.

Dershowitz's best shot, therefore, at reversal of Tyson's conviction would come from his argument concerning the exclusion of the three witnesses. Exclusion of any testimony by the trial court is considered a serious matter, and while the potential impact of the testimony may not have been all that significant, the difference between Desiree Washington's testimony and the three witnesses concerning physical contact between Washington and Tyson in the back of the limousine would relate to the credibility of Washington's testimony.

While legal observers pondered the weight of the defense arguments, much interest also centered on whether Judge Gifford would permit an appeal bond if Tyson were sentenced to an executed term in prison.

Prosecutor Jeffrey Modisett made the State's position clear prior to the hearing. Modisett said the pre-sentence investigation report concluded that "Tyson is capable of doing it [rape] again ... As a prosecutor, the number-one goal is safety." He also said the state would seek a six- to 10-year prison term, a $30,000 fine, and that Tyson would be required to reimburse about $150,000 for court and related costs.

Media interest in the hearing was even stronger than for the trial itself. Judge Gifford now had additional room in the courtroom through use of the 12 jury seats, and had arbitrarily designated seats for the *New York Times, Newsday, New York Daily News*, and Fox television. The others would watch from the media viewing room.

Spectators gathered early outside the City-County Building, hoping to obtain one of 17 public seats available. Chaos reigned in the hall outside the courtroom when some 25 supporters of Tyson decided they were going to be in the courtroom. All were denied, with the help of the deputy sheriffs.

The anticipated appearance of Dershowitz also caused quite a stir. The 53-year-old Dershowitz's passion for the downtrodden has made him known for taking on tough, hard-to-win cases. Such was the reason for the fact that over the last 20 years, published reports say that in some 57 appeals, the famed appellate advocate had only nine clear-cut victories (nine won, 39 lost, mixed results in nine). Dershowitz has made much of the inaccuracy of these statistics, stating that he and his brother, Nathan, have been successful in many more cases than have been reported in the media.

Dershowitz first became a Harvard professor in 1964, and was the youngest tenured law faculty member in its history by 1967. A graduate of Yale Law School (he finished first in his law class), Dershowitz became involved with the big time in 1964 when he assisted Supreme Court Justice Arthur Goldberg with a successful opinion that struck down existing death penalty laws that were unconstitutional.

Dershowitz has made it a point to defend unpopular clients. His recent work on behalf of evangelist Jim Bakker and

Helmsley ("only the little people pay taxes") has brought him much criticism, and many feel he is a better media lawyer than courtroom lawyer.

One judge has even gone so far as to say that Dershowitz makes his living by "conning his clients, and then writing books about them" (Dershowitz says this judge has since recanted the statement). Detractors also say he is bored with teaching, and more interested in high-profile cases where he can earn up to $1 million per case, as was reported in the Tyson matter.

Supporters of Dershowitz, however, call him "a methodical lawyer" who is "brilliant" and "unequaled as far as appellate counsel goes."

According to reports in the media, Dershowitz had apparently told colleagues that the "date rape" issue interested him very much, because of the need to balance "feminist interests with civil liberties issues." He also told a reporter that even while the trial was in progress, he felt he might be involved in the Tyson case "sooner or later," and that he would hone in on the "state of mind of Tyson as to whether the boxer possessed the requisite intent necessary to commit the crime."

After the trial, Dershowitz had been informed by several trial experts that there were questions regarding whether Tyson had been adequately represented due to the many blatant mistakes that had been made by Fuller and his colleagues.

Professor Dershowitz stated that he "had heard that they [the defense] were bad," but that he "didn't know they were *that* bad." However, Tyson's new appellate counsel apparently decided that an appeal based on incompetence of counsel stood little chance of success, and so, at the sentencing hearing, there was Dershowitz standing toe to toe with Vincent Fuller.

Just prior to the beginning of the same hearing, prosecutor Garrison and defense lawyer Beggs had a brief exchange that was anything but friendly. Apparently, the fiery Garrison, who had seemed to exhibit a dislike for the prim and proper Beggs all through the trial, had filed some document that Beggs hadn't received a copy of, and was upset with Garrison.

Beggs: "You ever hear of serving notice on counsel?"

Garrison: "Maybe you should return those phone calls at Williams and Connolly!"

Both cooled down, but then Beggs continued the dispute a couple of minutes later when she said something to Garrison about bringing the matter to the attention of the court. Garrison, now sitting at counsel table beside prosecutor Modisett, said in a tone loud enough for everyone, including the press and Tyson, to hear, "Well, you've been so successful thus far, go ahead, 'Grow up!'" Beggs was obviously embarrassed, and so it seemed were Fuller and even Modisett, who motioned for Garrison to take it easy.

While all the pre-sentencing matters were being completed, Tyson sat at counsel table talking to Voyles as he awaited his fate. Voyles had seemed closest to Tyson during the trial, and appeared to be deeply saddened by the disastrous outcome of the trial.

As he talked to Voyles, Tyson held in his hand a white sheet of paper about three by four inches in size. The paper had some indistinguishable words at the top, and a diagram with boxes containing the numbers 1 and 19 below the words.

Arnold Baratz, a public defender in Judge Gifford's court, thought the words indicated some sort of Islamic prayer, but no one in Tyson's defense team would elaborate on what the words or diagram meant. Tyson intently stared at the paper all through the hearing, and many times it appeared he was blocking everything else out by concentrating on the words on the paper.

Whatever comfort was provided by the sheet of paper, Tyson was now minutes away from learning his fate. Throughout his career, he had fended off strong, powerful, intimidating heavyweights who wanted to knock him out. On this day, however, it would be a slight, gray-haired, lightweight judge named Patricia Gifford who would deliver the knockout punch.

24

♦

GOING, GOING, GONE

by
ESPN's Charley Steiner

Forty-four days had come and gone since a jury of his peers had found Michael Gerard Tyson guilty of raping Desiree Washington.

At precisely 9:13 a.m. on March 26, 1992, Judge Patricia Gifford took the bench, gaveled her courtroom to order, and uttered the words that had begun each day's proceedings during the two-week trial that seemed so long ago: "State of Indiana vs. Michael G. Tyson, case number 91116245."

For Patricia Gifford, a well-respected judge, wife, and mother, the return to some sense of normalcy in her personal life was only hours away. She told friends she longed to get back into the kitchen. It was therapeutic for her.

But the judge had one final task at hand in dealing with the Mike Tyson case. Today Tyson would be sentenced, and after a trial in which millions of words were written and spoken by lawyers, witnesses, and the media, the judge would finally have her say. The final say.

Ultimately, it would be her words that would count the most and last the longest. Sentencing Mike Tyson, especially on the third leg of the sexual harassment / date rape triple crown (Clarence Thomas and William Kennedy Smith) would not be easy. Thomas had become a Supreme Court Justice. Smith would become a medical resident in an Arizona hospital. It seemed clear that Tyson was about to become a resident in an Indiana prison. But for how long? Only a 55-year-old Marion County Superior Court judge could answer that.

Ironically, from the opening statements by the prosecution and the defense to their closing comments, Greg Garrison and even Vincent Fuller kept reminding the jury that Mike Tyson must be viewed as just another citizen, not as a celebrity or a role model. But as Tyson's immediate future was about to be determined by Judge Gifford, that was precisely the dilemma she faced. Whether she cared to admit it or not, there would be a delicate balancing act of local politics, national repercussions, and of course judicial ethics.

To be sure, no one was indifferent about this case, because no one was ever indifferent about Mike Tyson. Nearly everyone had an opinion about what should happen. There were those screaming for the maximum. This was an animal poised to rape again, they believed, and the judge should throw the book at him. They wanted to teach him a lesson, let him know that he can't get away with raping a woman in Indianapolis.

There were those who believed Tyson had gotten a raw deal. What was that money-hungry bitch doing in his hotel room at 2:00 a.m., anyway? That was the key question going into the trial, and for some, it was still a question that remained unanswered. Tyson, in his own way, they argued, was just as much a victim as Desiree Washington. Tyson should be given a suspended sentence and probation, or perhaps a halfway house.

Judge Gifford had apparently already made up her mind about the exact sentence she would impose on Tyson. She would have to consider, however, any compelling last-minute arguments from either side. Gifford had read the pre-sentencing report that had been prepared by the Marion County Probation Department, and another one that had been prepared by a private consulting firm hired by Tyson's defense team. She had also received thousands of letters from around the world. But only one letter really counted.

That was the one from Desiree Washington, who decided against being in court for the sentencing. It was time for her to "get on with her life, and her studies."   Portions of the letter would be read at the sentencing hearing, and Washington's words would have a stronger, more emotional impact than if she had been present in the courtroom.

Both the defense and the prosecution would be permitted witnesses, with the hope of convincing the judge what they felt was an appropriate sentence. Vincent Fuller called only Lloyd Bridges, the executive director of the Riverside Correctional Facility in Indianapolis. Lloyd Bridges? Sea Hunt, thought some of the usually cynical members of the media; another fishing expedition for the Tyson defense team.

Bridges, an ordained minister, said he ran the Riverside Correctional Facility, which he compared to a half-way house. He called it a "minimum security" facility. Bridges also admitted that, in the 13-year history of the facility, the court had permitted only two convicted rapists to be admitted to his facility. Under questioning by Fuller, Bridges said that he spent three hours with Tyson, just five days earlier, at Tyson's mansion in Cleveland.

Bridges said they talked about "Tyson's background" and "his religious beliefs." According to a point system he normally used, Bridges determined that Tyson would most certainly be eligible for admission to his Riverside Correctional Facility. That was all Fuller wanted the judge to hear. Damage control. Keep his client out of jail. He knew it was a long-shot; probably no shot. But at $5,000 a day, Fuller had to come up with something. Anything.

Assistant prosecutor Barb Trathen smiled as she stood up from behind the prosecution table and began her questioning of Bridges. She knew this cross-examination would be a slam dunk. Hadn't there been four escapes recently at the Riverside Correctional Facility? Well, yes there had. But, Bridges said, he "didn't see Tyson as an escape risk."

Bridges also testified about his religious discussions with Tyson, and said that the former champion had been "truly touched by the Lord." With a disbelieving smirk, Trathen asked if that was nothing more than a "jailhouse conversion." Bridges said he felt Tyson was sincere. "If what Tyson expressed to me is real," he said, "and I believe it is, he will be okay."

Also under cross-examination, Lloyd Bridges admitted that it was Tyson or his defense team, who paid for his airline tickets to Cleveland for the interview. So much for the one and only defense witness at the sentencing hearing. Sea Hunt was dead in the water. Strike one.

Strike two then made his way to the batter's box. Vincent Fuller got up from behind the defense table and made his way toward his trusty podium. Maybe now he would pull some 11th-hour lightning from the bottle. Certainly the high-powered barrister, who had been shooting nothing but blanks since he was hired to defend Tyson, would finally hit a dramatic home run in time to save Tyson from hard time.

"Tyson came in with a lot of excess baggage," Fuller pleaded to Judge Gifford. "The press has vilified him. I have never seen an athlete that has so offended the press. Not a day goes by that the press doesn't bring up his faults."

When in doubt blame the press. It usually works in Washington. But this was Marion County, Indiana, a fact that Fuller never seemed to fully grasp in his nine months on the job.

"This is not the Tyson I know," said Fuller. "The Tyson I know is a sensitive, thoughtful, caring man. He may be terrifying in the ring, but that ends when he leaves the ring." This was an entirely different picture of Tyson than the one Fuller painted during the trial—a crude bore, from whom women should keep a healthy distance if they knew what was good for them. However, on the day his client was about to be sentenced, Mike Tyson had become "sensitive, thoughtful and caring."

Fuller then told the court about Tyson's early life of petty crime on the streets of Brooklyn, which landed him at the Tryon School for Boys in upstate New York. That was where Tyson was introduced to a guard named Bobby Stewart, who taught him the basics of boxing. At the age of thirteen, Stewart introduced Tyson to the legendary trainer Cus D'Amato, who lived an hour or so south of the reform school in the small town of Catskill, New York. D'Amato took a liking to and an interest in this man-child, and proclaimed, after watching him spar with Stewart, that he could make Tyson into "the youngest heavyweight champion of the world."

D'Amato had done that once before, with Floyd Patterson thirty years ago. Cus had a history, and he was determined that Tyson would have one too.

"But there is some tragedy in this," Fuller continued. "D'Amato only focused on boxing. Tyson, the man, was secondary to Cus D'Amato's quest for Tyson's boxing greatness."

Fuller may have been right, but the few people who had a genuine affection for Tyson and his adoptive mother, Camille Ewald (who had lived with D'Amato for almost 40 years), were stunned, anguished, and outraged. As if Fuller's performance at trial wasn't agonizing enough, he had effectively spit on the grave of the deified D'Amato.

"In 1985, Tyson became champion," Fuller continued, unaware of the pain he had inflicted on the few supporters the attorney had left. "And, except for Camille Ewald, he was in a male-dominant world. [He never had] peer interpersonal relationships with women. His entire world was that of boxing. This case calls for a suspended sentence with probation, and therapy, in a place like Riverside. To put Tyson in prison repeats the same experience he's gotten before. He needs to go into the work force with women, and see how he's expected to behave."

"You are in a difficult position," Fuller said, looking directly at Judge Gifford. "I am not asking for irrational leniency. Only for compassion."

Fuller would have been better served to have ended his statement, right then and there. Instead he invoked Desiree Washington, who, Fuller said, would no doubt join in asking that Tyson be "sent to a place like Riverside as well." Fuller, of course, hadn't consulted with Washington. The last time he had spoken to her, had been in this very courtroom, for three and a half hours almost seven weeks earlier, when he suggested that she had lied about her story and was trying to extort money from his client.

When all was said and done, the Riverside Correctional Facility was the only card that Fuller would play. It turned out to be a joker.

Fuller's plea for Tyson was as disjointed and confused as his presentation had been at trial. What was he getting at? What was he trying to do? Fuller never seemed certain of his purpose at this hearing, or of what the critical issues were that Judge Gifford would consider in evaluating Tyson's sentence. If Fuller and his team had done their homework, they would have realized that Gifford was interested in Tyson's attitude, his remorse (if any), and how receptive he might be to any psychological assistance that might be offered.

Instead Fuller talked in rambling generalities about Tyson's past and present, and little or nothing about his future. That left Judge Gifford few options with which to work, based on his presentation. Nothing that Fuller said on this pivotal morning in March helped to enhance Tyson's situation or to change the judge's mind. Judge Gifford, like those reporters covering the trial, kept waiting for something, anything, from Fuller, to help his client.

Twelve minutes is a relatively short period of time. It is four rounds in boxing, and it was the time it took to guarantee that the next few years of Mike Tyson's life would be spent behind bars.

When Judge Gifford asked Tyson if he had anything to say, he replied "Yes." Strike three.

The battered ex-champion got off his chair from behind the defense table and strode to the podium. It was like Tyson was getting off the stool in his corner, and heading out to the center of the ring in the final desperate round of a fight he was badly losing. He knew he needed a knockout to keep from going to jail. He would throw out all that he had, without fear of being hit. After all, it was well past the time of winning this fight on points. The next 12 minutes would be all or nothing for Tyson. It would turn out to be the latter.

Tyson, inexplicably, first apologized to the media. The reporters who were crammed into the courtroom furiously jotted down notes in their homemade shorthand. They looked at one another in disbelief, shook their heads, and shrugged their shoulders, with a collective "say, what?" written on their faces.

Tyson then apologized to the court, and to the other contestants of the Miss Black America pageant— but no apology to Desiree Washington was forthcoming. He admitted, "My conduct was kind of crass. I agree with that." Tyson said he "got carried away, ending up with a situation that got out of hand. I'm not guilty of the crime. The situation that occurred was not in a harmful meaning at all. I didn't hurt anybody. There were no black eyes or broken ribs," he said matter-of-factly, in his disarming voice.

The lisp. The almost fragile, high-pitched cracking sound with the New York accent. How does the self-proclaimed "baddest man on the planet" sound the way he does? That voice, the one that caused the kids in his second grade class, at Public School 178 in the Bedford-Stuyvesant section of Brooklyn, to laugh the first time he answered a question asked by his teacher, Doris Wilson. Wilson reprimanded the class, but it was a wound to Tyson that never has healed.

"I didn't rape anyone. I didn't attempt to rape anyone. I'm sorry. I agree, I've done something, but I didn't mean to."

Looking back over his left shoulder, he had a parting shot for the special prosecutor, J. Gregory Garrison, whom he referred to as "the big man," who had said "disdainful and distasteful" things about him.

"My personal life has been incarcerated. I've been hurt. I was humiliated. I expect the worst. I don't know if I can deal with it. I'm prepared for the worst." Tyson called the trial experience "one big dream. It was not real. I was quite devastated."

Tyson, though, maintained his bravado until the end, telling Judge Gifford, "I don't come here to beg you for mercy, ma'am. I expect the worst. I've been crucified. I've been humiliated worldwide. I've been humiliated socially. I'm just happy for all my support. I'm prepared to deal with whatever you give me."

Still clutching the magic sheet of paper, the one that he had been staring at earlier, Tyson was rambling, from one thought to the next. His train of thought never seemed to get on track. If he had a game plan in mind, or had one prepared for him through intense rehearsal, it wasn't evident.

It was so reminiscent of so many of his recent fights in the ring. So often his cornermen, Richie Giachetti or Aaron Snowell, would yell instructions at him, as he sat on the stool between rounds. "More head movement. Jab. Jab. Jab. Box. Box. Box," they would say. Quit going for the one-punch knockout. Set up your punches. Go to the body, then go to the head. Tyson would occasionally acknowledge, and then promptly go out and fight the way he wanted to fight. After all, in the end, Mike Tyson trusted only one person. And that was Mike Tyson.

Never was there any sense of sorrow or remorse. Tyson's friends, though, were quick to point out that there could be no sorrow or remorse if there was no crime. And in Tyson's mind there hadn't been one.

Tyson's comments, while barely heard by those in Judge Gifford's courtroom, weren't heard at all downstairs in the closed-circuit television room, which was packed with reporters who did not have the all-important "red pass" that would allow them into the courtroom. The sound system had gone dead in the basement. Reporters in the "tv" room were in a frenzy. It was bad enough that they weren't permitted into the courtroom, but now they couldn't hear anything Tyson was saying.

When informed of the technical difficulties that had nearly reduced the "tv" room into a free-for-all saloon scene, Judge Gifford ordered a recess until the sound system could be repaired. If nothing else, it bought Tyson a few more minutes of freedom.

It took nearly a half an hour to get the audio in the courtroom to travel from the second floor to the basement. When the session resumed, the judge began by posing questions to Tyson, who was now back behind the defense table. If Tyson could not make his plea lucid, it seemed as if Patricia Gifford would at least try to help him explain further.

Judge Gifford asked him about being a role model. Initially he responded about the difficulties of dealing with his "celebrity status." "I was never taught how to handle it," he replied. "I don't tell kids it's right to be Mike Tyson . . . Parents serve as better role models."

"Do you believe people look at you as a role model?" the judge persisted.

"Celebrity actions are different than other people," Tyson answered. Eventually he would get around to replying in the affirmative, but his responses and demeanor did nothing to lessen the sentence that would soon be pronounced.

Realizing this, Fuller asked Judge Gifford to understand that "he [Tyson] was not prepared for the responsibility of being world champion. He just made money for them [Tyson's promoters, managers, trainers, etc.]."

Tyson's final statement, like much of the defense strategy throughout the trial, laid a scrambled egg. It didn't make sense.

How could Fuller allow Tyson to go before the judge, in a last chance effort to keep him out of prison, without at least some notes at the podium? Instead, as a convicted felon, and an unpolished speaker, Tyson was wandering.

Tyson's plea of innocence, because of his ignorance of the "situation" and his contention that Washington "misunderstood" his intentions, did not impress Judge Gifford. She was looking for something, anything from Tyson except the "celebrity" attitude which he carried throughout the trial.

Aware of Judge Gifford's experience with sex crimes cases, and her authorship of Indiana's rape shield law that helps protect victims from embarrassing questions about their past, Fuller could have conjured up a strategy that would appeal to the judge's anticipated thoughts that Tyson must be prepared to answer for his conduct. In all likelihood, the judge must have been hoping that Tyson, by his own testimony or through Fuller, would provide a critical piece of information that would allow her to either decrease the sentence or find some alternative open to her. The defense simply miscalculated again, and it never happened.

Instead, Judge Gifford listened to a confused Mike Tyson, who could not or would not admit to any remorse. In the ghetto streets where Mike Tyson learned survival techniques, admitting mistakes is a sign of weakness. In his own mind, even if he felt like he had blundered, scratching the veneer of machismo is an even more unpardonable sin. "I gotta walk it like I talk it," Tyson explained in less turbulent times. This is the street talking.

If the judge expected Tyson to concede during the "Q & A" that he needed professional help (especially if in his own mind he had done nothing) she was badly mistaken. There was little question now that Tyson was a goner. Only one question remained. How long he would be gone?

One new observer watched Tyson's plea with fascination, Alan Dershowitz. The man who was about to become Tyson's chief appellate counsel was sitting against the wall, directly behind the defense table. On this Thursday morning, five days into spring, it still felt like winter outside, and Dershowitz's reaction to what was going on in front of him appeared to be chilly disbelief.

Dershowitz, in need of local counsel in the case, had brought in Indianapolis attorney Lee McTurnan to assist him. Along with Dershowitz, former law clerk for United States Supreme Court Justice Arthur Goldberg, McTurnan, in his turn, had asked his associate, Judy Woods, to accompany him to the hearing.

During Tyson's speech, Woods was absolutely flabbergasted that Fuller had allowed Tyson to be so unprepared for this last-ditch effort at some kind of leniency. Woods, who had read the daily accounts of the Tyson trial in the local papers and seen the myriad of television reports, would now see for herself Tyson's legal counsel at the end of the war. Woods couldn't believe the incompetence of an attorney with heretofore impeccable credentials (Vincent Fuller), the high priest of one of America's most prestigious law firms (Williams and Connolly). Her view matched that of most of the reporters (with and without legal backgrounds) who had been covering the story for the past nine months.

Once Fuller and Tyson had said what they had to say, it was the State's turn. Their speaker this day was Jeffrey Modisett, the first-term elected Marion County prosecutor. Tall, with a receding hairline, appropriately gray about the temples, Modisett had an impeccable posture. Born to wear a pinstripe suit, the canny Modisett knew that he had a gigantic political stake in all of this.

For most of the trial, Modisett had stayed behind the scenes, letting Garrison and Trathen do the up-front work. On this most important sentencing day, however, Modisett would rise to speak for the State of Indiana.

Not nearly as flamboyant as Garrison, the former aide to Governor Evan Bayh stepped to the same podium that Fuller had used throughout most of the trial. Clearing his throat, Modisett began his low-key, thoughtful soliloquy.

"Your honor, there are two different Mike Tysons. There is the Mike Tyson that's a nice guy, the one who only occasionally goes astray." But in "38 hours in Indianapolis, Tyson exhibited a pattern of behavior different from the nice-guy image. He displayed disrespectful behavior toward women.

"He had a capacity to be nice," the elected prosecutor told the judge, "just ask Desiree Washington. She saw the good side of him. She trusted him."

Whether he was being sarcastic, unduly generous, or was in a roundabout way giving his own victorious legal team praise, Modisett told the court that Tyson had "the best trial counsel anybody could ask for."

Whom was he kidding? Certainly not Greg Garrison or Barb Trathen. They had been astonished, as the trial proceeded, at the lack of competition they were receiving from the other side. And certainly not Judge Gifford, who would confide to her legal associates about how unimpressed she had been with Tyson's big-city, big-shot, high-priced legal team.

The county prosecutor told the court that he, like the judge, had been inundated with mail from all parts of the country. Each letter had its own spin.

"Many people," Modisett said, "tell me that a heavy sentence should be imposed to send a message to those who would commit rape. Others ask for a lenient sentence.

"Tyson was convicted of a violent crime, and the woman was tremendously victimized. It's an outrage to every person in the community, and I'm stunned that people say that she [Washington] got what she deserved for going to Tyson's hotel room." The first-term county prosecutor, sounding more like he was on the political stump than in a courtroom, told the judge, "There is no excuse for criminal behavior, but it is a time for healing."

His preliminary remarks now out of the way, Modisett headed into the heart of his commentary. "The defense wants you to handle this defendant differently, and allow probation or a trip to Riverside. They want to perpetuate the myth that males with money and power don't know how to deal with women.

"Draw the line," he implored the court. "The law says there's a presumption of 10 years, and that is then affected by either aggravation or mitigation.

"As to mitigation, the defendant doesn't have a prior record," Modisett said. "The 'he rose from the ghetto argument' is not a mitigator, and it is no comfort to Desiree Washington. It's not going to take away the nightmares. [She] is in prison permanently.

"From 1988 to 1990, Tyson made $34 million. He has millions left," said the prosecutor. (How many millions Tyson has left continues to be an unanswered question. Tyson's promoter Don King might be the only person who can answer that.) "But being rich and famous," Modisett continued, "doesn't make him a hero or a role model. Tyson had everything, but he continued to take what he wanted."

Modisett then read from Desiree Washington's letter. "In the place of what has been me for 18 years is now a cold and empty feeling. I can only say that each day after being raped has been a struggle to learn to trust again, to smile the way I did, and to find the Desiree Lynn Washington, who was stolen from me and those who love me, on July 19, 1991. Although some days I cry when I see the pain in my own eyes, I am also able to pity my attacker. It has been and still is my wish that he be rehabilitated." (The full contents of Washington's letter have never been made public.)

Setting her letter aside, Modisett then said the most forceful and memorable words of his 10-minute address. "From the date of his conviction, Tyson still doesn't get it. The world is watching now," Modisett said, his voice rising with intensity, "to see if there is one system of justice." With that, he stated that eight to 10 years was the sentence he would recommend, since anything less "depreciates the seriousness of the crime. It is his responsibility to admit his problem. Heal this sick man. Mike Tyson, the rapist, needs to be off the streets."

Not Mike Tyson, the baddest man on the planet. Not Mike Tyson, the former heavyweight champion of the world. Not Mike Tyson, even now a hero in some neighborhoods. But "Mike Tyson, the rapist."

The words were judicially correct, but they were nonetheless hard to fully fathom. It had been "Mike Tyson, the rapist," for 44 days. The headlines in the newspapers, the stories on television and radio told everyone as much, but somehow hearing it from the county prosecutor made it sound and feel so much more final.

Modisett's remarks were concise, to the point, and more passionate than Tyson's defense counsel, Fuller. Of course, the prosecution had seemed more fervent and compelling in the presentation of its case throughout the trial than the defense. Fuller and his team always seemed so matter of fact, so mercenary, so distant. There was never any evidence of heartfelt allegiance between lawyer and client, not even on this final day, this final chance to keep their rich employer from going to prison.

Modisett had done an impressive job of balancing his responsibilities of being prosecutor (in what had been the highest profile case he had ever had) with the political realities of having this case on his resume for re-election. He sought to offend no one, neither by demeaning Tyson (and even praising Tyson's legal team) nor by deemphasizing the serious nature of the crime. In the end, his request for an eight- to 10-year prison term for the former heavyweight champion of the world was right down the middle of Indiana's sentencing guidelines.

One of the most confounding aspects of the Tyson trial was Fuller's decision to keep James Voyles, the local defense counsel, under wraps. An enormously bright and successful attorney, Voyles, a good-humored, heavy-set Hoosier, appeared to be the only member of the defense team who had any sort of relationship with Tyson. He was the one attorney who put a reassuring arm around Tyson, and they would exchange words and smiles at the defense table during the trial.

Voyles, a criminal defense attorney, knew how the legal game was played in Indiana. He knew Judge Gifford. He knew and understood the 12 jurors more intimately than Fuller, the Washington outsider. He could have brought so much to the table, but Fuller never allowed him to even carry a tray.

Greg Garrison had been deeply relieved that Fuller had left the power-hitting Voyles on the bench throughout the trial. Garrison had worked with and argued against Voyles for years. The special prosecutor admitted to friends that if Voyles or another of Indianapolis's fine defense attorneys had been more directly involved in handling the case, a conviction would have been more difficult.

Voyles was a frustrated man. A competitor by nature, he wasn't given the opportunity to compete. And while he was a well-paid (said to be a quarter of a million dollars) member of the Fuller team, he might have been happier being a Fuller brush man. At one point during the trial he described himself to a friend as "one of the world's highest paid pencil carriers." But, as a ferocious sports fan, he also described himself as a "team player and loyal."

Alas, Voyles would finally have a chance to speak his mind before Judge Gifford. Perhaps he could provide the fire and brimstone on behalf of his friend that the legal eagles from Washington were simply unable to do. And, more importantly, perhaps he could present Judge Gifford with some strong reasons as to why Tyson should be spared prison.

Unfortunately, Voyles provided a bit of the passion, but the argument just wasn't there.

"Incarceration," Voyles said, "is the easy answer. You [the judge] can step up now . . . [and] do what's right for the person, Mike Tyson. We can't build enough prisons," he continued, "Plainfield, Westfield, the rehabilitation won't be there."

The halfway house idea, suggested Voyles, would be better for Tyson because, "What we can do as a society for people . . . is to deal with the problem. You have a unique opportunity, your honor, to do something for Mike Tyson."

Judge Gifford listened politely, probably wondering why in the world she should be put in the position of "doing something for Mike Tyson, the rapist."

Having said his piece, Voyles sat down. He had spoke with some of the fervor that had been so sorely lacking during the 14-day trial a month earlier. Even if he hadn't made points with the judge, at least there was a sense of passion and compassion coming from Voyles.

Voyles the competitor had finally had a chance to compete, even if it was, in basketball parlance, garbage time— when the outcome of the game has already been determined, the benches cleared, and the bit players get a chance to play. Voyles had always been a star player in the courtrooms of Indiana, and garbage time was something he did not like. He did his best, though, but it wasn't quite as impressive as most expected.

Somehow wanting to gain the last word for the defense, Fuller got up again, and offered the judge one final thought, and a compelling one at that.

"In the Department of Corrections, Tyson is a marked man," Fuller said. "A target of abuse. It's not the kind of environment where he should be," pointing out what everyone in the media had expected would be a critical argument from the defense at the sentencing.

Even Tyson's harshest critics wondered if such a high-profile prisoner could be safe. A "lifer" they said, with nothing to lose could test his machismo against the baddest man on the planet. In a prison environment, the Marquis of Queensbury rules do not apply. Prison officials, however, were not as concerned as the civilian population. Their thinking was that in prison there is a pecking order, and the baddest men in prison wouldn't be likely to risk their jailhouse titles against the baddest man on the planet. Prison officials were more concerned about their own security guards than fellow inmates making life even more miserable for Tyson. Prison officials knew that they could be burned by the glare of the media spotlight. As a result, meetings were held with security guards to remind them that if and when Tyson joined the prison population, he should be treated as "just another inmate."

Assessing the effectiveness of the respective counsel wasn't a difficult task.

Vincent Fuller had now said all that he was going to say, and everyone was still waiting for his special courtroom skills. In his final comments before Judge Gifford, in his opening statements two months earlier, in much of his cross-examinations, and in his closing statement before the jury 44 days earlier, Fuller rambled. He never, in his plea for leniency, talked about Tyson's current state of mind. Rather, he rehashed Tyson's well-chronicled past, and worried about his future; nary a mention of the present. Was his client sorry? If Tyson wouldn't admit it, perhaps Fuller could have or should have expressed some sense of remorse on his client's behalf.

Voyles had made a spirited plea for leniency, asking the judge to help Tyson when no one else would. While Voyles made points for his oratory, he made none in his appeal to the judge that she should somehow take Tyson under her wing and care for him.

Modisett had been low-key and out of the spotlight during the trial. Though he was rarely in the courtroom, he was involved in virtually every key strategic maneuver carried out by Garrison and Trathen. In his 10 minutes behind the podium, Modisett was efficient and specific, referring to the very guidelines that Gifford would utilize in making her decision.

Now it would be Patricia Gifford's turn to speak. Picking up the theme of Modisett, she too referred to the "two different Mike Tysons. Many fine things have been said about you, your work with the community, your treatment of children, and sharing your assets," she said in a strong, rhythmic, and even voice.

The former prosecutor, realizing that her audience was far larger (perhaps several million times larger) than the 70 people who were crammed into her tiny courtroom, was poised to make her feelings known about date rape. She wasted no time in saying the term "date rape" was a term she detested.

Gifford, who had been so official, so proper and so poised as she presided over the Tyson trial, displayed an emotion that she had been successful in keeping bottled when the evidence was being presented. Patricia Gifford, the woman and the mother who was also a judge, was speaking now.

"It is not all right to proceed if you are acquainted with or dating a person. The rape law doesn't mention anything about acquaintance." While her voice remained steady, an intensity about the judge became unmistakable. "We have managed to imply that it is all right to proceed to do what you want to do if you know or are dating a woman. The law is very clear in its definition of rape. It never mentions anything about whether the defendant and victim are related. The date, in date rape, does not lessen the fact that it is still rape."

Judge Gifford returned to the sentencing of Mike Tyson. "I feel he is a risk to do it again because of his attitude," she said as she stared sternly at Tyson. She then told the boxer, "You had no prior record. You have been given many gifts. But you have stumbled." After hesitating a few moments, the judge dropped the hammer on Michael Gerard Tyson, whose life was about to change forever.

"On count 1, I sentence you to 10 years," the judge said. Tyson winced.

"On count 2, I sentence you to 10 years," she went on. A half-dozen of Tyson's friends, including a subdued Don King, gasped.

"On count 3, I sentence you to 10 years" the judge concluded. Tyson stared intently at his precious white piece of paper.

"The sentences will run concurrently. I fine you a maximum of $30,000," the judge summed up.

Greg Garrison, Barbara Trathen, and their boss, Jeffrey Modisett smiled with satisfaction, knowing that their job was done successfully. Although they tried not to gloat, they knew that Tyson was actually going away. And soon.

"I suspend four of those years," Judge Gifford continued, "and place you on probation for four years."

Reporters not immediately familiar with legal jargon started counting fingers. Ten minus four equals six. Six years for the former heavyweight champion of the world. Not quite the length of his title reign.

"During that time [probation], you will enter into a psychoanalytic program with Dr. Jerome Miller, and perform 100 hours of community work involving youth delinquency."

Jeffrey Modisett had asked the court to make Tyson pay for the cost of the State's prosecution against him, which he estimated at $150,000. Judge Gifford, however, denied the State's position, because there was nothing in the law that could authorize her to force Tyson to pay for the State's legal fees, even though, she said, "the defendant had offered to do so."

The irony would have been overwhelming: Tyson paying his own legal fees of more than a million dollars to unsuccessfully defend him, and an additional $150,000 to convict him. Indiana law saved him from the embarrassing irony.

As for bail, there would be none, said the judge, who had admitted privately that in retrospect she should have sent Tyson to prison, back on February 10, the night of his conviction. Gifford, in setting no bail, thus agreed with the State's contention that with his money and his connections, Tyson was a legitimate risk to flee, and that he was a definite risk to commit rape again.

Tyson's new appeals attorney, Alan Dershowitz, along with his son, Jamie, loudly and abruptly left the courtroom. It was a rude and provocative departure, which Gifford would claim later she never noticed. The media horde, however, certainly did, and a comical caravan it was. Led by microphones, in hot pursuit, all did a snake dance down the stairs, into the lobby, and out through the revolving doors, which was no small feat for the camera people with their $20,000 high-tech, over-the-shoulder equipment.

Indiana law mandated that, with good behavior, an inmate's sentence can be cut in half. If Tyson therefore was to be a model prisoner he could be out of jail in three years. March 26, 1995. At the age of twenty-eight.

Of course, he would still be on probation for four more years and have to undergo court-ordered psychoanalysis, but Tyson could easily return to the profession he dominated for five years. But will Tyson go back to boxing? Of course he will. Tyson is a "gladiator" and a "warrior." Who used those words? Mike Tyson, that's who. And besides, what else would Tyson do?

Tyson most certainly will fight again. For the money.

But if Tyson's prison behavior is less than exemplary, he could remain behind bars for six years, until 1998, when he would be 31.

For the first time in Tyson's tortured life, he would finally have some control over his own destiny, even if the state of Indiana has taken away his freedom. For the first time, since the last time he was incarcerated (at the Tryon School for Boys in New York State as a pre-teen) Tyson wouldn't have the responsibility of making money for promoters, managers, trainers, and entourage.

As Judge Gifford remanded Tyson to the Indiana Department of Corrections and gaveled the trial to its conclusion, she stood up, turned to her left, and headed for her chambers.

Tyson stood up, removed his watch, his belt, and his wallet and gave them to his attorney, Vincent Fuller. Two women friends of Tyson, from the front row of the gallery, sobbed uncontrollably, and said loud enough for the former champion and everyone else in the courtroom to hear, "We love you, Mike."

Camille Ewald, stunned by the trial and devastated by the sentence, left her seat and made her way toward her fallen child. They hugged one another. Tyson then headed out the back door escorted by County Sheriff Joe McAtee, to the booking station.

Mike Tyson, the convicted rapist, was then searched, fingerprinted, and processed through. Once those tasks were completed, the ex-champ emerged with his handcuffs held high, and with a smirk on his face he headed for the prison in Plainfield, Indiana.

Camille Ewald, Rory Holloway, John Horne, Don King, and Vincent Fuller and his legal team would ho home.

While their beloved benefactor would go away.

25

◆

THE APPEAL BEGINS

During the bail hearing before sentencing, Vincent Fuller had reminded the Court that Tyson had appeared every time he was asked to do so. The defense counsel also took a jab at the prosecution's assertion that they had "pursued the truth," while denying the defense the right to call the three witnesses who had been excluded from testifying.

To this argument, Greg Garrison finally rose to speak. The media's designated "star" of the trial, Garrison had done every possible interview imaginable since the trial, including the famous one on ABC's "20/20" with Barbara Walters where he was made to look like a fool when the only question asked of him was to describe "criminal deviate conduct."

Silent in the hearing until now, Garrison resumed his attacks on Tyson. "He's a potential threat, possesses an on-going practiced pattern toward women." Tyson, he said, "possesses the desire of an opportunist."

Attacking Fuller's argument that the appealable issues implied that both "the State and the Court were incompetent," Garrison replied, "This defendant got a bucketful of due process."

Commending the Court, Garrison said, "We shouldn't let this defendant out when the issues for appeal are an exercise in fiction. It would depreciate and insult the case." Tyson is a "guilty, violent rapist who may repeat," Garrison went on. "If you fail to remove the defendant, you depreciate the seriousness of the crime, demean the quality of law enforcement, expose other innocent persons, and allow a guilty man to continue his lifestyle."

Judge Gifford then denied bail, citing the seriousness of the crime, risk of flight (she said five years earlier a drug dealer had fled to South America even when a very high bail was imposed), and the potential that Tyson would commit a similar act.

Even though Alan Dershowitz had made a mad dash for the State Capitol after the sentencing hearing was almost over, the Indiana Court of Appeals was not in as much of a hurry as the famous professor. In spite of his plea for an emergency hearing, the court set the matter for Friday, March 27, at 2:00 p.m.

At that time, Professor Dershowitz rose to address the court, made up of Honorable Judges Sue V. Shields, John G. Baker, and Patrick D. Sullivan. In a hearing that lasted about an hour and 45 minutes, Dershowitz not only argued that bond should be granted, but began his plea for reversal of the decision as well.

In a complete turnaround from the trial itself, the defense now had the passionate, articulate, and flamboyant attorney, while the state was represented by the quieter, low-key presence of deputy prosecutor David Dreyer.

With his flamboyant style and persuasive argument skills, Dershowitz seemed able to change the ground rules. When he pleaded for bail, he also was trying his case. In fact, it was as if he was saying, "I'm going to come into Indiana and snooker you," and the judges let him do it.

Dershowitz once told ESPN that he comes "into cases as a coroner doing an autopsy and tries to bring the patient back to life," but most everyone who attended the hearing was impressed with his argument. In a unique offer perhaps never made before, Dershowitz told the court Tyson would submit to house arrest "to allay fears that he would be a danger to women."

The professor then said, "Tyson would promise to live at his Cleveland estate under supervision of local law enforcement and keep out of trouble while on bail."

In an impassioned plea for his client, Dershowitz told the court that if Tyson violated the conditions of bail, he (Dershowitz) would drop the appeal.

David Dreyer countered by characterizing Dershowitz's statement as being "flamboyant hyperventilation," and asked "How would any of this help another rape victim?"

The judges asked the lawyers to hone in on the issues to be addressed by the appeal, since the potential for reversal of the decision is one criterion the court may use to determine whether bail is to be granted. "In my 28 years of practice, I've never seen a case with so many good issues for appeal, and I've never made that statement in any court about any client before," Dershowitz said.

Dershowitz now based his hopes for reversal on three main issues:

1) Exclusion of the three potential defense witnesses who allegedly saw Tyson and Washington "all over each other" in the back of a limousine outside the Canterbury Hotel. This was important because, if the witness's testimony were true, it would back up the defense contention that Washington consented to have sex with Tyson.

2) Exclusion of a defense submission of a jury instruction involving "implied consent." This was a defense if Tyson was "reasonably mistaken" that Washington wanted to have sex.

3) Gifford erred when she allowed prosecutor Garrison to read from a partial Supreme Court decision which says, "The job of a defense lawyer is not to seek the truth but to defend their clients." The defense believed this opinion indicated to a jury that they should not believe defense lawyers.

Of the three issues, the exclusion of the three witnesses issue was paramount. Dershowitz passionately argued that the exclusion violated Tyson's constitutional rights, and that the anticipated testimony "backed Tyson's claim that he believed that she had consented to have sex." Dreyer countered that the admission of the testimony would have severely prejudiced the State's case. Accusing Dershowitz of attacking Washington, Dreyer said, "She still continues to be battered by the defense. We still have Desiree Washington on trial here."

Judge Sue Shields recessed the hearing until a certified copy of the testimony from trial could be filed with the court.

Tyson, meanwhile, spent his first night in jail. "Tyson has been out of his cell," Kevin Moore, a prison system spokesman, said. "He is playing it very low key. There have been no confrontations or difficulties."

Monday, the 31st of March, however, was a different story. Prison officials announced that Tyson had refused to eat and was only taking liquids. He also had refused to participate in an educational assessment, which apparently he had the right to do. Tyson also faced his first disciplinary action after two inmates were found in possession of Tyson's autograph.

Prison spokesman Kevin Moore said Tyson "was warned that it is a violation of prison rules to give anything of value to another inmate, and his autograph is considered valuable. Mike Tyson was specifically counseled about this prison rule, and we found a couple of inmates who had autographs."

At the disciplinary hearing, Tyson received a reprimand, which would not affect his sentence.

On Tuesday, March 31, Judge Sue Shields issued a terse three-sentence opinion of the Appellate Court, to the effect that Tyson's request for the appeal bond was denied. Like Fuller before him, Dershowitz had failed.

26

♦

A JUROR
SPEAKS OUT

*Note: After the sentencing, Michael Wettig, juror #11 in the
Mike Tyson case, was interviewed in his hometown of Greenwood,
Indiana. None of the observations contained in this book were provided
to him prior to his interview, and none of the analysis or material in the
book was changed based on the interview.*

Speaking at length, Michael Wettig acknowledged that
serving on the Tyson jury was a very special experience for him.
He appreciated very much the support his employer, Indiana
Bell, had given him, and was proud of having served on the jury.

45-year-old Michael Wettig disclosed that he had never
served on a jury before. When he told his wife, Pat, a senior clerk
at Merchant's National Bank, that he might possibly be a juror in
the Mike Tyson case, she said she hoped he wouldn't because he
would be away too long while the jury was sequestered.

Michael Wettig had been notified by the Court that he
could be a potential juror on January 14, his birthday. He
reported to the jury room, and was given a 25-page jury question-
naire to fill out. When Judge Patricia Gifford popped in the room
and said, "You all know why you're here?" Wettig knew for the
first time that he might be a juror in the Tyson case.

On the 29th of January, Michael took the bus to the City-County Building in downtown Indianapolis and reported to room 260. It would be almost two full days later when he was called into the courtroom, where he took a seat in the front row as juror #631. Michael said he was "nervous, and didn't know what to expect." He remembers glancing at Tyson, who "didn't look as tall as I thought he would." Judge Gifford, on the other hand, "didn't seem as tough as she would later turn out to be."

Wettig was first questioned by prosecutor Greg Garrison, whom he described as being "very confident, and not intimidating." He remembers Garrison explaining to him "Tyson's right to be judged innocent until proven guilty," and also that "even if a person is in the wrong place at the wrong time, there is still a crime if that person is wronged."

As for defense lawyer Kathleen Beggs, Wettig said, "She wore the same thing all the time . . . skirt, blouse . . . It wasn't very attractive." He could not recall the questions she asked him.

Wettig did make a revelation regarding an issue that had been debated prior to trial concerning the potential racial makeup of the jury. The defense had argued that Tyson could not get a fair trial due to the fact that the system used in selecting blacks for jury service was improper.

While not being knowledgeable about the exact facts or figures that were being circulated about how many blacks or other minorities were actually on the jury panel, Wettig said he saw 10 to 12 blacks among the 50 potential jurors called with him. However, he pointed out the startling fact that "none of the black jurors wanted to touch the Tyson case with a 10-foot pole, apparently because they did not want to sit in judgment of one of their heroes." Wettig also believed that some of the black jurors were "scared" as well, and therefore did not want to be on the jury.

Wettig pointed to the case of one tall black man, with a beard, who told him that he was going to say that he "had a bad back" and thus couldn't serve. "If that doesn't work," he told Wettig, "then I'll tell them I have an opinion about the case." When that specific juror was called, he was true to his word, and was excused by the judge.

As he sat there with the other five potential jurors, Wettig wondered whether he would be selected. At about 1:30 p.m., all of the other five were excused, and only Wettig remained in his seat. The judge then asked him to return to the jury room, and Wettig said he went there in a "state of shock."

One of the bailiffs then asked him if he could be at the Indianapolis Athletic Club (where the jury was housed), by 3:00 p.m. Wettig said he called his wife and asked "her to pack a bag," and then took a taxi home. After calling his supervisor at work and another friend at Bell, Wettig was driven to the Athletic Club by his wife.

Wettig was directed to the sixth floor, where "Big Ed," the chief bailiff, assigned him room #651. Wettig described the room as "nice," and said that the jurors were allowed to watch television in the parlor, play pool, and enjoy the use of the basketball court and other athletic facilities. A deputy sheriff was always there when the television was on to make certain that no newscasts were shown, and Wettig said that only once during the entire trial did Tyson's name appear on the screen.

The jurors were allowed to read the newspapers, but they were cut up severely to exclude any mention of rape, Tyson, the Tyson trial, the Jeffrey Dahmer trial, or the subsequent fire. Wettig even said that one day the "picture of Indiana University basketball star Damon Bailey was cut out," and that the jurors "laughed because they couldn't figure out why." Wettig also disclosed that the bailiffs were so careful not to let the jury involve themselves with outside influences that they stopped some members of the jury as they were playing Trivial Pursuit when a boxing question came up.

Wettig said that family visits were allowed for two hours on Sunday, and that meant "exactly two hours and no more." He also discussed Chuck, juror #11, who was ultimately excused from the jury after the fire. "Chuck [a black man]," Wettig said, "was apparently married to a white woman, and it didn't seem like he wanted anyone to know. When they told us that we could have our families visit on Sunday, Chuck said that his kids had the chicken pox, and even after the bailiffs told him that they would find a separate area for them to meet, Chuck didn't have his family come down.

"Chuck was also really the only one who didn't get along with everyone else. He didn't seem to fit in with the others. He was a picky guy, didn't like cold sandwiches and other food we had. He also would just flip the channels on the television whenever he wanted to without asking," Wettig said. "Deep down, he seemed kind of scared."

Michael Wettig then talked about the fire at the Athletic Club on the fifth night of the trial. He said, "I was sleeping in my room, when I thought I heard something. I went to the door, but I didn't hear anything, so I went back to bed. I heard some commotion, but no alarm; it was some sort of a hum. I went out of my room and to the main area, and I smelled smoke," he went on, "and then I saw a fireman and a security guard.

"'Are you a member of the jury?' they asked me, and I replied that I was." Wettig said they led him down the stairs, and when they got to the third floor, "the smoke was very bad, and I couldn't see. I was the last juror out, and the other jurors across the street began clapping for me."

Wettig said that "a bailiff, a husky guy, wanted to go back in, but that a fireman wouldn't let him. Everybody was pretty calm, but juror #3, Beth, broke down and cried right there on the sidewalk."

The jury was then taken by bus (the jurors dubbed the bus a "prison wagon") to the downtown Hilton Hotel, where they spent the remainder of the trial. "We were allowed to have a drink [alcohol], per the judge's permission," Wettig said.

"The next day we were taken to the City-County Building, and one by one we were escorted into the judge's chambers. The judge was there, and Mr. Fuller, and Mr. Garrison, and a court reporter," Wettig said. "The judge apologized for the fire, and I told her 'it's not your fault.'

"The judge then told me that the preliminary investigation indicated that the fire started in the refrigerator on the third floor," Wettig recalled, "and then asked me whether the fire affected me in any way. I told her that there would be no more birthdays in our family this year, because I had been called for jury duty on my birthday, and then the fire occurred on my daughter Tanya's birthday. Fuller and Garrison and the judge all laughed, and neither Garrison nor Fuller asked any more questions of me. In fact, that very night, at about 7:30 [before the fire], the bailiff had called up Tanya, and a group of the jurors and I sang happy birthday to her," Wettig said.

After all of the questioning, juror #11, Chuck, was excused, and Michael, who had originally been juror #13 and an alternate, now assumed the position of juror #11 on the jury.

Returning now to the first real day of the trial, Wettig indicated that he "was impressed with Greg Garrison's explanation of what he was going to prove during his opening statement to the jury. He had a fluid delivery, was animated, and presented himself well. I knew that it was just his opinion, though," said Wettig, "because I've read a lot of books that are true stories about trials."

As for defense counsel Vincent Fuller, Wettig's comments were not so kind. "What is he doing here?, I asked myself," Wettig said. "He's stumbling and has lost his place a few times. He's also calling his own client a manic depressant, crucifying his own client [referring apparently to Fuller's portrait of Tyson as a 'bad boy']. He's starting off bad, I hope he's better at asking questions than giving statements."

Regarding the prosecution's case in chief, Wettig believed that "Desiree Washington made a very credible witness, and handled herself very well." He went on to say, "I believe she told the truth, that she was just going out to have a good time. She said she was just going to take pictures, and she took her camera. In my mind, she felt she was going out to see the city."

As for Fuller's cross-examination, Wettig said that he "didn't go after the jugular . . . didn't grill her . . . let her off easy . . . and therefore she only got rattled a couple of times. If she could handle cross-examination and stick to her original story, I figured she must be telling the truth.

"All along, it was a question of whether she consented to have sex or not, and if I had been Fuller, I would have come out more strongly. He more or less accepted her at face value," Wettig said. "She felt she was raped, and that part about her waiting two days to call 911, well, women think it's their fault. It takes a lot of courage to call 911 . . . and file charges against a guy of Tyson's stature."

In the two controversial issues at trial, Wettig said that Washington's explanation about the removal of the "panty shield" made sense, and that her answers concerning how she got "on top, and tried to escape," also seemed plausible to him. As for Tyson's demeanor during her testimony, Wettig said that "Tyson acted during the whole trial like he didn't give a shit. He had the same expression all the time. I glanced at Tyson, expecting a reaction, but he looked the same."

The state's most compelling witness, according to Wettig, was Tyson's limousine driver, Virginia Foster. "She was a strong witness," Wettig recalled. "In the end she made the case against him [Tyson], because she was hired by them to drive him around, and if anyone would have contradicted Desiree, it would have been Foster because she worked for them. She corroborated Desiree as far as the actions in the limo and the telephone call."

Wettig also said Foster contradicted what Tyson would later say about Washington's appearance when she left the hotel after the alleged rape incident. "When Tyson testified about how Desiree prettied herself up, that didn't coincide with what Foster said about her [Washington] looking like hell." Also impressive to Wettig was the testimony of the night manager at the Canterbury hotel. "He and Tyson's story didn't work. Tyson said the bodyguard was outside the room during the sex act, but the night manager said that the bodyguard was in the parlor making plane reservations," Wettig concluded. "Besides, they said they made the room reservations for the whole weekend, and there the bodyguard is making reservations to get out of town. Why are they cutting out within a few hours unless he [bodyguard] knew something was going on that shouldn't have," Wettig said.

Regarding the medical testimony at trial, Wettig said that only one doctor really impressed him, and that was the "young one from I.U. with glasses. He pointed out that injuries like she did have were very rare in case where there was consensual sex, but in the deliberations I don't think that really made a difference because there was at least a slim chance that injuries like that could be caused with consensual sex."

"One of the more ironic moments in the trial," Wettig said, "came when we found that one of the sequins from the garment worn by Desiree Washington was on the floor of the jury room. We called Ed, the bailiff, and told him we didn't know how it had gotten there and asked him what to do with it. He simply took it with him."

Surprisingly enough, though, while Wettig felt the State had presented a "strong case," he said that if the "case had ended there, he would be inclined toward guilty, but couldn't have said yes . . . couldn't have voted guilty."

As for the defense, Wettig first brought up the doctor that appeared in Tyson's behalf. "She kept changing her story as she went along . . . said she had seen all these injuries when there was consensual sex . . . and then would change her answer," Wettig recalled. "I never could figure out why they called her. . . . They could have called somebody better."

Overall, "the defense was boring," Wettig said. "They had a list of questions . . . the same questions . . . and if the answer differed from what they wanted to hear . . . it took all three defense attorneys to think of any retort. Heard [Lane Heard] couldn't think on his feet, and would walk back and forth. . . . He was nervous."

"Johnny Gill," Wettig recalled, "was the worst. Since they [he and Tyson] were good friends, I expected him to go along with what Tyson would say. But I didn't believe him because it was too close with what Tyson said, like taking a test in school, and looking over somebody's shoulder . . . word for word with Tyson."

As for Tyson's testimony itself, Wettig said, "He lied. That part about the bodyguard and where he was, and the fact that he couldn't remember screwing B Angie B. If it was me, I would remember B Angie B and not Desiree."

"Testifying before the grand jury was a mistake," Wettig asserted, "and the prosecutor made good use of it. They played it back and it so differed from Tyson's other testimony. That convicted him more than anything. Also, if Tyson is as crude as they [the defense] said he was, then why did he act so embarrassed when he had to say the F word in court? That didn't make sense at all."

As for the posttrial issue of the exclusion of the three witnesses who said they saw Washington and Tyson "all over each other" in the back of the limousine, Wettig said that he didn't think it would have made a difference since "the windows were so tinted . . . so dark . . . that if Virginia Foster couldn't see anything, then how could anyone see anything from the curb?"

Wettig also said that "he [Tyson] was all screwed up. If you take his story about getting all hot and bothered in the limo, and then stopping in the hotel for 15 minutes . . . that doesn't make sense. If you start something one place, you'll finish, and Tyson came across as that type . . . that he goes after something 100%."

The juror also said that "the fact that [Washington] didn't spend the night . . . If she was so interested in him . . . then she could spend the night and be around him [Tyson] and that type of life. . . . But she said no," was very important to him. "The defense painted him as a crude bad guy, but it worked in the wrong way for them . . . gave the impression . . . that no matter what . . . if she said no . . . he wouldn't take no from anybody. I wouldn't have degraded him as much as they did."

Wettig's observations as to the closing arguments of the respective counsels followed his previous assessments of Garrison and Fuller when they made their opening statements. As for Garrison, Wettig said that he used the blackboard to show us the percentages concerning Washington's vaginal injuries and whether they were possible with consensual sex or not, but that "the percentages did nothing for me, because they left room for doubt."

"I would have liked for someone to tape the rest of his argument, though," Wettig said, "because it would be good for law students to hear."

"Fuller," Wettig went on, "lost track too easily. He really got flustered when Steve [juror #5] asked to go to the bathroom. The rest of his argument was a waste. He also made Tyson out to be such a bad guy, and talked about Desiree's desire for publicity and money. That was a mistake." Wettig further stated that "Fuller stayed at his podium. He didn't seem to want to get close to the jury."

As for posttrial accusations that the verdict would have been different if the jury had seen a retainer agreement between Washington and Rhode Island lawyer Ed Gerstein, Wettig said, "We knew she had an attorney. . . . It made no difference. . . . More power to her if she can get money from him."

Concerning the jury deliberation process on the 10th, Wettig said that jurors began shortly after lunch. "The first order of business was to pick a foreman, and a couple of people said that Tim should be the foreman," Wettig went on. "He was one heck of a nice guy. Once we got his suit and tie off, he relaxed more, and was more like the rest of us."

"Right away," Wettig said, "I spoke up and said that we needed to get it out of our minds that this is Mike Tyson v. Desiree Washington. Look at it like it is John Doe v. Mary Smith. Some discussion was held," Wettig said, "regarding how we should discuss the evidence, but someone spoke up and said that we should take a vote first."

"Small slips of paper were passed around, and we all wrote down our verdicts," Wettig explained. "Then we gave them to the foreman, and he put them in a bowl. He undid the slips, and laid them on the table for everyone to see. Then he told us that the vote was six for 'guilty' and six for 'not guilty' on the rape charge, ten for 'guilty' and two for 'not guilty' on the first criminal deviate conduct count, and six for 'guilty' and six for 'not guilty' on the second criminal deviate conduct charge.

"We then decided that we would list a bunch of ideas on the blackboard that we wanted to discuss, but we weren't getting anywhere, so we decided that each of us would explain why we felt the way we did," Wettig stated. "One by one we went around the table, and eleven of us did that, but juror #5, Steve, wouldn't do it, so we didn't know how he had voted. I learned that besides me, the foreman, Tim, the T-shirt designer, Neil, [who was told by the bailiff that the judge felt he wasn't dressing professionally by wearing T-shirts in the courtroom], the Pizza Hut driver Walt, and Dave [nicknamed 'coach'] had voted 'guilty' on the first ballot.

"Later, I would find out that juror #5, Steve, had voted that way as well," Wettig explained. "He had apparently decided to play devil's advocate, and kept saying, 'I'm not changing my mind, give me some evidence,' whenever someone asked him where he stood, giving the impression that he favored 'not guilty.' I finally got tired of it, and said 'what do you want?,' but he wouldn't tell me."

As for the women on the jury, Wettig said, "They didn't care about the evidence, only that they wouldn't have gone up to the hotel room at that hour . . . wouldn't have put themselves in that position . . . . It was simply not the way they would have acted."

It apparently was juror #2, Ken, who ultimately changed the minds of those jurors who had voted "not guilty" on the first ballot. "He was against it [voting 'guilty'] on the first ballot, but only for a few minutes," Wettig said. "After that, he came over to our side and was very vocal. He helped to turn the others around when he broke down Tyson's testimony and his irregular answers with the grand jury testimony."

All of this discussion apparently took some two to three hours, and then the jurors decided to take a second vote. True to his word, Ken came around, and so did juror #3, Beth, and juror #12, Chuck, who worked for a medical equipment company. Now the vote was nine for "guilty," and three for "not guilty" as to the rape count, which was the only count the jury decided to vote on.

The last real holdout according to Wettig, was juror #8, Rosie, who was an insurance underwriter. "She was the last one to come around," Wettig said, "because she didn't care who it was, she wouldn't have gone out with him. When juror #2 started picking Tyson apart, however, it helped," Wettig went on, "and soon she came around too.

"The women weren't that strong, but we kept rehashing the evidence," Wettig said, "and Steve kept playing the devil's advocate, so no one was sure about where he stood although they thought he favored 'guilty.'"

"The jury then took the final vote, and after laying out the small pieces of paper on the table, Tim, the jury foreman, very calmly announced that the vote was 12 to 0 for conviction on the rape charge. I was surprised at the vote," Wettig said, "because I was very uncertain as to what Steve was going to do."

"It was now about ten o'clock," Wettig said, "and the bailiff came back and said that the judge wanted to send us home for the night. We told the bailiff that we were almost done, and that we would be done by eleven or we would go home.

"It took another half-hour or so to decide [the other two counts] once we got through with the big one," Wettig explained. "The 'finger' one [apparently the second charge of criminal deviate conduct] was iffy, but one of the jurors made the point that if he [Tyson] was guilty of the rape, then he was probably guilty of the other ones as well."*

The final vote was then taken, and it was twelve to zero for conviction on the two remaining counts. "Before the bailiff was summoned," Wettig said, "the foreman asked everyone if they were comfortable with the verdict, even after they had signed the papers. He told them they could go back and vote again if they weren't comfortable, but no one did.

"After the verdict was given, the judge came back to the jury room," Wettig said, "and she told us about the press confer-

---

Note: "Guessing" at a verdict on the final two counts against Tyson is contrary to law.

ence potential, and we asked her if she would do it if she were in our shoes. She told us she would just get it over with, and then a couple of jurors asked if they could get a lifetime exemption from serving on jury duty, but the judge said that was out of her control."

After the verdict, the jury was returned to the hotel. Wettig said he played pool with Ed, the bailiff, and most of the jurors went home, except Tim, the foreman, who went down to the bar in the hotel.

Regarding his overall impressions of the main characters in the trial, Wettig was most impressed with Judge Gifford, "who did a very good job, and never favored one side or another."

As for Greg Garrison, Wettig said he "was very well prepared for his questions and his arguments. He didn't use many notes, and didn't have a list of questions . . . only a list for cross-examination."

"Barb Trathen," Wettig said, "gave a good perspective from a woman's point of view. She was a good partner for Garrison. Vincent Fuller was out of his league. He lost his place and made Tyson look bad. He got flustered when he got answers he wasn't expecting, and it took him too long to rebound. His presentation was boring, and he spoke in a monotone."

Wettig thought that the sentence was "fair," and would have been disappointed if Tyson would have been put on probation. "Just because he was Mike Tyson . . . he shouldn't be [treated] differently. Tyson was in over his head with King and the others, and he's got all this money and thinks he can do whatever he wants to. I feel sorry for him in that regard. He has no control over his finances . . . he'll be broke when he gets out. But I feel the same about the verdict today as I did then," Wettig said, "Mike Tyson was guilty."

In early December, two more of the Tyson jurors spoke up during radio interviews with Philadelphia station WHAT-AM talk show host Ted Watley. Both discussed the verdict— based on the new evidence uncovered to the effect that Washington had discussed book and film deals with lawyers before the rape trial.

Speaking to the point made by Tyson's appellate counsel to the effect that Washington perjured herself by not revealing that information, Dave Vahle (juror #10) said "I cannot see her as a credible witness from what I know now. We [the jurors] felt that a man raped a woman. . . . In hindsight, it looks like a woman raped a man.

"Right now I wouldn't believe anything she said," Vahle went on. "I would sign an affidavit that if we had known about the money, I couldn't have voted to convict him. Mike Tyson deserves a new trial."

Juror Rose Pride (#8) said she "would have been more skeptical of Washington's testimony if I had known about the alleged book and movie deals and reports that the 19 year old had hung out in nightclubs since she was 16, and isn't the innocent young girl presented in court. When she [Washington] went on Barbara Walters, she said she wasn't looking to make any money. I thought then we made the right decision," Pride added. "I also think Tyson was poorly represented at trial by his high-powered Washington lawyer, Vincent Fuller. He [Fuller] wasn't very convincing," Pride said, "he was very aloof about everything, and had no rapport with Mike . . . his [Fuller] approach made me think his [Tyson] own lawyer thought he did it."

Both Vahle and Pride reported that they had sent letters to the Indiana Court of Appeals requesting that Tyson be given a new trial.

Michael Wettig's response to the allegations was to say, "For me, I don't think it would have made any difference. . . . To me, it had nothing to do with what happened that night . . . the rape in the bedroom. . . . If she was so greedy, why didn't she take the million and run, instead of taking the chance with the trial?"

27

♦

POSTTRIAL MATTERS

Most criminal cases end once the trial is over. Except for the continuation of the appeal process, the case fades from the headlines and goes away. The Mike Tyson case, however, is the exception, for not a day seems to pass without there being new information discovered that fuels the fire of controversy about the trial or those who participated in it.

Michael Tyson, Vincent Fuller, James Voyles, Jeffrey Modisett, Greg Garrison, Barb Trathen, and Alan Dershowitz were sent copies of a draft of this book. Subsequently, questionnaires were sent to Fuller, Modisett, and Dershowitz, but were unanswered.

Vincent Fuller initially sent back a terse letter, indicating that he and his firm would not comment, but that they would consider grounds for a possible lawsuit. To date, no lawsuit has been filed.

Marion County Prosecutor Modisett replied with a letter which stated that, while he did not agree with all of the observations in the book, he could now see why I was so tough on the defense in my coverage of the trial. He promised to forward the manuscript to Greg Garrison and Barb Trathen, but no reply has been received from either of them. Modisett also sent me a transcript of his remarks at Tyson's sentencing, and corrections were made in the book accordingly. Mike Tyson did not respond to either the manuscript or a copy of an excerpt article that appeared in *Indianapolis Monthly*. Jim Voyles telephoned right after he received the manuscript, but did not return the return telephone call to him.

Alan Dershowitz telephoned to report that he believes his appellate record has been misstated and that he and his brother Nathan have been successful with closer to 60 wins. Dershowitz said he had looked into the potential of filing for a reversal of Tyson's conviction based on incompetencies of trial counsel, but that the "Supreme Court guidelines make it nearly impossible to win on such grounds."

The posttrial media parade for the participants in the Tyson case began when Desiree Washington inexplicably revealed her identity to the world by not only agreeing to appear on the cover of *People* Magazine, but be interviewed by Barbara Walters on the ABC program "20/20."

In the television interview, the feisty Washington told Walters that a) she was offered $1 million to drop charges after Tyson was indicted for rape, b) she would have dropped the charges if Tyson would have apologized and said he would get help, c) called Tyson "sick" and said she agreed to prosecute Tyson not to destroy the former heavyweight champion's career but "because he needed help," and d) told Tyson "I did it [prosecute] because you need help, and if your so-called friends weren't big enough to tell you, at least I was."

While Dershowitz continued the appeal process on behalf of Tyson, the ex-champ settled into the routine of prison life. Reports indicated that Tyson was adjusting well, until an altercation occurred with two prison guards.

Apparently Tyson was returning from the visiting area (among his visitors have been Arsenio Hall, Whitney Houston, M. C. Hammer, Spike Lee, Malcolm X's widow, and Shaquille O'Neal) when he had an argument with one prison guard. Charges were then filed that Tyson allegedly threatened the guard. When Tyson was confronted with the charges, he supposedly again threatened another guard as well.

Tyson apparently admitted the first charge and denied the second. An administrative hearing was held, and Tyson was found guilty of the second charge as well. Prison officials found that Tyson had thus violated prison rules, and an additional 15 days were added on to his prison sentence.

Tyson broke his posttrial silence by agreeing to appear for an interview with correspondent Ed Bradley on CBS's "Street Stories." The interview was aired on June 18, and Tyson spoke freely about all aspects of his trial.

Tyson was especially outspoken with his comments about prosecutor Greg Garrison. "The prosecutor, I thought he was a racist, weak, publicity-happy, little weak man." When Bradley asked, "What do you say to the jury that convicted you? You think you got a fair shot?" Tyson replied, "Well, there was no way I could. I knew I was innocent. But I knew what I was in that court and when I was gonna get the verdict, I knew the verdict was gonna be guilty because of the mentality of the Court, the mentality of the prosecutor."

Garrison's response the next day was that he was "mystified by the charges of racism for prosecuting a black man for raping a black woman. It would have been racism not to prosecute him. That comment [by Tyson] is pretty consistent with the denial he has lived in ever since he committed the crime and probably before. Once in his life, he's been required to face up to his deeds and it wasn't until he got to Indiana."

Tyson also spoke about the alleged rape itself, saying "she just sat on my bed and she was talking. We started kissing. And she started pulling off her clothes. She was getting hot. She was getting aggressive." Tyson also stated that he couldn't understand why, if she had been raped, that she didn't immediately seek help at the hotel and report him. "And if she really screamed," he asked, "why didn't someone hear her? It's just astonishing what people will believe."

Responding to Bradley's question about Don King, Tyson said he supports his promoter despite a federal investigation in New York probing King's handling of Tyson's money. "He uses me. I use him. ... We'd never misuse one another. ... Don is my man," Tyson told Bradley.

Desiree Washington's response to Tyson's comments was one of disbelief and anger. Just four days after the interview, her Boston-based attorneys filed a civil suit for unspecified damages in the United States District Court in Indianapolis. The suit charged Tyson with having caused Washington "immediate and severe physical pain, serious and lasting physical harm, emotional distress, terror and trauma, and psychological problems." Washington's attorney, Deval Patrick, alluded in a press conference that an unspecified communicable disease had also been transmitted to Washington during intercourse with Tyson.

Washington's father, Donald, informed the Associated Press that the suit was filed because of a lack of remorse on the part of Tyson. He also told ESPN that his daughter "wasn't after money, but after you beat somebody and you continually beat them, they got to fight back, so she is going through the justice system.

"Don King and Alan Dershowitz keep coming on television, going into the news media, insulting her, embarrassing her and calling her all kind of names," Donald Washington said, "How much torment can a person take?"

Donald Washington repeated an earlier statement, that at a time prior to the trial his daughter was offered a bribe that started out as $100,000 and quickly rose to $1 million. "The bribe was done through a phone call," he said. "Rev. T. J. Jamison said, 'I have Don King sitting here in the room with me.'" Donald Washington asked Jamison, "'Is Mike Tyson going to apologize and plead guilty?' The Reverend said 'no,' and I said, 'End of conversation. All you want to do is insult my daughter.'"

Appellate lawyer Alan Dershowitz was quick to seize on the filing of the lawsuit to continue his attacks on Washington. He told reporters that the lawsuit "finally discloses Washington's true motive behind her accusation against Mike Tyson: money and lots of it." He also said that Tyson will not settle out of court, saying "we will fight it until the truth comes out."

Don King, Tyson's manager, issued a statement saying Washington "has been lying all along. . . . This is not a woman who was harassed, battered, confined, traumatized, terrorized, or, more important, raped."

Some three days later, another bizarre chapter was added to the story. Ed Gerstein, the Providence Rhode Island attorney who apparently represented Washington before and during the trial, received an opinion from the Rhode Island Supreme Court concerning his inquiry as to the status of his retainer agreement that he had with Washington. Gerstein had sought such an opinion because, while he knew he had such an agreement, he also knew that neither Washington nor the prosecution had divulged the written agreement at trial.

Normally, such matters of inquiry between an attorney and his client are kept confidential. However, because of the potential impact on Tyson's appeal, the Court had issued a public opinion stating that, while they were not ruling that Washington had committed perjury at trial, they did believe that the matter should be brought to the attention of the Indiana Court.

Dershowitz called the *Indianapolis Star* and other news organizations to say that this new piece of evidence was the "smoking gun" that would free his client. He also called Washington "a money-grubbing golddigger who is a liar to boot."

Such claims by Dershowitz were answered by Washington's attorney Deval Patrick, who said in a prepared statement that "the continued character assassination against Ms. Washington, which is being waged in the media, constitutes a second rape. It is a second rape that should not and will not be tolerated. Dershowitz's campaign to impugn Ms. Washington's character and motives is a transparent tactic to shift the focus away from the real issue: Mike Tyson's proven guilt of a terrible crime."

Almost a year to the day after the rape incident occurred, the 1992 Indiana Black Expo extravaganza opened in Indianapolis. Still under the leadership of the outspoken Rev. Charles Williams, who had encouraged Mike Tyson to visit the rehearsal session in 1991 where he met Desiree Washington, the 1992 Expo promised an upbeat event that would drown out the unfortunate events of the previous year.

On Thursday, July 9, almost 500 people attended a rally in downtown Indianapolis in support of Tyson. Organized by the "Justice Coalition for Tyson," its purpose apparently was to seek immediate release for Tyson on bond, ensure that he would obtain a new trial, and make certain that he would be given a fair opportunity to prove his innocence if a new trial were granted.

Although promoter Don King and Tyson's former girlfriend B Angie B did appear at the rally, controversial black leaders Louis Farrakhan, the minister who leads the Nation of Islam, and the Reverend Al Sharpton, the activist from New York City, did not appear as promised.

Los Angeles city councilwoman Patricia Moore of Compton, California, a suburb that was torn apart by riots after the Rodney King trial, did appear and said, "The African-American women throughout the United States are not happy about what's happened to Mike Tyson. . . . We will not let Desiree get away with using us as a tool to destroy one of the greatest men we've ever known."

On Thursday, July 23, the Rev. T. J. Jamison, president of the National Baptist Convention, U.S.A., the nation's largest black Baptist Denomination, was indicted for perjury in Shreveport, Louisiana for lying in front of a grand jury when he said he never offered up to $1 million dollars to Washington to drop the charges against Tyson.

In early August, former Tyson bodyguard Rudy Gonzalez told the *New York Post* and Fox Television News that the ex-champ was a man with such "intense sexual appetites that he would have four to five girls, sometimes 10 to 15 a night."

Gonzalez went on to say that Tyson "had 1,300 names of sex partners filed on a pocket computer, including women whose names would be recognizable. "He knew how to please women . . . It was very important to Mike to make each woman feel special . . . to remember her name . . . her birth date," Gonzalez said.

Regarding an explanation of why Tyson was left alone to fend for himself when he was in Indianapolis during the Desiree Washington incident, Gonzalez said that "King [Don King] and his employees insisted Mike get on the plane by himself. . . . I had no choice. . . . While I was arguing with them downstairs . . . the plane was boarding and ready for take-off."

Gonzalez said, "Tyson returned home to Cleveland from Indianapolis earlier than expected, and depressed. . . . He finally told me 'I met a girl . . . we really hit it off . . . we went out . . . we had sex . . . but I really messed up. . . . I didn't walk her to the car.'"

On August 17, Judge Patricia Gifford put a temporary end to Tyson's hope for a new trial. In an eight-page opinion, the judge denied Tyson's motion for a new trial, and affirmed an earlier ruling denying Tyson's attorneys the right to question Washington in a deposition hearing about the disputed fee retainer agreement issue. Judge Gifford also personally rebuked Alan Dershowitz for misleading statements about the fee-retainer agreement issue, stating, "this Court is both appalled and shocked that such an attempt to perpetrate a fraud upon the Court has occurred."

In September 1992, Tyson's attorneys defending him in the civil suit being brought in federal court by Desiree Washington made a counterclaim against her, seeking an unspecified amount of compensatory and punitive damages. The counterclaim alleged, "Washington made false and misleading statements about the boxer with the intent to obtain money or property, and that such statements were made with an ulterior purpose and motive and not in the interest of enforcing Indiana criminal law. . . Tyson has been and continues to be injured by Washington's statements."

Shortly thereafter, Washington's lawyers filed documents alleging that during the rape, Mike Tyson had transmitted a certain "venereal disease." Dershowitz was quick to deny such claims.

In October, as the Tyson case continued its path to the Appellate Courts the popular rap group Public Enemy denounced Tyson's conviction and the Indiana Judicial System in general by comparing Tyson's plight to the 1930 lynching of two black men in Marion, Indiana.

The cover of "Hazy Shade of Criminals" shows two black men, who were convicted of killing a 23-year-old white man, dangling from ropes while a mob of smiling white Hoosiers looks on. Rapper Chuck D uses the following lyrics in one of the cuts from the album: "Never liked what I saw in the law/Indiana trees hangin' us instead of leaves/we hangin' from the rope."

On the back cover of the record, the rapper writes that the picture on the cover depicts men "hanged for bulls . . . that they didn't do based on cracker racism, jealousy, envy and greed. In 1992, by no coincidence, in the State of Indiana, a good friend of mine, Mike Tyson, was hanged the same G . . . way. Some things never change. Free Mike Tyson and all the hundreds of thousands of black men and women who are political prisoners in the jail cells of the United Snakes of Amerikkka . . . Hell is on Earth."

One Tyson supporter, looking at the record cover, said "It's not as physical or as drastic . . . but the way they did Mike Tyson . . . they lynched him through the legal system. The only difference is he's not dead. Yet."

In early December, Deval Patrick, the attorney who represented Desiree Washington in her civil suit said that, in his opinion, Alan Dershowitz "continues to infect and taint prospective jurors in the civil case by attacking Washington's character and motives." The Boston-based attorney said, "This is the same man who has written books about using the media and manipulating public opinion to influence the minds of prospective jurors—or to beat down the other side to make it back down."

Alan Dershowitz responded to Patrick's remarks, saying, "Washington and her father talked about how she could get movie and book rights," citing a radio interview with Donald Washington as proof of the intentions.

USA Today also reported in December that Rosie Jones, the 1990 Miss Black America, had reached a settlement with Mike Tyson regarding her $100-million lawsuit that claimed that Tyson propositioned her and acted lewdly toward her in a pageant ceremony at the Black Expo in July of 1991. No financial terms were announced.

In keeping with a three-year tradition, representatives of Mike Tyson passed out 1,500 free turkeys to needy families just prior to Christmas in the Indianapolis area. The turkeys were distributed through the Indiana Black Expo "We Can Feed The Hungry" program. Tyson had been criticized for the same thing the previous year, with critics saying he was trying to influence prospective jurors.

Also in December, Dershowitz filed a second appeal with the Indiana Court of Appeals alleging that "Desiree Washington had a financial interest in the criminal trial's outcome," and that the "trial court erred in summarily dismissing the petition for postconviction relief without permitting discovery, holding an evidentiary hearing, hearing oral argument, or even permitting the defense to respond to the factual claims and legal arguments set forth in the State's motion for summary disposition."

Dershowitz also alleged that "if the jury had been aware that the complainant and her parents had lied and misled to conceal their financial interests in a conviction, it probably would have reached a different verdict."

Meanwhile, Alan Dershowitz reported that Tyson was occupying himself in prison by exercising and reading. "He has been reading biographies like that of showman Florenz Ziegfield and others involved in New York City in the 1920s," Dershowitz said. "He is also reading a lot about ancient Egypt, and we have had a number of intellectual discussions about these things."

Sources at the Indiana Youth Center said that Tyson was also doing a lot of sit ups and other exercises, and that he had lost nearly 40 pounds since the trial. Dershowitz said he believed that Tyson had thrown himself into an exercise program to take his mind off the death of his father in October. Tyson was not allowed to attend the funeral, and Dershowitz said that since "you can't grieve in prison, you can't show emotion, you can't shed tears, and you can't show any sign of weakness, even if you are Mike Tyson," he felt that Tyson was working harder than ever on the exercise program.

On January 2, 1993, reports confirmed the sale of Mike Tyson's 17-room, all-stone castle in Bernardsville, New Jersey, to Richard Hall, the mayor of nearby Bound Brook, for a reported $3 million. Once listed for $8 million, the Victorian Gothic mansion was occupied by Tyson when he was married to Robin Givens.

The January issue of *People* magazine reported that Desiree Washington "spends most of her time alone in her room at Rhode

Island's Providence College where she is plagued by nightmares that have been worsened by the split-up of her parents in June 1992. Her attorney, Deval Patrick, said Washington still dreams of going to law school, but "her plans these days are to get through tomorrow."

The infamous *Globe* magazine presented statements from some of Washington's acquaintances in their January 12th issue that shed a different light on Tyson's accuser. "Desiree was very sophisticated when it came to boys and sex," said longtime pal Heather Anderson, 18. "Very early on in our friendship she told me she was not a virgin, and she spoke in intimate terms about her lovers . . . to be frank, I was shocked." The *Globe* stated that another "friend" said that Washington only cried "rape" when her furious father found out that she'd had sex with Tyson.

Juror Dave Vahle was also quoted in the article, saying, "at the time, we all felt a man had raped a woman, but now I believe a man was raped by a woman. I would sign an affidavit that if we had known about the money, I couldn't have voted to convict him. Mike Tyson deserves a new trial."

Fellow juror Rose Pride allegedly commented, "The panel was taken in by Desiree's performance," and that ". . . it's she who committed a crime."

In response to these statements, juror Michael Wettig stated to reporters that the evidence about the potential book and movie deals "wouldn't have made a difference. . . . It had nothing to do with what happened that night . . . the rape in the hotel room. If she [Washington] was so greedy, why didn't she take the million and run?"

Legal scholar Henry Karlson of the Indiana University School of Law told the *Indianapolis Star* that in his opinion, the jurors' statements "are totally inappropriate and that their testimony is not admissible. . . . No jury's decision would ever be final if the jury were permitted to go back and change their minds."

Also in late January, Alan Dershowitz continued his media parade in Tyson's behalf by appearing on "The Maury Povich Show," "The Morton Downey Program," ESPN, and "This Week in Indiana" on the local Indianapolis ABC affiliate, as well as being quoted in every newspaper and magazine that would provide him with a forum. Marion County prosecutor Jeffrey Modisett remained in the background until he finally faced off with Dershowitz on "This Week in Indiana," where he said, "Enough is enough" and began to defend Washington against attempts by Dershowitz to "drag her through the mud."

On that program, Alan Dershowitz reiterated his belief that the exclusion of the three witnesses by the Court (who allegedly saw Tyson and Washington "necking" in the back seat of the limousine), and the perjury allegedly committed by Desiree Washington regarding a pretrial retainer agreement with Ed Gerstein were his main arguments for reversal of Tyson's conviction. Dershowitz took issue with Prosecutor Modisett's statements that the case did not have "compelling" issues, arguing that the appellate court's granting of oral argument must mean that the court believes that there are indeed potential grounds for reversal.

When asked whether the potential perjury issue was weaker than he had been expressing in public due to the wrong questions being asked by counsel Vincent Fuller to Desiree Washington at the trial, Dershowitz was steadfast in his belief that the appellate court would decide that she had lied about the retainer agreement. Fuller also said that, in Indiana, the defense is not required to prove technical perjury, only that "the testimony misled the jury."

Modisett said that Dershowitz's statements regarding the "three witnesses" who were excluded from testifying were an exaggeration since "only one person said they [sic] saw Tyson and Washington necking in the back of the limousine prior to their entering the Canterbury Hotel, and that the other two only said that the one witness told them of what she saw."

In response to a question I asked during the program, Modisett denied that the prosecutor's office withheld its knowledge of the retainer agreement allegedly signed by Washington prior to trial, even though it was discussed with Greg Garrison, Barb Trathen, and local Indianapolis counsel David Hennessey during a mock cross-examination of Desiree Washington by attorney Robert Hammerle one month before the trial began.

Asked whether Mike Tyson would be retried if the conviction were reversed, Modisett replied that it "would be up to the victim, Desiree Washington, to decide that, because we cannot go forward without her."

In response to a question about his chances of having the conviction affirmed by the court now that Alan Dershowitz was in the case and not Vincent Fuller, Modisett replied, "No one thought we could beat Fuller either."

Responding to arguments that the Tyson jurors had said most of the "new" evidence wouldn't have made any difference in their decision to convict Tyson, Dershowitz stated that there were now "four jurors who had come forward who said that they would have changed their vote . . . two who had appeared on a radio program in Philadelphia, one on the Povich show, and one who had telephoned me."

Modisett countered by saying that, regardless of the jurors' statements, he did not believe that the development would in any way influence the decision of the appellate court. He also said that he understood why "the Tyson case is a very difficult one. Mike Tyson was a hero, and still is to many. There is a sense of loss, not only in the country, but in our community. We never singled out Mike Tyson for prosecution."

In her first interview since the Barbara Walters television appearance, Desiree Washington spoke out on WISH-TV, Channel 13, Indianapolis, during the week of January 25. At the urging of prosecutor Jeffrey Modisett, and her civil attorney, Deval Patrick, Washington told reporter Jane Harrington that she felt trapped by the publicity surrounding her since the trial one year ago.

"I think I was also tried and convicted," Washington said in the interview, "and as long as Tyson is in prison, and maybe even longer, I will be in prison." She continued by saying, "I look at people my age having a good time, enjoying their lives . . . and I can't do that . . . I basically just lost my life. I know it [pressing charges against Tyson] was the right thing to do, but I can't say it was the easy thing to do."

Washington said the publicity has made it difficult for her to resume her private life. "I was attacked once, and now I'm attacked over and over and over again," she said. "I can't heal, and I can't get better. I'm finding it hard to love and to open up."

Washington was also highly critical of Alan Dershowitz over his personal attacks on her, and asked him "to think about what it would be like if it were his daughter who had been raped like I was, and how she would feel."

Alan Dershowitz responded by saying, "I think it's in her financial interest to come forward now. . . . Maybe she thinks . . . she'll have a better opportunity to get movie and book rights."

Dershowitz also said it was unfair to blame him or other Tyson supporters for the publicity surrounding Washington. The Harvard professor said that Washington lost her right to privacy when she agreed to disclose her name after the guilty verdict.

"She made the decision to go public, and so she and her lawyers take any responsibility for her being in the public eye." He added, "She is home free and going to college, and Mike Tyson is in prison. Who's the one who's been attacked?"

Documents filed by Dershowitz and his co–counsel, Lee McTurnan, prior to the hearing in front of the Indiana Court of Appeals, indicated that the two lawyers would argue that Tyson should be given a new trial because Desiree Washington was motivated to testify against him by a "well-developed financial agenda." Dershowitz also wrote in a brief filed with the Court of Appeals that "when the allegation is that the state knowingly, recklessly, or negligently promoted false testimony, a new trial is required . . . so long as the testimony could have affected the jury's verdict."

For the first time, Tyson's lawyers also said that, if a new trial was granted to the ex-champ, Patricia Gifford should not be allowed to preside, citing concerns about Gifford's comments that the impact of publicity in the case and the public's costs for prosecuting are factors for deciding whether there should be a new trial.

NBC announced that it would air a documentary, "Fallen Champ: The Untold Story of Mike Tyson" on February 12. Oscar-winning writer-director Barbara Kopple and executive producer Diane Sokolow told the press that they had put together a montage of interviews, home videotapes, and old news footage that give "a coherent insightful view of the whys and wherefores of Tyson."

Kopple and Sokolow also said that there are videotapes of Tyson crying in trainer Teddy Atlas's arms before winning the 1982 Junior Olympic heavyweight title and the famous Robin Givens interview with Barbara Walters in which she calls him a manic depressive and characterizes her marriage to him as "pure hell."

The producers also said that in an interview for the special, Desiree Washington's father told them, "I idolized him [Tyson]." After his daughter told him she had been raped, Donald Washington said, "Tears welled up in my eyes, my heart sank, and I went and put my arms around her. She used to give me a really tight hug. . . . but no more. She just held her hands like this, to her chest. I want my little girl back, I just lost her, and I'm not getting her back. She will try to come back to me, but I don't think I'll ever have the little girl I sent to Indiana back."

The documentary also apparently was intended "to put into perspective the enormous amount of sympathy that was given to Tyson after his conviction, and explodes a 'lot of myths' about black athletes and their infallibility."

On Super Bowl Sunday, January 31, the television tabloid program "Hard Copy" ran a one-hour special entitled "Reasonable Doubt," which featured an analysis of the Tyson case. The special recounted Tyson's days as a young fighter, with a former middleweight boxing champion telling the interviewer that "Tyson was a master at cheating in the ring," an apparent reference to Tyson's ability to fool his opponents into believing he was going one way when he was going another.

Former Tyson trainer Kevin Rooney described Tyson as "a black ghetto kid who moved to a white household" when he was taken in by the legendary Cus D'Amato. "He made $82 million in his career," said Rooney, "and today, he's broke because of cars, women, and King."

The special also featured ex-wife Robin Givens's accusation against Tyson during the Barbara Walters interview that "he shakes, he pushes, he swings . . . trying to scare me."

Alan Dershowitz and Greg Garrison traded words on the special as well, with Dershowitz reiterating his allegations that Desiree Washington was less than truthful with the jury regarding her intention to pursue book and movie rights.

Garrison defended his client, saying she was a "Joan of Arc" on the witness stand, and would have passed a lie detector test if given one. Dershowitz was especially strong in his remarks regarding Washington's statement to ABC's "20/20" that she would have never brought charges if Tyson would have called and apologized. Dershowitz said, "Can you imagine anyone saying they'd accept an apology for being raped?"

The two combatants also squared off regarding Dershowitz's contention that the prosecutor's office knew about the retainer agreement that Washington allegedly signed prior to the trial, yet withheld such information from the defense. Garrison said that he had no such knowledge, and that the jury knew from the beginning of the trial that "Washington had a lawyer."

Dershowitz discounted Garrison's remarks, saying that he had two witnesses who he had personally spoken with who would contradict Garrison's statements, and that the behavior of the prosecutors would amount to "prosecutorial misconduct."

On the eve of heavyweight champion Riddick Bowe's first defense of his title against Michael Dokes (Bowe knocked him out in the first round), ESPN reported that Mike Tyson had sent a letter to Bowe that in effect reprimanded him for "weighting too much" to fight. The letter also stated that Tyson would look forward to doing "some fighting" against Bowe, the very first reference to Tyson's intention to fight when released from prison.

On February 7, news reports stated that Tyson's days in prison go by rather routinely. Phil Slavens, assistant superintendent for operations, told reporters that Tyson awakes at six a.m. for breakfast, and then either watches television, reads, or receives visitors before heading for the gym where he makes 65 cents an hour for handing out gym equipment. "The fewer exceptions we make for him the better," Slavens said. He also told reporters that Tyson gets more than 100 letters per day, all of them subject to searches and prison restrictions. "Tyson can't have the many pieces of women's lingerie sent to him by fans because it would create jealousy among the prison inmates," Slavens said.

The Rev. Charles Williams, who visits with Tyson regularly, reported that "the trial was kind of a turning point in the sense that I think Mike is more focused on who he is. . . . His salvation, his piece of mind, and his relationship with God are the most important things to Mike Tyson right now."

Boxing promoter Bob Arum told the press, "Tyson doesn't need to worry about being replaced in the boxing ring . . . [because] nobody in the current crop of fighters has been able to match Tyson's skill in the ring or his celebrity status outside of it. Tyson was probably the premiere attraction in boxing while he was champion. . . . He had that ferocity . . . and a menacing charisma when he came into the ring that people can't get enough of.

"If he comes back and right into a title fight, I think there would be high interest," Arum said. "The public would be fascinated to see him fight the current champion."

28

---◆---

ANOTHER DAY IN COURT

On February 15, 1993, the Indiana Court of Appeals convened to hear oral argument regarding the two appeals that counsel for Mike Tyson had brought in his behalf.

Under Court of Appeals #49A02-9203-CR-129, Tyson attorneys Alan Dershowitz, Lee McTurnan, Judy Woods, James Voyles, Nathan Dershowitz, and Jamin Dershowitz filed the appeals based on both the Tyson conviction at trial and on a denial for postconviction relief (request for a hearing to decide if a new trial is warranted) concerning new evidence involving Desiree Washington and the attorney retainer agreement.

Newly elected Indiana Attorney General Pamela Carter chose her chief deputy, Larry Reuben, to argue the State's case against Dershowitz and his colleagues.

The direct appeal of Tyson's conviction listed seven main points for argument. Foremost among them was Judge Patricia Gifford's refusal to allow three witnesses to testify at trial that, counter to the testimony of Desiree Washington, they saw Tyson and Washington necking in the back of a limousine prior to entering the Canterbury on the night of the rape.

Tyson's lawyers had also included arguments pertaining to: 1) the judge's refusal to permit a jury instruction concerning mistake of fact and reasonable belief of consent, 2) an error involving prosecutor Greg Garrison's reading from an Indiana court decision dissent during final argument, 3) the admission of the 911 tape into evidence at trial, and 4) the selection process under which Judge Gifford was chosen to preside over the trial.

In the briefs that accompanied the arguments, Tyson's counsel argued that the trial court had committed reversible error as to each of these points. The State countered with arguments that many of the issues had been waived at trial through inadequate objection, or that even if error had taken place, the error was harmless and would not have affected the final outcome of the trial.

Regarding the appeal from the denial of postconviction relief, the Tyson attorneys pinned their hopes on the belief that the trial court erred when it summarily denied the relief petition even though newly discovered evidence had been presented for the Court's review. Dershowitz and company argued in their brief that the State knew of the existence of a written fee retainer agreement between Washington and lawyer Ed Gerstein, but concealed its existence and promoted false testimony from Washington as a result.

Because of this concealment, Tyson's attorneys argued that they were prevented from proper means of filing a motion for discovery, and therefore could not bring the document to the attention of the jury at trial. The lawyers also argued in the briefs that Judge Gifford's ruling was based on false information, and that they should have been permitted a hearing in order to present their case for relief.

To these arguments, the State specifically argued that the Court was correct in denying the petition for postconviction relief since the defense had never asked in discovery for the retainer agreement even though they knew Washington had a private attorney. Further, they argued that regardless of whether there was an agreement or not, Washington never perjured herself at trial, because she was not asked the right questions, and any discussion by her of the agreement would have been privileged under the attorney-client privilege.

In its argument, the State also set out for the appellate court the nine-point test for considering new evidence:

1. Evidence must be disclosed since trial .
2. The material is relevant.

3. The evidence is not cumulative.
4. The evidence is not merely impeaching.
5. The evidence is not privileged or incompetent.
6. Due diligence was used to secure new information.
7. The evidence is worthy of credit.
8. The evidence can be reproduced at trial.
9. The evidence will probably produce a different result.

Besides the main points of argument, the brief disclosed other interesting information. The defense presented evidence that Donald Washington, Desiree's father, believed that the jury in the criminal case could award her damages (only done in a civil case), and that any criminal conviction would be utilized in a civil case as proof.

My name was also included in a defense brief, in which it was pointed out that in a television interview with prosecutor Jeffrey Modisett, he responded to my questions by saying that indeed the prosecution team of Garrison and Trathen knew of the existence of the written fee agreement before trial. The defense argued that this admission supported their contention that the prosecution hindered their efforts to secure access to discovery of the document.

Star Jones, NBC's legal correspondent, who is a former prosecutor, was especially vocal in her criticism of Modisett's office for not revealing the existence of the retainer agreement. "That's sleazy," she said, "A prosecutor has a duty to turn over all the evidence."

Most surprising in the briefs, though, was the fact that issues II and III of the brief had been filed under seal of the court, and thus were not specified in the documents. Close scrutiny of the briefs indicated that these issues might be further accusations by the defense that Washington had lied about her reasons for charging Tyson with rape.

Hearing the appeal was Presiding Judge Sue Shields, the first woman appointed to the Court of Appeals; Jonathan Robertson, perhaps the most liberal of the three justices; and Patrick Sullivan, known as the legal technician of the three. Dershowitz and the defense team would need to convince two of the three of their way of thinking in order to gain a new trial for Tyson.

The opposition from the State would come from Larry Reuben, a 1973 graduate of the Indiana University School of Law. His former law partner, James Atlas, described Reuben as a "tenacious lawyer who is often retained by other attorneys as co-counsel, and who has handled numerous federal civil rights cases." In 1982, Reuben successfully argued for integration of the private Riviera Club in Indianapolis.

With the briefs as the basis for the appeals, Alan Dershowitz rose to address the Court at promptly 10:00 a.m. Justice Sue Shields sat between her fellow judges, and looked down at the bespectacled Harvard professor as he began to argue for his client's freedom.

With more than 200 people looking on, including repre-sentatives of more than 50 media organizations, friends and associates of the court, and Tyson's promoter, Don King, Dershowitz quickly launched into high gear by attacking Patricia Gifford's decision to disallow a proposed defense instruction regarding Tyson's state of mind at the time of the alleged rape.

The proposed instruction would have allowed the jury to acquit Tyson if they found that he reasonably believed that Desiree Washington wanted to have sex with him. Dershowitz's argument and the justices' questions dealt with whether there was sufficient evidence at trial to permit the jury to draw that inference.

Dershowitz argued that several witnesses at the trial testified that Washington's actions would have made Tyson think that she wanted to have sex with him. He pointed especially to the testimony of a chaplain who said that from what Washing-ton told her, she presumed that there was "some participation" between the two prior to the alleged rape.

Chief Deputy Larry Reuben countered Dershowiz's ar-gument by pointing out that just the opposite had occurred since Washington made it crystal clear through her actions and her comments ("I don't want to have a baby; I have a future"), that she had no intention of having sex with Tyson.

The three justices seemed especially concerned with this issue. Judge Patrick Sullivan pointed out that a "jury needs rules to work with," and seemed to indicate that the absence of the instruction prevented the jury from considering whether Tyson could be acquitted if he reasonably believed that Washington wanted to have sex with him.

That point covered, Dershowitz turned his attention to the issue involving Judge Gifford's refusal to allow the three witnesses to testify. Operating on the assumption that the three witnesses would have testified in direct opposition to Washington's story, Dershowitz argued that the defense had done everything in its power to bring the existence of the witnesses to the Court's attention as soon as possible. Reuben countered this argument by noting the defense interviewed the witnesses at least four times before alerting the Court to the possibility that they would testify.

The justices seemed to question whether the defense had, in fact, done everything it could to alert the Court to the existence of the witnesses, explaining that while the attorney that interviewed the witnesses wasn't directly a part of the trial defense team, he perhaps should have been more diligent in his pursuit of the witnesses.

The defense next pursued the question of the admissibility of the 911 tape, which allowed Washington, as Nathan Dershowitz put it, to "testify twice." Dershowitz pointed out that the tape was admitted even though it was hearsay, and contained very prejudicial comments by the dispatcher who talked to Washington as she spoke.

The prosecution argued that the tape was admissible since the defense had brought into question the money motives by Washington, and thus the tape served to show that her motives were pure.

The justices seemed to be sympathetic to the argument of the defense regarding the dispatcher's comments, and to the fact that the statement was given almost 48 hours after the alleged rape had taken place.

The fourth major argument of the defense had to do with the selection process by which Judge Gifford was selected. Tyson's appellate team argued that the process allowed the prosecution to "judge-shop," and in effect choose the judge most sympathetic to their trial strategy. The State countered by pointing out that Judge Gifford was selected through the normal county court procedures, and asked why the defense had never taken a change of judge when the case came before Gifford in the first place.

Determining who had won this round of arguments was most difficult, but it did appear that the justices were more in tune with the defense's way of thinking. Most observers still believed that, due to the tremendous burden that the defense faces in reversing a decision by a jury and the small number of reversals that do occur, Tyson's chances were slim. Other observers, including me, believed that there was enough reversible error in the record for the justices to award Tyson a new trial if politics were not involved with the decision.

In order to reverse the conviction and provide Tyson with a second trial, Dershowitz would have to convince two of the three justices that there was sufficient reversible error in the trial record. A two-to-one vote against Tyson would allow Dershowitz to take the case to the Indiana Supreme Court, but if the vote were three to zero, the Supreme Court could deny the appeal once and for all in Indiana. Dershowitz's only recourse in that case would be to attempt to appeal the case through the federal courts up to the Supreme Court, only if he could find a sufficient "constitutional issue" on which to appeal.

From the start, Dershowitz had faced an uphill battle to free Tyson from prison. Now that decision rested with the Court of Appeals, and it remained to be seen whether they would decide the case based solely on the legal issues, and perhaps stab trial judge Patricia Gifford in the back by reversing the conviction, or possibly allow politics to intervene in their decision by backing Gifford and denying Tyson a new trial.

Prior to the hearing, the justices had released to the defense the attorney retainer agreement signed by Washington and attorney Ed Gerstein before the criminal trial began. Whether that decision by the Court indicated their concern about the issue involving the document was unclear, but now the defense had the document that they swore would have changed the verdict of the jury if they would have seen it at trial. After the hearing, promoter Don King told the press, "I just hope the brother gets out, but it's probably a snowball's chance in hell."

On February 26, Tyson's lawyers filed a "Second Verified Petition for Postconviction Relief," alleging that Tyson's conviction should be reversed due to new evidence that Washington had falsely accused a high school boy of rape in 1989. Court documents stated that Wayne Walker, a high school classmate, alleged that Desiree Washington once told her father that Walker raped her, and later told him (Walker) that she did it "to cover myself . . . or I would have been in big trouble." Walker told ESPN radio that when he heard that Washington accused Tyson, "the first thing that came to my mind is she's doing it again."

An angry Deval Patrick said, "The charge is . . . categorically false and is totally irrelevant to the central issue of what happened in that hotel room with Tyson in July of 1991."

Besides the new allegations against Washington, Tyson personally requested for the first time in the petition a change of judge due to his belief that Judge Patricia Gifford was biased against him. The defense also charged that prosecutor Greg Garrison, in television interviews with NBC and ABC, contradicted previous statements made about whether he personally knew of the existence of the written attorney fee agreement between Desiree Washington and attorney Ed Gerstein and thus was guilty of concealing the document from the defense.

On March 25, Karen Grau, an Indiana Department of Corrections spokesperson issued a press release reporting that Mike Tyson had been ordered by a prison board to spend at least 30 and perhaps as many as 60 additional days in prison for allegedly disobeying an officer. Sources close to the prison indicated that Tyson apparently was "buying" other inmates' telephone time, and then argued with a guard when confronted over the rules violation.

That same week, prosecutor Greg Garrison, apparently utilizing inside information, told a reporter that the decision on Tyson's appeal would be forthcoming in "five to six weeks." He also predicted that the vote would be "3-0 against Tyson," and that Justice Patrick Sullivan would write the opinion "since Judge Sue Shields has decided to take a vacation."

On March 23, Judge Larry McKinney of the United States District Court in Indianapolis ruled in the civil case between Tyson and Washington that all discovery proceedings in that case would be suspended until the outcome of the appeal of Tyson's rape conviction was known.

Besides prohibiting the defense from interviewing witnesses, and obtaining further evidence regarding Washington's past, the judge also ruled that certain personal information regarding Washington's private life would remain confidential to the public.

In late March, the *New York Post* reported that Desiree Washington's relationship with her father, Donald, may have been a violent one. The report stated that in October of 1989, Mary Washington, Desiree's mother, had Donald arrested and charged with assault and battery against Desiree.

Utilizing police reports, the *Post* quoted Desiree as saying that her father "hit me and pushed me under the sink . . . He continued slamming my head into the wall and the floor. I freed myself and reached for a knife to protect myself."

The article also said Mary Washington stated in a deposition that Donald "flew off the handle" when Desiree told him "she had lost her virginity," and that she (Mary) "arranged for Desiree to undergo psychotherapy, because of severe depression and suicide threats."

In response to the defense's second motion for post-conviction relief in state court regarding their allegation that a hearing should be held concerning Washington's alleged "cry rape" incident with fellow student Wayne Walker in October of 1989, the State of Indiana filed a motion that included a strict denial that Washington had ever had sex with Walker at all.

In the affidavit that accompanied the motion, Desiree Washington swore that:

> "Although Wayne and I have known each other since junior high school, and briefly dated in high school, I categorically and unconditionally deny that Wayne and I ever had sexual intercourse with penetration. I also categorically and unconditionally deny that I ever accused Wayne of having raped me. I have never said such a thing or made such a charge to my father or to anyone else."

The defense then filed a motion alleging that Washington's statement was contrary to testimony given by her mother in a deposition prior to Tyson's rape trial. In that deposition Mrs. Washington is quoted as saying, "Desiree lost her virginity in October of 1989," which is precisely when Wayne Walker swore he had sex with Washington and she falsely accused him of rape.

In the motion, the defense also produced the March 26, 1993 affidavit of one Marc Colvin, a schoolmate of Washington's who stated that

> "I am very reluctant to come forward with this information because I still consider Desiree Washington to be a friend. She [Washington] called me on the telephone toward the end of 1989 and confided in me that she had sexual intercourse with Wayne Walker. ... She also said that after it happened she went into the bathroom and cried."

In the motion, the defense also once again accused the Marion County Prosecutor's office of misconduct at trial by pointing out that Barb Trathen had argued in final argument that "Foster (the limousine driver) knew Washington had just been raped ... she knew it and felt it and she tried to describe it to you ... " when in fact a review of Foster's testimony at trial revealed no such thing.

On April 1, Florence Anthony and Tim McDarrah reported in the *New York Post* that Mike Tyson had decided to embrace the Muslim religion, and change his name to Malik Abdul Aziz (Servant Of The Almighty). Tyson was not available for comment, but his appellate attorney Alan Dershowitz denied the story, stating that "Mike Tyson will continue to be known as Mike Tyson."

In a phone interview on April, Juror Michael Wettig reported that the jury was planning a reunion for the weekend of April 4. All of the jurors were expected to attend, although Wettig said that "they are having a hard time finding Kenny," the young black juror who made headlines after the trial by saying "the case was rigged."

On April 10, 1993, 14 months to the day after the jury convicted Mike Tyson of rape, 12 Los Angeles Federal Court jurors returned a guilty verdict against two of the L.A.P.D. officers charged with violating the civil rights of Rodney King.

Sgt. Stacey Koon, who was in charge of the arresting officers, and Officer Lawrence Powell, who pounded King with the most severe blows to the body and head, were found guilty of using excessive force in apprehending King. Federal prosecutors were able to convince the jury that the famous videotape of the incident clearly indicated that Powell was already in a "batting stance" position ready to beat King before the motorist rose to confront him and the other police officers.

While the prosecution was aided by several key mistakes by the defense, legal experts pointed out that the convictions were the result of the jurors being able to learn much more about what really happened during the crucial moments when the officers were attempting to subdue King.

In the May issue of *Penthouse* magazine, appellate attorney Alan Dershowitz continued his p.r. campaign to free Mike Tyson. Dershowitz is quoted as saying, "Mike Tyson was convicted of rape on the basis of testimony that we believe we can now prove was known to be false and incomplete by the prosecutors."

In addition to presenting a biased, one-sided view of the facts in the case, he also provided a new glimpse into the mindset of the imprisoned ex-champ.

In the article, Dershowitz writes that: "the one subject Mike does not discuss is his future." He quotes Tyson as saying, "My life is in prison now, and dealing with prison one day at a time is a full-time job."

Dershowitz also quotes Tyson as saying, "How could she [Washington] have done this to me? She knows that I didn't rape her; she knows she agreed to have sex. How can she do this to another human being?"

The Harvard professor goes on to write that during the day Mike is allowed to walk around in a fenced-in field that is part of the prison. According to Dershowitz, Tyson said that "That's the worst . . . if I were locked in a cell all day, at least I wouldn't get myself into thinking I was free. But when I walk in the field, I can sometimes forget for a minute or two that I'm not free, that I can't make any decisons on my life in here. I'm dying in here a little at a time."

29

◆

POSTSCRIPT

Much can be learned from the one hearing and four trials that have been discussed in this book. There are many similarities and as many differences in these important events that reflect not only on the guilt or innocence of the men and women involved, but also on the state of affairs in the United States during the time period when the events occurred.

The Clarence Thomas/Anita Hill case, even though it was held outside the normal channels of the judicial system, permitted the world to see that every man who aspires to one of the highest positions in the land will have his mettle strongly tested. Because of Hill's courage in coming forth with her allegations, attitudes have changed regarding sexual harassment, and a woman's right to say "no" to mental or physical abuse from men.

While the shocking outcome of the Rodney King state court trial unfortunately caused deadly riots on the one hand, it may also have had a positive effect on the other. The conduct of police officers toward those they arrest has been closely examined, and in many areas new police procedures have been instituted to replace archaic rules of conduct.

From the trial of William Kennedy Smith, it was proved once again that, while many celebrities may enjoy a grandiose lifestyle, there are prosecutors who will not hesitate to bring them to justice if they break the law. Fortunately, for Smith, there are also juries who will not send a man to prison unless there is proof beyond a reasonable doubt, even if he is related to a famous (or infamous) family.

The Bensonhurst case points out that an eye for an eye attitude cannot and will not be tolerated, but that the police must rise to the occasion and prove their credibility to a jury before justice can be done. Hopefully, Lemrick Nelson will make something of his life, and the family of Yankel Rosenbaum will find peace in his memory.

And what of Mike Tyson? What can be learned from his trial? Even though the evidence against him was perhaps less powerful than that brought forth against the accused in other cases, Tyson is the only one to have been convicted.

In his short, but explosive career as a boxer, Tyson never met an opponent as tough as the criminal justice system. Even his shocking K.O. by boxer James "Buster" Douglas in Tokyo must seem mild in comparison with the knockout punch delivered to Tyson by the judicial system. To his dismay, that system hit Tyson with a proprosecution judge, prosecutors who may have withheld critical evidence, a borderline-incompetent trial defense attorney, a jury that paid more attention to Tyson's bad-boy public image than to the incompleteness of the case's facts, and a loud-mouthed appellate counsel who publicly ridiculed the Indiana courts and judges.

Even if Mike Tyson's advisers are responsible for many of the decisions that led him directly to prison, the former heavyweight boxing champion of the world must sit in his prison cell today and wonder what the hell happened to him. From the moment fate brought him in contact with beauty contestant Desiree Washington, to February 15 when his appeal was heard in Indianapolis, Tyson has taken more shots to the jaw than a has-been fighter.

Tyson's fall from grace began when he somehow convinced the 18-year-old Washington to accompany him to a hotel room in downtown Indianapolis at 2:00 in the morning on July 19, 1992. After some harmless chit-chat, Washington and Tyson then had sex, either consensually or forcibly, depending on which version of the story one believes. The circumstances surrounding that sex act thus set up the only critical legal issue to be decided—whether Mike Tyson was guilty of the crime of rape.

Tyson truly believed he was innocent. Learning from past mistakes involving his celebrity status and altercations with "groupies," he made his sexual intentions perfectly clear several times to Washington, by telling her "I want to f . . . you." When she accepted his invitation, left her hotel room in the middle of the night, and then kissed him in the limousine when they met, Tyson thought he and Washington were on the same wavelength.

When Washington voluntarily came in and sat on the bed in his hotel room, Tyson was even more sure of himself. After the beauty queen went to the bathroom (where she removed a panty shield) and then returned to the bed, he was positive that her intention was to have sex with him.

Desiree Washington truly believed she was raped. In spite of Tyson's blatant sexual innuendoes both to her and other beauty contestants during preliminary competition for the 1992 Miss Black America Pageant, Washington had only joined Tyson to see the sights of the city. When Tyson said that he had to pick up something at the hotel, Washington went up to Tyson's hotel room, intending to stay briefly and leave. Washington also thought she made her intentions clear by telling Tyson she "wasn't that kind of girl" when he tried to kiss her while they sat on the bed. She had merely removed the panty shield because her "time was coming," and was shocked to see Tyson sitting on the bed wearing only flimsy briefs when she came out of the bathroom. When Tyson grabbed her and pulled her down, Washington told him "no," that "I have a future," and "I don't want a baby." Nevertheless, Tyson, Washington alleged, forced himself on her, and raped her in spite of her cries for him to stop.

Putting aside all of the peripheral issues, and based simply on the differing facts in the two stories, this was a classic case of "he-says, she-says," with the outcome of the case hinging upon who a jury would believe.

Both Washington and Tyson testified that when Washington came out of the bathroom, Tyson was sitting on the bed. What happened next is anyone's guess. Incredibly, none of the attorneys in the case provided the jury with a "truth lies somewhere in the middle" version of the facts as is so often the case involving such matters.

Based on this possible theory, Washington removed her panty shield in readiness for sex with Tyson. When the beauty queen then reentered the bedroom, Tyson had removed all of his clothes except for the tiny briefs. Some foreplay occurred, but then Tyson offended Washington by treating her less like a lady he cared for romantically, and more like a "slam-bam, thank you ma'am" sexual plaything.

Washington repeatedly objected to Tyson's behavior, but Tyson paid no attention to her pleas, and continued to treat her more roughly than she had anticipated. At some point, Washington may have even told Tyson to stop, but Tyson was used to getting his way, and probably either ignored Washington's strong words or merely tried to soothe her hurt feelings as he performed oral sex, and allowed her to sit on top of him.

Washington may very well have warned Tyson of her fear of pregnancy and of her desire to "have a future," and so Tyson ejaculated on her stomach. Too quickly for Washington, the sexual interlude was over, and what Washington had expected to be a beautiful experience with the rich and famous Tyson ended up being a nightmare.

Heartbroken and in tears, Washington now at least expected some consideration from the man who had just used her. When Tyson refused to even walk her down to the limousine, Washington felt even more like a one-night stand. By the time she saw Virginia Foster in the limousine, Washington was growing angrier by the moment, and when she finally arrived at her hotel room, she was utterly convinced that she had been raped.

Embarrassed by the shocking turn of events, Washington told her roommates, "Tyson's such a creep, such a jerk, he tried to rape me," and then told them varying accounts of what had happened. When she finally talked to her mother, and especially to her father, Desiree Washington had convinced herself that rape had indeed occurred.

And maybe it had. Even if this scenario is accepted, Tyson still would be technically guilty of rape if at <u>any</u> point before the sex act took place Washington said "no." Whether a jury would have found him guilty of rape under these circumstances will probably never be known, since both Tyson and Washington seemed to either tell partial truths or to exaggerate during their testimony at trial.

Since the real truth may never be known, Mike Tyson, convict #922335, remains in prison where he mops the floor and passes out equipment in the weight room to his fellow inmates. The rich and famous have come by to console him, while Dershowitz, like Fuller before him, drains the former champ's bank account.

Besides the obvious, Tyson's case might well be remembered as one that brought many difficult and important social issues to a public that is often reluctant to even admit that these issues exist.

To begin with, was a rich celebrity singled out by overzealous prosecutors because of his fame and fortune, and was he wrongfully accused by a woman who simply sought fame and fortune herself? Did a young black woman go from being the accuser to the accused, as her name was dragged through the mud by those who felt she falsely accused the celebrity of rape?

Whether his conviction is reversed or not, Tyson has had to pay the piper for his unfortunate acts. In truth, however, he has been represented by a trial defense counsel who should have never taken the case and an appellate counsel who has gone way beyond the boundaries of accepted judicial ethics. Further, Tyson's case was heard by a well-intentioned judge who either should have removed herself from presiding over the trial due to the potential for bias, or have been recused by the defense based on sound arguments regarding her pro-prosecution/rape case background.

Tyson, of course, was also up against win-at-all-costs prosecutors who apparently withheld a critical piece of evidence, and against a jury that may have been prejudiced against him and arrived at his guilty verdict contrary to law.

On the other hand, Washington may very well have fallen prey to a private attorney who had Tyson dollar signs dancing in his head, and to headline-seeking prosecutors who led her down a path of half-truths concerning the attorney fee agreement. In the end, both Tyson and Washington have suffered greatly from their fateful encounter. He has lost his freedom and, most likely, his career, and she, her dignity and privacy.

Perhaps most important, both people put their trust in a legal system that promises truth and justice for all. Unfortunately, most of the critical participants in that very system used both Tyson and Washington as mere pawns, and concentrated on either filling their pockets with gold, or enhancing their own careers.

Mike Tyson and Desiree Washington both sought simple justice, but instead became victims themselves, caught in a criminal justice system that denied them the very justice they sought.

In the final analysis, the set of unfortunate circumstances that came together to topple the ex-champ may turn out to be the saving grace for Iron Mike. Seemingly hell-bent for self-destruction, Tyson now has the opportunity to turn his life around and become a powerful influence on not only the black community, but on the millions of young kids who believe that Mike Tyson is still the champion of the world.

INDEX

EXHIBITS

The Indictment

Michael G. Tyson was indicted by the Marion County Grand Jury in Indianapolis, Indiana on 19, 1991. The indictment read as follows:

THE STATE OF INDIANA, MARION COUNTY, SS:
        In the Marion Superior Court,
        Criminal Division Four
        Special Grand Jury -August, September, October 1991

THE STATE OF INDIANA

INDICTMENT FOR:
        VS.
        MICHAEL G. TYSON

COUNT I: RAPE IC 35-42-4-1
          CLASS B FELONY
COUNT II: CRIMINAL DEVIATE CONDUCT
          IC 35-42-4-2
COUNT III: CRIMINAL DEVIATE CONDUCT
          IC35-42-4-2
          CLASS B FELONY
COUNT IV: CONFINEMENT IC 35-42-3-3
          CLASS D FELONY

The Grand Jury for the county of Marion in the State of Indiana, upon their oath presents:

Count I

        Michael G. Tyson, on or about July 19, 1991, at and in the County of Marion in the State of Indiana, did knowingly or intentionally have sexual intercourse with Desiree L. Washington, a member of the opposite sex, by use of force or imminent threat of force;

Count II

        Michael G. Tyson, on or about July 19, 1991, at and in the County of Marion in the State of Indiana, did knowingly or intentionally cause Desiree L. Washington to submit to deviate sexual conduct, by inserting Michael G. Tyson's finger or fingers into the sex organ of Desiree L. Washington, when Desiree L. Washington was compelled by force or imminent threat of force to submit to such deviate sexual conduct;

Count III

        Michael G. Tyson, on or about July 19, 1991, at and in the County of Marion in the State of Indiana, did knowingly or intentionally cause Desiree L. Washington to perform or submit to deviate sexual conduct, on act involving a sex organ of one person and the mouth or anus of another person, when Desiree L. Washington was compelled by force or imminent threat of force to submit to such deviate sexual conduct;

Count IV

        Michael G. Tyson, on or about July 19, 1991, at and in the County of Marion in the State of Indiana, did knowingly or intentionally confine Desiree L. Washington without her consent by restraining her on a bed in Room 606 of the Canterbury Hotel, 123 South Illinois Street;

all of which is contrary to the statute in such case provided and against the peace and dignity of the State of Indiana.

                                JEFFREY MODESETT
                                Prosecuting Attorney
                                Nineteenth Judicial Court

AFFIDAVIT

I, Wayne Walker, the undersigned, being duly sworn upon my oath, state and depose as follows:

1)   Desiree Washington and I were friends in high school. I was on the football team and she was a cheerleader.

2)   Sometime in October of 1989,

3)   About a week later, her father, Donald Washington, called my house. He was very agitated, and he said that Desiree had told him that I raped her. He threatened to go to the police, but my mother and I persuaded him that it wasn't true. The police were never called.

4)

5)   The following school day, after the call from Donald Washington, I cornered Desiree during "passing time" at school. I said, "Why the fuck did you tell your father that I raped you?" She said, "I had to say something to cover myself  or I would have been in big trouble." I said, "Why the hell did you have to tell him that? Couldn't you tell him something else?"

At that point, she just walked away.

I have read both pages of this affidavit and it is true and accurate.

Further the Affiant says not.

Wayne Walker
Wayne Walker

SUBSCRIBED AND SWORN TO before me this _18th_ day of _February_ , 1993.

Mark C. Hodson
Notary Public   MARK C. HODSON
My Commission Expires _6/23/93_

MICHAEL G. TYSON,   )
)   TRIAL COURT NO.
     Appellant,   )   49G04-9109-CF-116245
     (Defendant Below))
)   The Hon. Patricia J. Gifford
     v.   )
)   Marion Superior Court
STATE OF INDIANA,   )   Criminal Division, Room No. 4
)
     Appellee.   )

AFFIDAVIT OF DESIREE LYNN WASHINGTON

I, Desiree Lynn Washington, being duly sworn upon my oath, state and depose as follows:

1.   I was raped by Mike Tyson on July 19, 1991 in Indianapolis. I was 18 years old at the time of that rape. As a result of that rape, I testified in a criminal trial of Mr. Tyson in January, 1992. Mr. Tyson was convicted of raping me. I am now 20 years old.

2.   I have reviewed and am now familiar with the affidavit of Wayne Walker dated February 18, 1993 and filed in this Court as an attachment to a document entitled "Second Verified Petition for Post-Conviction Relief." I make this affidavit in response to Mr. Walker's "claims" and for no other purpose.

3.   Although Wayne and I have known each other since junior high school, and briefly dated in high school, I categorically and unconditionally deny that Wayne and I ever had sexual intercourse with penetration. I also categorically and

unconditionally deny that I ever accused Wayne of having raped me. I have never said such a thing or made such a charge to my father or to anyone else.

4. In his affidavit, Wayne describes an encounter with me during "passing time" at school after my father made a telephone call to his home. I deny Wayne's account of such a conversation. The only confrontation between Wayne and me at school occurred in the fall of 1989 when I confronted him after learning that he was writing racist graffiti of a sexually explicit nature about me on the walls of the boys' locker room and saying horrible and hurtful things about me to other students. Wayne never said anything to me about any supposed accusation that he raped me during that conversation or at any other time. Wayne and I have had no substantial conversation since that time.

Signed under the pains and penalties of perjury this _18th_ day of March, 1993.

Desiree L. Washington
Desiree Lynn Washington

SUBSCRIBED AND SWORN TO before me this _18th_ day of _March_,
1993.

Rosmary Probasco
Notary Public
My commission expires _7/10/93_

MICHAEL G. TYSON,   :
                                               :   TRIAL COURT NO.
    Appellant,   :   49G04-9109-CF-116245
    (Defendant Below)   :
                                               :   The Hon. Patricia J. Gifford
    v.   :
                                               :   Marion Superior Court
STATE OF INDIANA,   :   Criminal Division, Room No. 4
                                               :
    Appellee.   :

AFFIDAVIT

I, Marc Colvin, the undersigned being duly sworn upon my oath state and depose as follows:

1. I was a close friend of Desiree Washington while we were in high school and beyond. In the latter part of 1989 I had just graduated and she was a junior.

2. I am very reluctant to come forward with this information because I still consider Desiree Washington a friend.

3. However, she is now calling Wayne Walker a liar about a matter I know she is not being truthful about.

4. She called me on the telephone toward the end of 1989 and confided in me that she had had sexual intercourse with Wayne Walker. She said that it was her first time and that she had bled. She also said that after it happened she went into the bathroom and cried.

I have read this affidavit and it is true and accurate.

_Marc Col__
MARC COLVIN

Subscribed and sworn to before me in the County of Kent, State of Rhode Island this
___26th___ day of March, 1993.

_Marc C. Hadden__
Notary Public

MARC C. HADDEN
My Commission Expires: 6/23/93